From Anti-Judaism to Anti-Semitism

From its earliest days, Christianity has viewed Judaism and Jews ambiguously. Given its roots within the Jewish community of first-century Palestine, there was much in Judaism that demanded Church admiration and praise; however, as Jews continued to resist Christian truth, there was also much that had to be condemned. Major Christian thinkers of antiquity – while disparaging their Jewish contemporaries for rejecting Christian truth – depicted the Jewish past and future in balanced terms, identifying both positives and negatives.

Beginning at the end of the first millennium, an increasingly large Jewish community started to coalesce across rapidly developing northern Europe, becoming the object of intense popular animosity and radically negative popular imagery. The portrayals of the broad trajectory of Jewish history offered by major medieval European intellectual leaders became increasingly negative as well. The popular animosity and the negative intellectual formulations were bequeathed to the modern West, which had tragic consequences in the twentieth century. In this book, Robert Chazan traces the path that began as anti-Judaism, evolved into heightened medieval hatred and fear of Jews, and culminated in modern anti-Semitism.

Robert Chazan is Scheuer Professor of Hebrew and Judaic Studies at New York University, where he was the founding chair of the Skirball Department of Hebrew and Judaic Studies. He has published many books on medieval Jewish history and numerous articles in American and foreign academic journals. His two recent books are *The Jews of Medieval Western Christendom* and *Reassessing Jewish Life in Medieval Europe*, both published by Cambridge University Press. He is a Fellow of the Medieval Academy of America and the American Academy of Jewish Research.

From Anti-Judaism to Anti-Semitism

*Ancient and Medieval Christian
Constructions of Jewish History*

ROBERT CHAZAN
New York University

CAMBRIDGE
UNIVERSITY PRESS

CAMBRIDGE
UNIVERSITY PRESS

One Liberty Plaza, 20th Floor, New York, NY 10006, USA

Cambridge University Press is part of the University of Cambridge.

It furthers the University's mission by disseminating knowledge in the pursuit of education, learning, and research at the highest international levels of excellence.

www.cambridge.org
Information on this title: www.cambridge.org/9781316606599

First published 2016

Printed in the United States of America by Sheridan Books, Inc.

A catalogue record for this publication is available from the British Library.

Library of Congress Cataloging-in-Publication Data
Names: Chazan, Robert, author.
Title: From Anti-Judaism to Anti-Semitism: ancient and medieval christian constructions of Jewish history / Robert Chazan, New York University.
Description: New York NY: Cambridge University Press, [2016] |
Includes index. Identifiers: LCCN 2016016149 |
ISBN 9781107152465 (hardback) | ISBN 9781316606599 (pbk.)
Subjects: LCSH: Antisemitism – Europe – History. | Antisemitism – History. |
Christianity and antisemitism. | Judaism – Relations – Christianity – Middle
Ages, 600–1500. | Christianity and other religions – Judaism – Middle Ages, 600–1500.
Classification: LCC DS146.E85 C43 2016 | DDC 305.892/4040902–dc23
LC record available at https://lccn.loc.gov/2016016149

ISBN 978-1-107-15246-5 Hardback
ISBN 978-1-316-60659-9 Paperback

Contents

Prologue

The Holocaust was a traumatic event for all of Western civilization, as it exposed depths of inhumanity that the Western world had assumed lay far back in the distant past. The Holocaust constituted a monumental tragedy first and foremost for the West's Jewish minority, which was the target of the Nazi genocide. Secondarily, it impacted the West's majority, which was confronted by painful evidence of ongoing savagery that it thought had been eradicated from its midst. Within the Western majority, this impact was especially distressing for the various Western Christian churches. Since Christianity has long been the dominant religion in the West, and as observers have pointed increasingly to the influence of Christian anti-Jewish stereotypes on Nazi thinking, the diverse Western Christian churches of the post–World War II period have been forced to confront their possible culpability for sowing the seeds that resulted in the murder of millions of Jews by the Nazis and in the silence of much of the rest of the European populace during the genocide.

In the immediate aftermath of the war, many projected the Nazi movement as non-Christian or even anti-Christian – a tendency that has been mitigated considerably with the passage of time.[1] Despite the effort at distancing Christianity from the Nazis, important observers suggested that Christianity – although not directly implicated in modern anti-Semitism generally and in Nazi anti-Semitism more particularly – nonetheless played an important role in the germination of these anti-Jewish movements and their thinking. One of the first such observers was James Parkes, an English clergyman and historian, who was deeply distressed over the emergence of Nazi anti-Semitism in the 1920s and 1930s and turned his scholarly attention to the history of Christian–Jewish relations and especially to the Christian tradition of anti-Jewish thinking that established the foundation for widespread modern European antipathy toward Jews.[2]

Subsequent to World War II and the Holocaust, Parkes's concern with the Christian roots of European animosity toward Jews and of the especially virulent Nazi variety of this animosity intensified. A leading spokesman for the view that traditional Christian thinking played a dominant role in modern European fear of, and hostility toward, Jews was Jules Isaac, a renowned French intellectual. Isaac was a highly respected historian, who before World War II had little association with Judaism and Jewish life, but who suffered deeply nonetheless during the war years, losing his wife and daughter during the Holocaust. As Isaac turned his scholarly attention and formidable academic skills to the anti-Jewish themes that shaped Nazi thinking, he focused on the centrality of traditional Christian perceptions of Judaism and Jews.

Isaac's pithiest and best-known work has been translated into English as *The Teaching of Contempt*. In this widely cited and influential work, Isaac highlighted three central Christian teachings about Judaism and Jews:

1. The degenerate state of Judaism at the time of Jesus
2. The crime of deicide
3. The dispersion of the Jews as providential punishment for the Crucifixion[3]

All three doctrines, which Isaac considered the cornerstone of the Christian "teaching of contempt" and thus the core out of which the anti-Jewish Nazi program developed, involve aspects of Jewish history as constructed by Christians – the allegedly debased state of Judaism at the time of Jesus, the role purportedly played by the Jews in the crucifixion of Jesus, and the projected impact of that role on subsequent Jewish fortunes. According to Isaac, these negative characteristics of Jewish history and thus by extension of Jews over the ages – regularly projected by traditional Christian thinkers and widely accepted by Christian masses – shaped much of the nineteenth- and twentieth-century European imagery of modern Jews.

As a prominent French academic, Isaac was able to command a far-reaching audience for his views. His writings were especially influential with the leadership of the Roman Catholic Church, played a considerable role in the innovative policies of Pope John XXIII, and eventually impacted the Second Vatican Council and its concern with historic anti-Jewish thinking in the Church.[4] The promulgation of the *Declaration on the Relationship of the Church to Non-Christian Religions* by the Second Vatican Council acknowledged – at least to an extent – the reality of destructive anti-Jewish Church teachings and articulated a commitment to purging the Church of this baneful legacy.[5] This commitment on the part of the Roman Catholic Church was paralleled by similar concerns and efforts in many other Christian churches as well.

With the passage of time, consideration of the role of Christian imagery of Judaism and Jews in anti-Semitic and Nazi thinking has given rise to further examination, clarification, and nuance. A sense of varying degrees of Christian anti-Jewish thinking has crystallized. Since Christians and Jews disagree with respect to key theological issues, Christian negativity toward Judaism and Jews is grounded in significant measure in standard interreligious theological disagreement. The term "anti-Judaism" has been utilized to designate such theological disagreement, and it has been argued that this normal interreligious contention should not be adduced as an element in murderous Nazi imagery and policy. At the same time, however, many observers have urged that Christian hostility toward Judaism and Jews has often moved well beyond the bounds of what is projected as theologically grounded anti-Judaism.

A leading researcher in distinguishing varieties of Christian negativity toward Judaism and Jews was Gavin I. Langmuir. Langmuir attempted to differentiate among three levels of Christian anti-Jewish imagery – what he called the rational, the nonrational, and the irrational.[6] For Langmuir, Christians and Jews sometimes disagreed over issues that could be and were approached rationally. More common and important, however, were issues that divided the two communities but were not amenable to rational discussion. Langmuir fully accepted the notion of Christian anti-Judaism. For him, Christian anti-Judaism constitutes nonrational Christian disagreement with Judaism and Jews, that is to say disagreement involving issues of far-reaching metaphysical principles that cannot be adjudicated through the use of reason. While such disagreement can engender a significant level of frustration and even hostility, it does not – according to Langmuir – account for the intense and radical quality of modern anti-Semitic and Nazi fear and hatred of Jews.

For Langmuir, the intense and radical modern fear and hatred of the Jews that marked Nazism was a different phenomenon, which drew its strength from irrational – rather than nonrational – perceptions of Judaism and Jews. While pre-medieval Christian disagreement with and argumentation against Judaism and Jews was nonrational according to

Langmuir, medieval European civilization created irrational perceptions that produced extreme fear and hatred of Jews and became contributing factors to Nazism and the Holocaust. For this more intense hostility toward Jews, Langmuir used the term "antisemitism," although he was fully aware that the term carries overtones of modern racial pseudoscience. For Langmuir, "antisemitism," despite its problematics, was the only term available to signal the difference he sought to establish between religiously grounded and nonrational Christian disagreement with Jews and the virulent anti-Jewish imagery that emerged in medieval Christian Europe, that became a destructive element in modern European thought, and that eventually played a central role in Nazi projections of the dangers allegedly posed by modern Europe's Jews.[7]

According to Langmuir, the history of medieval antisemitism began during the middle decades of the twelfth century in western Christendom. The claim first leveled in Norwich in 1150 that the Jews of that town crucified a Christian youngster constitutes for Langmuir the onset of irrational Christian thinking about Jews – antisemitism in his view – and the beginning of its long and destructive history.[8] Although he acknowledges the earlier roots of this antisemitic thinking in prior Christian imagery, his position represents as it were a gloss on the Isaac claims. For Langmuir, the traditional assertions identified by Jules Isaac as the core of Christian teaching of contempt do indeed entail potential dangers. However, for over a thousand years these dangers did not materialize. Although pre-twelfth-century Church spokesmen often spoke harshly of Jews, they did not – in Langmuir's view – cross over from the nonrational to the irrational. It was only in medieval Christian Europe that this momentous leap was made. Thus, early Christian imagery was potentially dangerous, but the dangers were not actualized until the twelfth century, exerting a frightful toll thereafter.

Langmuir's work has attracted considerable criticism. His definition of irrationality has been widely challenged, and irrationality is the key to his distinction of levels of anti-Jewish hostility. Irrationality has proven difficult for the mental health profession to define, and Langmuir's proposed definition has seemed to many observers primitive. Moreover, Langmuir identified the grounds for the emergence of irrationality in medieval western Christendom as growing rational doubts regarding key Christian beliefs, such as transubstantiation. In his view, the effort to suppress these rational doubts fostered heightened irrationality within the Christian populace.[9] This grounding for the proposed new irrationality has been severely questioned. Finally, many have been uncomfortable with the term "antisemitism" for the intensified medieval anti-Jewish sentiment that Langmuir has proposed, although alternatives have not been forthcoming.

Despite these criticisms, the direction pioneered by Langmuir has proven fruitful and has been pursued by a number of subsequent scholars. R. I. Moore has projected twelfth-century Christian Europe as the scene of persecutory tendencies that were maintained and in fact intensified over the succeeding centuries. Not closely focused on the Holocaust, Moore has been concerned with a wide range of twentieth-century persecutions and has – like Langmuir – identified their roots in the generally expansive and creative environment of twelfth-century Europe. The factors projected for these persecutory tendencies by Moore are socioeconomic and differ considerably from those suggested by Langmuir.[10] Anna Sapir Abulafia, highlighting the accelerating emphasis on the rational in twelfth-century Europe, has concurred with Langmuir and Moore regarding the accelerating antipathy toward Jews during this period. She has argued that the deepening conviction of Christianity's total rationality transformed the Jews, as deniers of Christian truth, into irrational and hence subhuman creatures.[11]

In *Medieval Stereotypes and Modern Antisemitism*, I joined this chorus of voices urging that medieval western Christendom spawned a sequence of destructive stereotypes that projected the Jews as malevolent toward their Christian neighbors, as bent on harming these neighbors, and as having the power to inflict serious damage on the Christian societies that hosted them.[12] The destructive stereotypes included the allegation of gratuitous Jewish murder of Christians, of ritualized Jewish murder of Christian children, of utilization of the blood of Christian youngsters for Jewish ritual purposes, of Jewish desecration of the host wafer, and of Jewish poisoning of the wells of Europe. I suggested that these stereotypes were absorbed into the folklore of western Christendom and, under the intense pressures generated by the process of modernization, emerged as the core projections of the anti-Semites, who identified the Jews as sources of radical danger to the Christian majority of modern Europe.

Recently, Sara Lipton, in her *Dark Mirror: The Medieval Origins of Anti-Jewish Iconography*, has advanced considerably the case argued by Langmuir, Moore, Abulafia, and me.[13] Like these predecessors, Lipton argues for the deterioration of the image of the Jews in medieval Europe. Using representations of Jews in medieval Christian art, she is able to marshal an enormous quantity of source material to support her claim of deterioration and to present a series of steps in this process. In effect, she is able to construct a six-stage chronology of deterioration that begins in the eleventh century and concludes at the close of the fifteenth century.

Lipton argues that, during the three earliest stages of Christian representation of Jews, the focus was on the Jews of antiquity and their short-comings.[14] Lipton suggests that, beginning early in the thirteenth century, the focus shifted from the ancient to the contemporary:

In moralizing imagery in various types of artwork, coins and coin-filled bags signified moneylending or avarice; cats, which were associated with hunting and nighttime and symbolized heresy, were shown with Jews; and crows, which collected shiny objects, and toads, which swelled themselves up, signaled greed and usury, the illicit amassing of wealth. Through these and other images, Jews, traditionally used to signify the outdated past, came to be identified with the most "modern" of activities and tendencies – moneylending, philosophy, heresy, curiosity.[15]

The transformation of European Jews from a relic of the outdated past to a source of present-day danger was a giant step in the deterioration of the imagery of medieval European Jewry.

Lipton's book, in addition to its copious source material and its specification of stages in the deterioration of the imagery of Jews, offers yet another important advantage. Because of its nature, much of the Christian artwork upon which she draws survived into modernity and continued to convey its negative messages to succeeding generations. Even Christians no longer fully committed to the Church continued to view these works of art, be moved by them, and absorb their anti-Jewish messages, the most dramatic of which involved the broad dangers that Jews posed to their European contemporaries. While I suggested in my earlier study the absorption of the new and more damaging imagery of Jews into European folk wisdom, Lipton's study of medieval Christian art opens up more identifiable channels of transmission of what Langmuir dubbed medieval antisemitism into modern Europe.

The present study focuses on yet another channel through which the increasingly negative perceptions of Jews were transmitted into modernity. Like artwork, intellectual achievements maintain their impact over the generations. Important European authors were read and pondered into modernity. In this book, I shall move beyond the popular perceptions of Jewish enmity and the dangers purportedly flowing therefrom that developed in medieval western Christendom and examine the buttressing of these popular perceptions in the writings of key thought leaders on the medieval and early modern scene. These thought leaders were profoundly influenced by the innovative popular perceptions of the dangers posed by Europe's Jews, but they moved beyond the popular focus on Jewish contemporaries and addressed what they perceived to be the essential nature of the Jews, who were allegedly so consumed by hatred and malevolence.

These reflections on the essential nature of the Jews addressed the broad history of the Jewish people. As is normally the case, the conviction of these Christian thinkers was that the essential nature of human communities is clearly reflected in their histories. Thus, these medieval Christian thinkers undertook a reconstruction of the entire trajectory of Jewish history – the Jewish present, the Jewish past, and the Jewish future. In so doing, they engaged a very complex aspect of Christian thinking about Judaism and Jews and skewed the generally balanced complexities of ancient Christian thinking in a decidedly negative direction, bequeathing to modern Europe a more broadly grounded pejorative perspective on Jews than that embodied in the popular and somewhat limited slanders.

The normal tendency to identify the essence of a human community through its history touched on an especially sensitive element in Christian thinking, which flowed from the unique evolution of Christianity itself. Christianity began its lengthy and rich history as a small dissident Jewish group in tumultuous first-century Palestine. Slowly, it broke away from its Jewish matrix and assumed independence as a separate and increasingly powerful religious community. This curious evolution meant that Jewish history and identity formed an integral element in Christian history and identity. Thus, the history of the Jews has necessarily played a central role in Christian self-perception and self-understanding.

For Christians, the history of the Jews has had to include elements both of commendation and condemnation. The commendation was mandatory. By the lifetime of Jesus, Jews had developed a monotheistic system that posited one divine being, divine control of human history, a covenant between that divine being and a human community, the significance of this human partner community for the workings of all of human history, and a series of revelations bestowed upon his human partners by the beneficent God. Out of these early Israelite/Judean/Jewish views emerged a small group of Palestinian Jews who perceived in the Jew Jesus of Nazareth a divinely mandated figure sent by God to shape the next stage of human history. The emergence of the Church that built upon Jesus and his initially small band of followers can be understood only against the backdrop of prior Jewish history and thought. Without this prior Jewish history and thought, the emergence of Christianity is incomprehensible.

At the same time, condemnation of Jews has been mandatory as well. In the Christian view, rejection of Jesus by the first-century Jews of Palestine was a stunning sin, exacerbated by their responsibility for his condemnation and crucifixion. God had sent his Messiah to the Jewish people, as he had promised he would do. The Jewish people, however, had spurned him and occasioned his demise. In the face of this breathtaking failure, God replaced his original covenant people – the Jews – with the Christian Church, perceived as more loyal and trustworthy. Thus, in this sense as well, Jews and Judaism laid the foundation for the emergence of Christianity and its eventual successes. Once again, but this time in a negative sense, Christianity cannot be understood without reference to the Jews.

This double grounding of Christianity in the prior history of the Jewish people – in both a positive and negative sense – has meant that the subsequent Christian Church has had to be intensely focused on the history of the Jewish people, as played out before, during, and after the brief mission of Jesus. A sure grasp of Christian history has meant concern with and comprehension of the history of the Jewish people – its pre-Jesus history, its engagement with Jesus, and its post-Jesus trajectory. An understanding of Christianity requires attention to and knowledge of the history of the Jews that extends from the hoariest antiquity down through the present and in fact into the future as well. The trajectory of Jewish history – in both positive and negative terms – must be known and its meaning grasped, if Christianity itself is to be properly comprehended.

To be sure, there has been one constant in Christian views of Judaism and Jews over the ages, and that is negative assessment of Jewish contemporaries for not acknowledging the truth of Christianity, which for Christians has been so obvious. Although this negative view of contemporary Jews has been standard, its evaluation has varied widely. For some Christians, the failure to accept Christianity has constituted a critical shortcoming of the Jews and reflects their profound disabilities – intellectual, spiritual, and moral; for other Christians, this failure reflects a Christian lack of the charity and the reasonable argumentation that would prove convincing to Jews and creates a challenge to provide that sympathy and reasonable argumentation.

Alternative assessments of the Jewish present have led ineluctably to divergent constructions of the Jewish past and future. For some Christian observers, the failures of the Jewish present are rooted in a past characterized by unceasing Jewish inability to perceive religious truth and to act in accordance with that religious truth; for others, the Jewish past has been splendid, with the Jews bringing the vision of one true God into the world and thus in effect civilizing primitive humanity. These divergent views of the Jewish past are paralleled by alternative projections of the Jewish future. For one set of Christians, Jews will be punished decisively by God for their recurrent failures; for another set of Christians, the richness of the Jewish past and Jewish service to God and humanity will be suitably rewarded at the end of days.

Christian constructions of the Jewish present, past, and future have by no means been internally consistent. As noted, assessment of the Jewish present is inherently negative, grounded in the fact that Jews have chosen to remain Jews. However, this brute fact can be and has been evaluated by Christians in multiple ways. Negative evaluation of the Jewish present can readily be combined with the positive evaluation of the Jewish past and future (as was the case for Paul, for example). Thus, breaking down global and undifferentiated Christian impressions of Judaism and Jews into constructions of the Jewish present, past, and future opens the possibility of a more nuanced understanding and a surer grasp of the complexities of Christian stances toward Jews over the ages and will allow us to assess more carefully the shift from the balanced Christian constructions of Jewish history bequeathed from antiquity to the increasingly negative views generated in medieval western Christendom and passed on to the modern West.

In the present study, I shall begin by engaging ancient Christian constructions of the trajectory of Jewish history and note the tendency in these early constructions toward balance between the negative and the positive. In the second part of the book, I shall turn our attention to a number of medieval Christian constructions of the trajectory of Jewish history, which turn far more thoroughly pejorative.[16] These more intensely negative constructions of Jewish history complement the emergence of the popular slanders generated in medieval western Christendom. The more intellectually grounded and expressed constructions of Jewish history reinforced powerfully on the medieval scene the broad popular negativity identified by a number of recent researchers; at the same time, these negative and damaging constructions constitute yet another important channel through which the medieval anti-Jewish imagery was transmitted to modern Western civilization.

Notes

1 There is now a growing literature on the role of German Catholicism and Protestantism in Nazi Germany. As an introduction to the topic, see the recent and important studies of Richard Steigmann-Gail, *The Holy Reich: Nazi Conceptions of Christianity, 1919–1945* (Cambridge: Cambridge University

Press, 2003), and Susannah Heschel, *The Aryan Jesus: Christian Theologians and the Bible in Nazi Germany* (Princeton: Princeton University Press, 2008).

2 James Parkes, *The Conflict of the Church and the Synagogue* (London: Soncino, 1934); idem, *The Jew in the Medieval Community* (London: Soncino, 1938); idem, *Antisemitism* (Chicago: Quadrangle Books, 1963). For a valuable study of James Parkes, see Robert Andrew Everett, *Christianity without Antisemitism: James Parkes and the Christian-Jewish Encounter* (Oxford: Pergamon Press, 1993).

3 Jules Isaac, *The Teaching of Contempt*, trans. Helen Weaver (New York: Holt, Rinehart and Winston, 1964), 37. I have (with apologies) reordered the sequence presented by Isaac.

4 Marco Morelli, "Jules Isaac and the Origins of *Nostra Aetate*," in *Nostra Aetate: Origins, Promulgation, Impact on Jewish Catholic Relations*, eds. Neville Lamdan and Alberto Melloni (Berlin: Lit Verlag, 2007), 21–28.

5 See the valuable study by John Connelly, *From Enemy to Brother: The Revolution in Catholic Teaching on the Jews 1933–1965* (Cambridge, MA: Harvard University Press, 2012).

6 Langmuir's most important and innovative essays were collected and published as *Toward a Definition of Antisemitism* (Berkeley: University of California Press, 1990). The synthesis of his work was published at the same time as *History, Religion, and Antisemitism* (Berkeley: University of California Press, 1990).

7 Langmuir attempted to avoid the pseudo-scientific overtones of the term "anti-Semitism" by consistently utilizing the strange orthography of "antisemitism," feeling that "anti-Semitism" suggests there is something that can be labeled Semitism. For the purposes of this study, I have taken a slightly different track. When speaking of the modern political and cultural phenomenon, I have used the normal orthography of "anti-Semitism"; however, when using the term to signify radical medieval anti-Jewish imagery, which Langmuir projected as essentially irrational, I use the strange orthography of "antisemitism." This is hardly an ideal procedure, but it enables me to build on the insight of Langmuir and others that suggests extreme anti-Jewish perspectives that began to crystallize in twelfth-century Christian Europe and intensified thereafter.

8 Gavin I. Langmuir, "Thomas of Monmouth: Detector of Ritual Murder," *Speculum* 59 (1984): 822–846, reprinted in *Toward a Definition of Antisemitism*, 209–236.

9 Idem, "Peter the Venerable: Defense against Doubt," in *Toward a Definition of Antisemitism*, 197–208.

10 The first edition of Moore's book had enormous impact – R. I. Moore, *The Formation of a Persecuting Society* (Oxford: Blackwell, 1987). In 2007, he published a slightly revised second edition.

11 Anna Sapir Abulafia, *Christians and Jews in the Twelfth-Century Renaissance* (London: Routledge, 1995).

12 Robert Chazan, *Medieval Stereotypes and Modern Antisemitism* (Berkeley: University of California Press, 1997).

13 Sara Lipton, *Dark Mirror: The Medieval Origins of Anti-Jewish Iconography* (New York: Metropolitan Books, 2014).

14 Ibid., chapters 1 through 3.
15 Ibid., 132.
16 It is not my intention to suggest that all medieval constructions of the trajec-
    tory of Jewish history were negative. Just as the popular anti-Jewish slan-
    ders were not universally embraced among medieval Europeans, so too was
    medieval Europe diverse enough to generate a variety of constructions of
    the Jewish present, past, and future. Nonetheless, the negativity we shall
    encounter on the part of the major thought leaders upon whom we shall
    focus is extremely important for understanding the emergence of modern
    anti-Semitism.

PART I

JEWISH HISTORY: CLASSICAL CHRISTIAN CONSTRUCTIONS

I

The Synoptic Gospels

Modern scholarship has reached the consensus that no sources whatsoever from the earliest days of the Jesus movement have survived. Neither Jesus nor his immediate Galilean followers have left us a firsthand depiction of the lifetime of Jesus, of his preaching and healing, or of the Jewish and Roman reactions to him. There is a second consensus as well – that the group that coalesced around Jesus was one of several such dissident movements in the tense and polarized environment of first-century Roman Palestine. Precisely the position taken by Jesus and his followers on the burning issues of the day – war against or accommodation to Rome, the key demands of the divine–human covenant, and authoritative leadership within the Judean community – is unfortunately not available to us today.

In the view of modern New Testament scholars, the four canonical Gospels were composed during the second half of the first century or perhaps even a bit later, many decades after the events they depict. In those intervening decades, much had happened in Jewish Palestine and within the small but rapidly expanding Jesus movement. Two developments are especially noteworthy – the first in the larger Jewish ambiance and the second within the young Jesus movement itself. In the year 66, the Jews of Palestine mounted a major rebellion against their Roman overlords. This rebellion was a serious affair; suppressing it necessitated Roman deployment of vast resources and took four years to complete. Nonetheless, by the year 70, the rebellion was suppressed, with large-scale loss of Jewish life and property, with the capital city and religious center of Jerusalem destroyed, and with the Jerusalem temple in ruins.

3

The implications of this uprising and defeat for subsequent Jewish life and for the budding Jesus movement were profound.

Within the Jesus movement itself, the significant development was the emergence of Paul – not a member of the original Jesus circle – into a position of leadership and the development of a distinctively Pauline approach to the movement and its objectives. Paul – whose views will be closely analyzed in Chapter 2 – saw the mission of Jesus in new and more universal terms. God had sent Jesus to implement an expanded covenant that would encompass gentiles as well as Jews. The results of this internal development were momentous for the growing Jesus movement, for the Palestinian Jewry that by and large rejected Jesus, and ultimately for the successors of this Palestinian Jewry over the centuries.

The Gospels were composed subsequent to these two developments and were undoubtedly influenced by them, although precisely how constitutes the great dilemma of modern New Testament scholarship. The four Gospels are generally divided by scholars into two subgroups: the Synoptic Gospels – Mark, Matthew, and Luke – on the one hand, and the rather distinct Gospel according to John, on the other. Mark – it is widely agreed – is the earliest of the three Synoptic Gospels and served as one of the foundations for Matthew and Luke. In addition, Matthew and Luke are said to depend on a now-lost collection of the sayings of Jesus, with both Matthew and Luke working their preexistent materials into somewhat divergent compositions.[1] While all four Gospels, and especially the Synoptic Gospels, strive to locate Jesus firmly within his immediate Palestinian Jewish ambiance, their narratives were surely impacted by the subsequent developments we have noted, although the precise nature of this impact cannot be ascertained. We shall focus on the three, more straightforward and interrelated, Synoptic Gospels.

The earliest of the three Synoptic Gospels – it is now widely agreed – is Mark, generally dated to the late 60s or early 70s of the first century, that is to say, approximately four decades subsequent to the Crucifixion. The locale for the composition of Mark is uncertain, although few scholars identify Palestine as the author's home base. What is relatively certain is that the author was not an eyewitness to the events he depicts, meaning that his sources were oral or written testimonies to the lifetime of Jesus. The far longer Gospel according to Matthew – which draws heavily on Mark – is generally dated during the 80s of the first century and was almost certainly composed outside of Palestine. It is often suggested that the author of Matthew may have been a Jewish-Christian. This suggestion is grounded in the author's extensive concern with and knowledge of

Jewish traditions and attitudes. Matthew has historically been the most popular of the Gospels, the most widely used in Christian liturgy, and thus the most influential. Scholars have dated the Gospel according to Luke to about the same time as Matthew. The author of the Gospel according to Luke in fact composed a two-volume opus, with the second volume devoted to the decades immediately following the Crucifixion.[2]

The Synoptic Gospel narratives are in most respects simple, telling a fairly direct tale. There are, to be sure, internal discrepancies within each of the three Synoptic Gospels and among them as well. Although these discrepancies are interesting and will be noted, they do not create serious issues for our purposes; rather, the Synoptic Gospels create an overall portrait of Judaism, Jews, and Jewish history that is relatively straightforward and relatively consistent in its negativity toward the leaders of Palestinian Jewry, although mitigation of this negativity is important and will be duly indicated.

The Synoptic Gospels are tightly constricted in space and time. They take place almost exclusively in the Galilee and Judea, with a special focus on Jerusalem. One of the results of this tight spatial focus is that Jews play a dominant role in the Gospels. Gentiles make almost no significant appearance in them. When gentiles are portrayed, as in the Crucifixion accounts, they appear essentially as dupes of the Jewish leadership in Jerusalem. What is true spatially and ethnographically is true chronologically as well. There is only minimal rumination on the Jewish past and future, which is dwarfed by the Gospels' focus on the immediate and intense opposition manifested by Jesus' Galilean and Judean Jewish contemporaries and especially their role in his crucifixion.

The close focus on limited space and time results in a rather minimal interest in the overall trajectory of Jewish history. Although reflections of the Jewish past and Jewish future are by no means totally absent, for these Gospel authors Jewish history is encapsulated in the thinking and behaviors of Jesus' Jewish contemporaries, especially in the opposition and enmity of the leaders of the Jewish community of first-century Palestine to Jesus and his message. That opposition and enmity more or less define Jewishness for these Gospel authors, although again the complications they introduce are important for our purposes.

Scholarly consensus places the time of composition of the Gospel according to Mark toward the end of the 60s or the beginning of the 70s of the first century and the place of composition somewhere in the eastern half of the Roman Empire, and not in Palestine itself. Mark is the shortest of the Gospels and is effectively spare in its narrative style. It opens with a brief account of John the Baptist, who appears as a prophetic precursor of the far greater Jesus. Very quickly, the mature Jesus occupies center stage, which he does not relinquish thereafter. The narrative stresses the obvious greatness of Jesus, expressed in multiple ways, and the recalcitrance of his Jewish contemporaries in understanding and acceding to his message. Mark is in many ways a tale of failure, which was ultimately of course a stunning success. In this respect, it is much like the earlier Pentateuchal narrative of Moses, who brought God's message and was subjected to incessant questioning and rejection by the Israelite people to whom and on behalf of whom he had been sent.

The sources of opposition to Jesus described in Mark were multiple. The least of these sources of opposition was his band of immediate followers. Although portrayed as understanding overall his nature and mission, Jesus' immediate followers recurrently disappointed him. This is especially prominent toward the end of Mark, at the point of arrest, condemnation, and execution of their leader, but there are earlier incidents of such disappointment as well. Similarly minor opposition is mounted by the shadowy forces of Satan, which regularly recognize, attempt to seduce, or challenge Jesus and his powers. Unquestionably, however, the dominant oppositional force in Mark – and the other Gospels as well – is Palestinian Jewry, precisely the community that Jesus was sent to lead. From the beginning through the end of Mark, it is the Jews who mount the most intense objections to Jesus and do the greatest damage to him and his cause. This tendency reaches its climax at the dramatic close of Mark, as the Jews use their power to have Jesus condemned, deflect Roman efforts to save him, and revile and mock him on the Cross.

Thus, once again – as in the Hebrew Bible – internal enemies are by far the most significant factors on the historical scene. Since history is presumed by the Hebrew Bible and subsequently by the New Testament authors to revolve around fulfillment or nonfulfillment of the divine–human covenant, the covenantal community itself is the most potent factor in historical causation. The Jews to whom Jesus had been dispatched were his most consistent, vociferous, and aggressive opponents. Because of the Jewish sense of the nature of historical process, fully shared by Jesus and his followers, with fulfillment or neglect of divine command the operative force in history, the Jews were Jesus' most important adversaries, on both the spiritual and terrestrial levels.

Modern scholarship has concluded that Jesus appeared as a Palestinian Jew, addressed his fellow Palestinian Jews, and projected himself as their divinely mandated leader. There is powerful support for this conclusion in the terminology employed in Mark. The locution "Jew" or "Jews" is not employed in the first-person statements attributed to Jesus or in the third-person narration of events by the author. Indeed, the only times the term appears are in Chapter 15, which is the Crucifixion chapter, and the only ones to use the terminology are Romans. Pilate asks Jesus: "Are you the king of the Jews?"[3] In addressing the assembled crowd, the Roman procurator again uses the same term twice.[4] In mocking Jesus, Roman soldiers "dressed him in purple and, plaiting a crown of thorns on his head, placed it on his head. Then they began to salute him: 'Hail to the king of the Jews!'"[5] The titulus on the Cross invoked the same designation one last time.[6] For Romans to use this term of course makes perfect sense. They were outsiders, speaking to and of Jews as a separate and alternative group.

The fact that Jesus' first-person statements and the narrator's third-person account do not invoke the locution "Jew" or "Jews" is highly significant. Reportage of American election campaigning would not note that the audience addressed was American, since all such campaigning involves American audiences. So too the author of Mark does not desig-nate Jesus' audience as composed of Jews, since such was so obviously the case. Rather, reportage of American election campaigning focuses on subgroups in American society. Audiences are depicted as midwestern, southern, middle class, Latino, old, or young. So too does Mark iden-tify subsets of Palestinian Jews – scribes, priests, Herod's men, Pharisees, Sadducees, or the crowd. The audiences were all Jewish; only the sub-groups of Palestinian Jewry were important to note and specify.

The key points conveyed by this specification of Jewish subgroups are two. In the first place, the leaders of the diverse sectors of the tense and fragmented Jewish community of Palestine were united in their oppo-sition to Jesus, the divinely appointed messenger. Despite the deep dis-agreements among these leadership groups on a wide range of political and religious issues, they came together in their rejection of Jesus. The second impression created is that the opposition to Jesus was by and large the responsibility of these leadership groups. The Jewish people on their own were responsive to Jesus' message, but were regularly led astray by their misguided and self-interested leaders. To be sure, we shall see that the author of the Gospel of Mark occasionally undercuts these broad impressions.

The grounds for the opposition of the various leadership groups in Palestinian Jewry were numerous and diverse; they ranged from understandable uncertainty through what Mark perceives to be excessive legalism and ultimately to reprehensible self-interest. Some of the questions posed by Jewish leaders opposed to Jesus seem to have been motivated by a relatively straightforward desire for clarification. Of course, the author of Mark sees even such straightforward questioning as problematic. Jewish observers should have been convinced by the power of Jesus' miracles, the brilliance of his teaching, or his fulfillment of well-known prophetic predictions. Nonetheless, these straightforward questions are the least offensive of the lines of opposition. Chapter 2 of Mark begins with the incident of the paralyzed man who was lowered through the ceiling into Jesus' presence. "When he saw their faith, Jesus said to the man: 'My son, your sins are forgiven.'" This touched off anxiety among some of the scribes in attendance. They thought to themselves: "How can the fellow talk like that? It is blasphemy! Who but God can forgive sins?"7 Again, from the perspective of the author of Mark, this anxiety was unfounded, but the response of the scribes was not in and of itself obnoxious.

The most regularly recurring motif in the opposition of the Jewish leadership revolves around the legal demands of Jewish tradition. Recurrently, the Jewish leaders, especially the scribes and Pharisees, are distressed with what seemed to them Jesus' flaunting of Jewish law. Thus, in the same chapter of Mark, shortly after the incident involving the paralyzed man, Jesus was having a meal in his own house, in the company of many of his disciples, who included in their ranks a considerable number of tax collectors and sinners. This reality agitated some of the scribes present. "Some scribes who were Pharisees, observing the company in which he was eating, said to his disciples, 'Why does he eat with tax-collectors and sinners?'"8 Instances of questioning based on considerations of Jewish law abound throughout Mark.9

In some cases, like the one just now cited, the questioning arose in the normal course of events; in other cases, the questioning based on legal considerations was contrived, constituting a premeditated effort to embarrass and expose Jesus. Thus, the question about taxes found in Chapter 12 is introduced in the following way: "A number of Pharisees and men of Herod's party were sent to trap him with a question. They came and said, 'Teacher, we know you are a sincere man and court no one's favor, whoever he may be; you teach in all sincerity the way of life that God requires. Are we or are we not permitted to pay taxes to the Roman emperor?'"10 Although the question was a legitimate one, in this instance it was intended as a trap. This intention makes the flattering introductory observations about Jesus' sincerity all the more irksome in their obvious insincerity.

Perhaps the most negative questioning is grounded in blatant self-interest. Although many of the questions may be reasonably inferred as emerging out of self-interest on the part of Jewish leaders who would be displaced by the divinely mandated authority of Jesus, in a number of instances the author of Mark asserts this self-interest overtly. A major example of this blatant self-interest is contained in the famous passage in which Jesus entered the temple and drove out the merchants buying and selling there and the moneychangers. His actions are described by the author of Mark as deeply upsetting to the chief priests and scribes. "The chief priests and the scribes heard of this and looked for a way to bring about his death; for they were afraid of him, because the whole crowd was spellbound by his teaching."[11] This episode shows the forces of opposition planning the most drastic of measures. Moreover, there is here no sense of opposition grounded in principle. Rather, it is the fear of popular acceptance of Jesus and rejection of their own leadership that is portrayed as moving the chief priests and the scribes to their extreme plans.

In contrast, there are recurrent references to public support on the part of Jesus' audiences, which were – as we have noted – composed totally of Jews. Mark reports repeatedly enthusiastic responses from crowds of Jews to Jesus – his appearance, his miracles, and his teachings. The report on Jesus' entry into Jerusalem is a particularly impressive depiction of such popular enthusiasm. "Many people carpeted the road with their cloaks, while others spread greenery which they had cut from the fields. Those in front and those behind shouted, 'Hosanna! Blessed is he who comes in the name of the Lord! Blessed is the kingdom of our father David which is coming! Hosanna in the heavens!' "[12] This is an especially rich description of adulation on the part of the general Jewish population.

The broad paradigm of opposition to Jesus on the part of the vested leadership of Palestinian Jewry and acceptance of his message by the common folk in and of itself portrays Jesus' Jewish contemporaries in a balanced way. Jewish opposition to Jesus is by no means depicted as total. Indeed, the implication is that the majority of Palestinian Jews acknowledged him and his teachings. Occasionally, however, Mark undercuts this simple paradigm, complicating the picture of first-century Palestinian Jewry considerably.

On the one hand, leadership figures on the individual level are portrayed as recognizing the divine mission of Jesus and accepting it. The rambling incident involving a synagogue president, depicted in Mark 5, offers one such instance. In this case, the distraught man pleaded with Jesus for help with his grievously ill daughter. While on their way to the daughter, word arrived of the little girl's death. Jesus continued to the home, where he was successful in raising the girl to life. The confidence reposed in Jesus by the distraught father indicates that not all Jewish leaders were in opposition.[13]

The same point is made by the post-Crucifixion activities of Joseph of Arimathaea. Joseph is described by the author of Mark as "a respected member of the Council, a man who looked forward to the kingdom of God."[14] Thus, Joseph is depicted as a member of the leadership of Palestinian Jewry who was responsive to the message of Jesus or was at the very least in agreement on the nearness of the kingdom of God. Joseph seemingly used his position to make his way to Pilate and ask for the body of Jesus. This request was granted, and Joseph respectfully wrapped the body and buried it. Again, not all leaders of Palestinian Jewry ranged themselves in opposition to Jesus.

Conversely, not all members of the broad Jewish community accepted Jesus. There are interesting instances of rejection by Jewish onlookers, even without the intrusion of leadership figures. A relatively benign example of such rejection comes in Jesus' own hometown. On the Sabbath, he preached in the synagogue and elicited the following reaction: "'Where does he get it from? What is this wisdom he has been given? How does he perform such miracles? Is he not the carpenter, the son of Mary, the brother of James and Joses and Judas and Simon? Are not his sisters here with us?' So they turned against him."[15] While this rejection is attributed by Jesus to the special issue of acceptance of a prophet in his own original environment, it shows popular rejection, without the intrusion of Jewish leadership figures.

A far more significant instance of crowd rejection is associated with the scenes of condemnation and execution of Jesus. When Pilate offered the crowd the opportunity to have Jesus released, the assemblage chose instead to ask for the release of Barabbas, thereby in effect condemning Jesus to the cross. In this instance, Mark attributes the crowd response to the incitement of the chief priests.[16] However, during the crucifixion itself, Mark reports crowd derision of Jesus, with no reference to incitement on the part of leadership figures. "The passers-by wagged their heads and jeered at him: 'Bravo!' they cried, 'So you are the man who was to pull down the temple and rebuild it in three days! Save yourself and come down from the cross.'"[17] Here, the Jewish crowd seems ranged in self-generated opposition, indeed derision. While Mark presents a broad portrait of Jewish leadership opposed to Jesus contrasted with Jewish masses that accepted him, from time to time the author of Mark upsets this simplistic portrait, suggesting that the Jewish reactions to Jesus were – like all important human reactions – exceedingly complex.

Jewish opposition to Jesus reached its climax in his crucifixion. Mark advances a fairly straightforward sequence of events, in all of which the Jewish leadership plays the dominant role. Although the Roman official Pilate formally decreed the execution of Jesus and although Roman soldiers carried out the decree, Mark makes it abundantly clear that the Romans had no quarrel whatsoever with Jesus and that the execution was a bow to insistent Jewish demands. In fact, the Roman procurator Pilate is portrayed as having attempted to save Jesus by invoking a traditional custom, whereby one prisoner could be released at the request of the crowd assembled to witness executions. According to Mark, this Roman attempt at saving Jesus failed, due to the agitation of the Jewish crowd, stirred up by its leaders. Subsequently, the Jewish mob turned negative on its own, as we have just seen.

[margin note: cruci-fixion w/ Jewish opp.]

Thus, Mark provides an essentially balanced portrait of Jewish responses to Jesus, with general acceptance by the Jewish population at large and rejection by the Jewish leadership. He further balances his portrait by indicating instances of acceptance of Jesus by Jewish leaders and rejection by the masses. Nonetheless, this general balance is dwarfed by the portrait of the monolithic and negative Jewish role in the Crucifixion. The execution and resurrection of Jesus constitute the high point of the Gospel according to Mark, the denouement toward which the drama of Jesus' life had been leading. In this dramatic high point, the Jews – leaders and masses alike – play an unrelievedly destructive role.

To be sure, the portrait of Jewish responsibility for the death of Jesus was undercut to a significant extent by another major theme in Mark, which was Jesus' forewarning that he was to suffer and die in accordance with prophetic prediction. At about the mid-point of the Gospel according to Mark, Jesus warns his disciples of the reality of Jewish opposition, of his death, and of his resurrection. "He began to teach them that the Son of Man had to endure great suffering, and to be rejected by the elders, chief priests, and scribes; to be put to death; and to rise again three days afterwards. He spoke about it plainly."[18] From this point on, Jesus recurrently reminded his followers of what was to happen to him. Now, the notion that God had planned for Jesus to be put to death and then resurrected complicates considerably the

Marcan portrait of Jewish culpability for the Crucifixion. However, in dramatic terms, the hostile role of the Jews – both leaders and followers – tends to overwhelm the theological niceties. The Crucifixion account is exceedingly powerful, drawing much of its narrative force from the contrast between an innocent victim and gratuitously malevolent enemies, who are the Jews.

The Jewish opposition to Jesus so totally reflected in the Crucifixion narrative must be seen against the backdrop of Palestinian Jewish life during the days of Jesus and likewise against the realities of the slightly later period during which the Gospel according to Mark and the other Gospels were composed. As noted, Palestinian Jewry was beset by major political and spiritual rifts, which set groups of Jews intensely and often violently against one another. This intensity surely influenced the Marcan portrait of virulent Jewish opposition to Jesus at the time of his crucifixion, as the Gospel authors were surely well aware of the polarized Jewish environment within which Jesus appeared.

At the same time, the internal developments in the Jesus movement we have noted certainly played a role as well. As the Pauline version of Jesus' message began to spread among the gentile population of the Roman Empire, the spectacle of Jesus executed at the hands of the Roman authorities raised serious problems. The solution to these problems was to create a portrait that effaced all traces of tension between Jesus and Rome. In order to achieve this, it was necessary to shift culpability for the crucifixion of Jesus from the Romans to the Jews. As a result of these needs, Mark's relatively balanced depiction of Jewish reactions to Jesus prior to the Crucifixion gives way to the wholly negative portrait of the Jews at the time of Jesus' execution. Overall, the drama of the Crucifixion narrative has shaped much of Christian popular thinking about Jews. More thoughtful observers, however, have not overlooked the complexities and nuance of the broader Marcan narrative.

Mark's focus in depicting Jews is almost wholly on the Jewish contemporaries of Jesus. This focus flows from the nature of the narrative, which is concise and limited to the immediacy of Jesus, the Galilee, and Jerusalem. There is only one significant instance in which Mark explicitly extends its purview beyond the immediate and into the Jewish past and future. Interestingly, that introduction of Jewish past and future is achieved in the form of a parable, a favorite mode of teaching on the part of Jesus in the Synoptic Gospels. This is the well-known parable of the vineyard owner and his rebellious tenants. It was clearly intended by the author of the Gospel according to Mark as a reflection on the past and future of Jesus' Jewish contemporaries, who were in the process of rejecting him and causing his death.

The parable begins with the creation of an elaborate and well-equipped vineyard. "A man planted a vineyard and put a wall round it, hewed out a winepress, and built a watch-tower; then he let it out to vine-growers and went abroad."[19] Since we know that the parable will eventually apply to the relationship between God and the people of Israel, the sense is that God had made a major investment in his vineyard/covenant and had reposed considerable confidence in the people he had chosen as overseers of the vineyard/covenant, out of the conviction that they would carefully tend it and be loyal to him as their patron. In this, he was to be sadly disappointed.

"When the season came, he sent a servant to the tenants to collect from them his share of the produce. But they seized him, thrashed him, and sent him away empty-handed. Again, he sent them another servant, whom they beat about the head and treated outrageously, and then another, whom they killed. He sent many others, and they thrashed some and killed the rest."[20] These messengers who were so badly mistreated in the parable are of course references to the prophets sent by God to chastise his errant people. Jewish opposition to Jesus was to be understood – in the view of the Gospel according to Mark – as a continuation and in fact culmination of problematic patterns of Jewish behavior long in existence.

The most significant reflection on the Jewish past in Mark is extremely negative, highlighting the historic Jewish rejection of God's messengers. Yet once again, matters are not all that simple. There is much that is positive about the Jewish past that is clearly implicit in Mark. The most obvious is the simple fact that God's message is delivered within Palestinian Jewry through a Palestinian Jew. At no point does Mark deny or diminish the Jewishness of Jesus and his followers. Moreover, Jesus is projected as fulfilling the predictions of the prophets of Israel, whose rejection by their Jewish contemporaries is highlighted in the parable of the vineyard. For the author of Mark, the Jewish people were obviously God's initial chosen people. Although this exalted status was diminished by the ongoing Jewish failure to respond properly to divine demands, the reality of Jewish uniqueness underlies much of the tale told in Mark.

Mark's treatment of the Jewish future is limited and monochromatic; it lacks the complexity and nuance of his treatment of the Jewish present and past. Again, the key source is the parable of the vineyard. Mistreatment of the messengers/prophets moved the vineyard owner/God to a more extreme and desperate step. "He had now no one left to send except his beloved son, and in the end he sent him. 'They will respect my son,' he said, but the tenants said to one another: 'This is his heir; come on, let us kill him, and the inheritance will be ours.' So they seized him and killed him and flung his body out of the vineyard."[21] This part of the parable explains, as it were, God's decision to send his son and deepens the sense of the wickedness of the tenants/Jews. Rather than accept the son of the vineyard owner/God, they opted to seek to control the vineyard in its entirety. This reflects the sense noted earlier of the leaders of Palestinian Jewry rejecting Jesus out of self-interest, the desire to buttress their own humanly grounded authority.

"What will the owner of the vineyard do? He will come and put the tenants to death and give the vineyard to others."[22] While the early part of the parable sets Jewish opposition to Jesus in the context of a prior history of Israelite/Jewish recalcitrance, this last segment addresses the Jewish future. Jewish errors and crimes would result in divine rejection of the miscreants and appointment of replacement tenants for the vineyard.[23] At this point, we have reached the stage of gentile Christianity as a replacement for the original Jewish partners to the divine–human covenant. This view in Mark is redolent of aspects of the Pauline thinking reflected in the Acts of the Apostles; it diverges, however, from the position expressed by Paul himself in his epistles, which we shall examine in the next chapter.

Thus, the narrative structure adopted by Mark, which set the framework for Matthew and Luke as well, is heavily negative, dominated by a focus on the Jewish role in the crucifixion of Jesus. The Jewish past is portrayed – albeit briefly – as a sequence of failures, and the Jewish future is sketched out in bleak terms. Nonetheless, for attentive readers, there is considerable mitigation of this negativity. Jewish rejection of Jesus is attributed to the Jewish leadership, with the suggestion that the Jewish masses accepted him. Even within the ranks of Jewish leadership, there are exceptional figures who recognize Jesus' greatness and role. The aspect of the Jewish past highlighted is the failure to heed God's voice, but the underlying reality is that God had selected the Jewish people to be his human partners. The one unrelievedly negative feature of Jewish history is the future, but we shall see that was altered strikingly in the thinking of Paul.

The Gospel according to Matthew, while introducing considerable additional material to the framework established by Mark, hews closely to the basic Marcan story line and perspectives. Vis-à-vis Jesus' Jewish contemporaries, the portrait is once more dominated by opposition to Jesus, led by the disparate but unified Jewish leadership groups against the inclinations of the positively inclined Jewish populace. Again, there are occasional indications of leaders who are sympathetic to Jesus and Jewish popular groupings that are hostile to him. Once more, the broad balance of this picture of Jewish reactions to Jesus is overturned by the overwhelmingly negative role assigned to the Jews – both leaders and followers – in Jesus' crucifixion.

Indeed, the most significant shift in Matthew's portrayal of Jesus' Jewish contemporaries is its intensification of the theme of Jewish animosity at the time of the Crucifixion and thereafter. This intensification begins in the account of the proceedings before the Roman procurator Pilate, where Matthew adds further details that deepen the sense of Roman innocence and Jewish culpability. Mark indicated already Pilate's negativity toward the execution of Jesus, thus laying full responsibility on the Jewish leaders. Matthew proceeds further, making the Roman governor a yet more sympathetic figure and the Jews yet more reprehensible.

According to both Mark and Matthew, Pilate asked the assembled crowd whether it wished the release of Barabbas or Jesus. At this suspenseful moment, Matthew introduces the wife of Pilate.

While Pilate was sitting in court, a message came to him from his wife: "Have nothing to do with that innocent man; I was much troubled on his account in my dreams last night."[24]

The Jews, who should have been sensitive to Jesus' uniqueness, were not; rather, it was a Roman lady who received and absorbed a divine message about him.

In Matthew, when the crowd asks for the release of Barabbas, Pilate takes the public step of distancing himself from what was about to happen.

When Pilate saw that he was getting nowhere and that there was danger of a riot, he took water and washed his hands in full view of the crowd. "My hands are clean of this man's blood," he declared. "See to that yourselves."

The Pilate gesture and his insistence that the assembled Jews accept responsibility for the death of Jesus elicited, according to Matthew, full acknowledgment by the Jews of their role – and more.

With one voice the people cried: "His blood be on us and on our children."[25]

This purported acceptance of responsibility for all time has echoed down through the ages.

The crucifixion of Jesus was the first half of the culminating drama of the Gospels; the second half of the drama involved his resurrection. The Mark narrative is spare in details, with no intrusion of Jews into the story. In contrast, Matthew tells a far fuller tale, with the Jews making an appearance again designed to portray them in a profoundly negative light. Building on Mark, Matthew indicates that "a wealthy man from Arimathaea, Joseph by name," sought and received permission from Pilate to take the body of Jesus. Permission was granted, and "Joseph took the body, wrapped it in a clean linen sheet, and laid it in his own unused tomb, which he had cut out of rock. He then rolled a large stone against the entrance and went away."[26]

With Jesus thus buried, the leaders of the Jews came before Pilate and requested that they be allowed to secure the gravesite, out of the following concern.

We recall how that impostor said, while he was still alive, "I am to be raised again after three days." We request you to give orders for the grave to be made secure until the third day. Otherwise, his disciples may come and steal the body and then tell the people that he has been raised from the dead. The final deception will be worse than the first.[27]

The deadly opposition of the Jewish leadership extended beyond the Crucifixion. These Jewish leaders are portrayed as pursuing their animosity yet further.

According to Matthew, on the third day, "there was a violent earthquake; an angel of the Lord descended from heaven and came and rolled away the stone and sat down on it," frightening the guards deeply.[28] The angel announced to the two Marys seated nearby that Jesus had been raised from the dead and ordered them to share the news with the disciples. Meanwhile, the frightened guards reported these events back to the Jewish authorities.

After meeting and conferring with the elders, the chief priests offered the soldiers a substantial bribe and told them to say: "His disciples came during the night and stole the body while we were asleep." They added, "If this should reach the governor's ears, we will put matters right with him and see that you do not suffer." So they took the money and did as they were told. Their story became widely known and is current in Jewish circles to this day.[29]

Matthew thus projects Jewish enmity to Jesus even subsequent to his death, deepening the message of overall Jewish opposition and malevolence.

Because of the historical popularity of the Matthew version of the life and message of Jesus, this intensified portrait of Jewish malevolence at the dramatic highpoint of the Gospel narrative has occupied center stage in subsequent Christian imagery.

Although Matthew intensifies the negativity of Mark toward Jesus' Jewish contemporaries in the closing episodes of both Gospels, it portrays the pre-Jesus Jewish past more positively than does Mark. As noted, many recent scholars have come to see the author of Matthew as a Jewish-Christian. Key elements that have led to this conclusion are Matthew's focus on Jesus' genealogy and the recurrent citation of Hebrew Bible verses that Jesus episodes are taken as fulfilling. Both these sets of evidence show Matthew as more keenly attuned to the Jewish past than Mark and Luke, which is important for our purposes.

Matthew opens its account of Jesus by presenting "the genealogy of Jesus Christ, son of David, son of Abraham."[30] It proceeds to trace the generations from Abraham to Jesus through David, noting that that there was a significant symmetry in the numbers of these generations: "There were fourteen generations in all from Abraham to David, fourteen from David until the deportation to Babylon, and fourteen from the deportation to the Messiah." In tracing this genealogy, Matthew is asserting that Jesus is descended from David, the founder of Israel's true dynasty that was to culminate in the Messiah, and that the threefold sequence of fourteen generations suggests that Jesus' place in this sequence was of obvious significance. Matthew embeds Jesus firmly in the distinguished history of Israel.

Beginning with the second chapter of Matthew, the author presents a string of incidents in the early life of Jesus, each of which represents fulfillment of a major prior prophecy. Once again, Matthew – perhaps a Jewish-Christian – is highly sensitive to the greatness of earlier Jewish history, in the form of prophetic vision, and links Jesus to that greatness. Indeed, Jesus is the culmination and fulfillment of the prophetic uniqueness that is the glory of earlier Jewish history.

With respect to the future of the Jews, Matthew's most important observation is to repeat the parable of the vineyard, with its sharply negative reflection of the punishment to be dispensed by God for the mistreatment by the vineyard tenants of the messengers of the owner and eventually – and most reprehensibly – of the owner's own son.

Like Matthew, Luke also is grounded in the Mark narrative. Although it offers only limited alterations of its Marcan source, these alterations are once again interesting and valuable. In addition, it is useful to compare Luke's version of events to that of Matthew. The differences between Luke on the one hand and Mark and Matthew on the other reinforce the sense that the Gospels left a legacy of diversity as regards the Jewish present, past, and future.

The first significant addition to the Marcan substructure comes at the very beginning of the Luke narrative. Alone among Gospel authors, Luke opens with a brief but illuminating introduction.

Many writers have undertaken to draw up an account of the events that have taken place among us, following the traditions handed down to us by the original eyewitnesses and servants of the gospel. So I in my turn, as one who has investigated the whole course of these events in detail, have decided to write an orderly narrative for you, your excellency, so as to give you authentic knowledge about the matters of which you have been informed.[31]

Patent here is the late date of composition of the Gospel according to Luke and the author's commitment to examining the multiple sources at his disposal in order to fashion the most reliable account possible.

The Gospel according to Luke is in fact the first of a two-volume opus. The second volume begins with the post-Crucifixion activities in Jerusalem of Jesus' immediate disciples and shifts midway through the book to a focus on Paul that abandons the original band of Jesus' followers, that leaves Palestine altogether, and that claims displacement of the Jews as the recipients of Jesus' message. The author of Luke was late, was fully aware of the changing nature of the Jesus movement, and was conversant with the efforts of Paul to reach out to a gentile audience. Despite this knowledge of later developments, he nonetheless chose to tell as carefully as possible the story of Jesus, his Palestinian environment, and his uniquely Jewish setting. This serves to reinforce the sense that the Gospel authors, despite their later dates, sought to reconstruct – with whatever level of success – Jesus' original setting and pattern of thinking about Jewish history. Once again, it is of course likely that Luke was influenced by the non-Palestinian environment in which he penned his account and by the new set of gentile readers for whom he wrote. Again, exactly how this environment and these needs shaped Luke's narrative cannot be known.

The major substantive contribution of the Gospel according to Luke for our purposes is found in his account of the Crucifixion. In the first place, Luke did not add the episodes adduced by Matthew that deepened the sense of Jewish culpability. Pilate's wife and Jewish acceptance of guilt down through the generations make no appearance in the Luke account, which is highly significant.

Moreover, Luke's account of the Crucifixion adds two items not found in Mark and Matthew, both of which serve to diminish the image of Jewish cruelty and hatred toward Jesus. The first of these two additions comes at the point of the crucifixion of Jesus and the two criminals.

There were two others with him, criminals who were being led out to execution; and when they reached the place called The Skull, they crucified him there, and the criminals with him, one on his right and the other on his left. Jesus said: "Father, forgive them; they do not know what they are doing."[32]

Since Luke – like Mark and Matthew – portrays the condemnation of Jesus as a Jewish responsibility, this mitigation of Jewish behavior is of great significance.

In addition, Luke adds an important detail at the aftermath of Jesus' death. "The crowd who had assembled for the spectacle, when they saw what had happened, went home beating their breasts." The crowd indicated can only mean the crowd of Jews that had gathered. Thus, Luke replaces the Matthew imagery of defiant Jewish acceptance of guilt for the Crucifixion with a portrait of remorse on the part of the Jewish crowd that had assembled to witness Jesus' execution. For our purposes, the differences between Matthew's depiction of Jesus' Jewish contemporaries and Luke's description of these same Jewish contemporaries are significant. Above all, they suggest that there was hardly unanimity in the portrayal of Jewish guilt for the Crucifixion. Differences of emphasis in the Gospels set the stage for later diversity in the assessment of what became, with the passage of time, key moments in the Jewish past.

Within the New Testament corpus, the Gospels dominated in fashioning broad popular perceptions of Jesus, his activities, and the reactions to him. Within the Gospels, the most influential scenes involve the condemnation, crucifixion, and resurrection of Jesus, which is the dramatic culmination of the well-crafted narratives. The impact of these culminating scenes – especially the extreme portrait in Matthew – on subsequent Christian perceptions of Judaism and Jews has been decisive over the ages. Recalling the claims of Jules Isaac, we note that the three key elements in what he designated as the Christian teaching of contempt are clearly adumbrated in the dramatic tales of Jesus' crucifixion and resurrection.[33] Over the ages, the popular Christian sense of Jewish contemporaries has regularly projected them as the heirs of the Jerusalem Jews who – according to Matthew – accepted upon themselves and these heirs responsibility for the death of Jesus, has understood the past of their Jewish contemporaries as fundamentally flawed, and has envisioned the future of these Jewish contemporaries as cursed by their prior and sullied history.

Yet our closer look at the Gospel narratives has disclosed a considerably more complex picture. Jewish opposition to Jesus is surely a central Gospel motif, but this opposition is portrayed in a more nuanced way than the popular, Crucifixion-centered imagery might suggest. There were positive pre-Crucifixion Jewish responses to Jesus alongside the negative, and there were positive elements in the pre-Jesus Jewish past alongside the shortcomings. Indeed, there are even substantial differences between Matthew and Luke in the portrayal of Jewish behavior during the Crucifixion and its aftermath. Popular readings and reenactments of the Gospels tended to efface this complexity and nuance, but careful readers – and there were very many such careful readers in the Church – could hardly remain unaware of the more complicated picture of Jesus' Jewish contemporaries and their lengthy past incorporated in the diverse Gospel narratives.

Careful readings of the Gospels were complemented by – and indeed were often stimulated by – changing environments and the needs they generated. During the lifetime of Jesus, the environment was Roman Palestine, with its intense intra-Jewish political and spiritual tensions. As a result of Paul's innovative thinking and policies, the locus of Church growth and evolution shifted to the vast reaches of the Roman Empire. The intense interactions within the Palestinian Jewish community gave way to a young Christian Church seeking to reach out to a diverse gentile audience. In this new setting (as we shall shortly see), Jews were no longer a dangerous opposition group. To the contrary, Jewish opposition was essentially irrelevant in this new setting. Indeed, Jews – despite their rejection of Jesus – could prove extremely useful to a Church addressing a largely gentile audience. The new environment and the needs of the young Church very much encouraged more careful reading of the Gospels and the absorption of the more nuanced perspectives embedded therein. As new views of the trajectory of Jewish history emerged, they could claim solid grounding in the core literature of the Church, despite the overwhelmingly negative portrayal of Jews in the Crucifixion narratives.

Paul himself introduces us to this new and more nuanced perspective on the trajectory of Jewish history. From a later date, Eusebius provides a fascinating example of acknowledgment of this complexity, composed at the moment of the triumph of the Church and its establishment as the ruling religion of the heretofore hostile Roman Empire. Augustine – the dominant thinker among the Church Fathers, whose formulations of Church doctrine became normative – provided an authoritative and highly nuanced view of Jewish present, past, and future. These complexities often made little headway against the normal popular desire for clear and simplistic messages. For our purposes, however, the complications are illuminating and important. They reinforce for us the sense we have gleaned of Gospel narratives that – despite an emphasis on Jewish short-comings – they actually present a broadly balanced portrait of Jewish history. Paul, Eusebius, and Augustine served over time as strong reinforcement for the internal Gospel evidence of diverse perspectives on Judaism and the Jews.

Notes

1 For a full and reliable introduction to the Gospels, see Raymond E. Brown, *An Introduction to the New Testament* (New York: Doubleday, 1996; Anchor Bible Reference Library), 97–383.
2 On each of these three Gospels, see ibid., 126–170 (Mark); 171–224 (Matthew); 225–278 (Luke). For full analysis of Matthew's possible Jewish-Christian identity, see Anthony J. Saldarini, *Matthew's Christian-Jewish Community* (Chicago: University of Chicago Press, 1994).
3 Mark 15:2. Citations from the New Testament are taken from Revised English Bible with Apocrypha (Oxford and Cambridge: Oxford University Press and Cambridge University Press, 1989).
4 Mark 15:9 and 15:12.
5 Mark 15:18.
6 Mark 15:26.
7 Mark 2:5–7.
8 Mark 2:16.
9 This may well reflect some of the Pauline views that will be discussed in Chapter 2.
10 Mark 12:13–14.
11 Mark 11:18.
12 Mark 11:8–10.
13 Mark 5:21–43.
14 Mark 15:43.
15 Mark 6:2–3.
16 Mark 15:11.
17 Mark 15:29–30.
18 Mark 8:31–32.
19 Mark 12:1.
20 Mark 12:2–5.

[Handwritten annotation: Mark = balanced until crucifixion / Matt = wildly anti-semitic / Luke = not at all]

21 Mark 12:6-6-8.
22 Mark 12:9.
23 Interestingly, Isaiah had created a parable of a vineyard as well – Isaiah
    5. In the Isaiah parable, God plants the vineyard, which is the people
    Israel, and they disappoint him. According to Isaiah, this vineyard/human
    community will be ravaged and destroyed by an angry God, but in the
    Isaiah vision there is no suggestion of replacement of the miscreants with
    another people.
24 Matthew 27:19.
25 Matthew 27:24–25.
26 Matthew 27:57–60.
27 Matthew 27:63–64.
28 Matthew 28:2.
29 Matthew 28:12–15.
30 Matthew 1:1.
31 Luke 1:1–4.
32 Luke 23:32–34.
33 See the Prologue.

Luke of Mark prob. AND non-Jew
Matt = Jew
Jesus movement = poor ppl's movement
on the fringer

2

Paul

The Gospels, although written well after the lifetime of Jesus and outside of Palestine and its tensions, attempted to re-create the constricted and fractious environment of Jesus' setting. The result is a set of narratives that are narrowly focused on the Jewish present, with little breadth of view across the broad scope of Jewish history. Paul, a diaspora Jew from Asia Minor, made his way to Jerusalem and seems to have imbibed – for a time at least – the intensity of the Jewish life he encountered there, pursuing zealously the post-Crucifixion followers of the Jesus movement. Ultimately, however, Paul's roots asserted themselves, as he returned to the diaspora to pursue what he perceived to be his unique mission and as he speculated broadly on the Jewish past, present, and future.

Paul was steeped in the traditional view of history adumbrated in the Hebrew Bible. At the same time, his diaspora upbringing moved him to see this legacy in ways different from those of his early Palestinian Jewish confreres and his eventual Palestinian Jewish partners in the Jesus movement. Paul's special perspective led him to formulate eventually an innovative and wide-ranging sense of covenant history. This view of covenant history proposed that the advent of Jesus as Messiah was set in motion not by divine concern for the Jews, but rather by God's broader commitment to initiating a new phase of covenant history, which was to include all of humanity. To be sure, prior Jewish thinking posited the notion that all humanity would eventually acknowledge the one true God, but this was to happen as a by-product of the redemption of Israel. In Paul's view, universal acceptance of God was to be an independent development, one that God had always intended and had begun to implement through Jesus.

In Paul's innovative sense of covenant history, the place and role of the Jews became problematic, rather than axiomatic. The centrality of the Jews in the universal phase of covenant history was not necessarily clear. Rejection by the Jews of Jesus as the divinely dispensed messianic initiator of the outreach to all humanity and their persecution of him complicated the Jewish role in the new and universal order. Paul's innovative conceptualization of the stages of covenant history led to complex and ambivalent perspectives on the Jewish past, present, and future and added a powerful new element to subsequent Christian perspectives on Jewish history.

Paul was a Jew from Asia Minor who made his way to Jerusalem. He reports himself and is reported by others to have been an ardent and zealous Pharisee, attracted in particular to combating what he perceived to be the serious threat emanating from the post-Crucifixion followers of Jesus. At some point, Paul was transformed – he believed through divine intervention – from a persecutor of the young movement into an intense adherent of it and eventually a major spokesman for it. From his new perspective, he perceived that he had been appointed by God to a special role in the nascent community – the role of apostle to the gentiles. While the original followers of Jesus seem to have continued to preach their message to Jesus' original audience, that is Jews, Paul saw himself as commissioned to address quite a different audience, gentiles. This shift in target audience – which followed from his innovative view of the covenant – raised complex issues that regularly brought Paul into serious conflict with Jesus' original disciples.

Paul – the diaspora Jew whose views were shaped by the breadth of his diaspora experience and always involved very wide-ranging perspectives – looked out over humanity and discerned four groupings: pagans, whose religiosity was totally erroneous; Jews who denied the divine mission of Jesus, who seem to have constituted the overwhelming majority of Palestinian Jewry; Jews who accepted the divine mission of Jesus, led by Jesus' original followers; and formerly pagan gentiles who acknowledged the divine mission of Jesus, for whom Paul viewed himself as a divinely appointed emissary. The last three of these four groupings were involved in some sort of relationship with the one true God, and the nature and rectitude of these relationships were of paramount importance to Paul. Under the pressures of recent twentieth-century events, the complexity, obscurity, and ambiguity of Paul's writings have made these issues – complex enough in their own right – even more contentious, the source of protracted, vigorous, and polarized scholarly dispute.[1]

The view of Paul projected in the second part of Acts is straightforward: Paul brought the message of Jesus to the Jews, was rebuffed, and eventually gave up on them. According to the second part of Acts, Paul castigated the Jews whom he encountered, indicating that – just as they had rejected God – God was rejecting them. Paul's actual views – as reflected in the seven epistles now considered Pauline – are far more complicated.[2] It is widely agreed that the language of these epistles is extremely difficult, as is often the precise pattern of thinking advanced by Paul. In addition, these epistles were by and large addressed to specific issues on which Paul held very strong positions. This could lead to a lack of moderation and extreme formulations generated by the contention involved.[3] All these problems have contributed notably to the dispute already indicated as to Paul's views of Judaism and Jews.

The traditional view of the Pauline position is that Paul projected the first of the groupings genuinely related to the one true God – Jews who denied the divine mission of Jesus – as mired in a superannuated religiosity that had been rendered obsolete by the appearance of Jesus in his divinely appointed role as the initiator of the new stage in covenant history. According to this view, Paul saw Jews in the post-Jesus era as outmoded relics, and their only avenue to salvation – which would eventually materialize through God's grace – had to involve renunciation of their Jewish emphasis on the law and acceptance of faith in the risen Christ as the divinely mandated alternative.[4]

[handwritten margin note: Jew law was useless now, faith is everything]

More recent views – by and large reflecting the post-Holocaust concerns noted earlier – begin with deep discomfort at the thoroughly pejorative position on Judaism attributed to Paul.[5] In addition, as scholars of Paul have immersed themselves more deeply in first-century Jewish sources, they have come to see that the tradition of Pauline opposition to an arid and desiccated Jewish legalism simply does not fit the reality of early rabbinic Judaism, which Paul knew intimately. As a result, recent Paul scholars have portrayed him as far more respectful of his Jewish coreligionists who rejected Jesus.

Daniel Boyarin provides a review of five of the new perspectives on Paul, which are followed by his own view. For Boyarin himself,

I read Paul as a Jewish cultural critic, and I ask what it was in Jewish culture that led him to produce a discourse of radical reform of that culture. This question, moreover, raises two closely related but different points: What was wrong with Jewish culture in Paul's eyes that necessitated a radical reform? And what in the culture provided the grounds for making that critique? The culture itself was in tension with itself, characterized by narrow ethnocentrism and universalist monotheism. I thus contend that Paul's motivation and theory were genuinely theological, but that his practice and preaching were directed toward radical change in Jewish society.

My fundamental idea, similar to Dunn's – and, as I have said, ultimately going back to Bauer – is that what motivated Paul ultimately was a profound concern for the one-ness of humanity. This concern was motivated by certain universalist tendencies within biblical Israelite religion and even more by the reinterpretation of these tendencies in the light of Hellenistic notions of universalism.[6]

This study does not aspire to solve the "Paul problem." Our focus is Christian constructions of Jewish history. As it happens, however, analysis of Paul's complex construction of Jewish history reaches a set of conclusions more or less identical to Boyarin's (and others') sense that the striving toward universalism is the cornerstone of the Pauline system/ reform. Our concern with Paul's sense of the Jewish present, past, and future ends up dovetailing with some of the key directions in the contemporary analysis of the "new Paul."

Far more exposed to the larger Greco-Roman world than Jesus and his Palestinian followers, Paul's eye was focused on the broadest possible range of humans and human destinies. Paul was convinced that he was living at a pivotal juncture in cosmic history. The appearance and resurrection of Jesus were viewed by Paul as bringing to fruition divine promises to humanity as a whole, extending far beyond the Jewish matrix out of which both he and Jesus had emerged. Moreover, Paul was certain that Jesus' appearance and resurrection were in fact preludes to the imminent *eschaton*, with the world poised on the brink of monumental change, in fact on the eve of ultimate and universal redemption.

The combination of mundane awareness of the larger Greco-Roman world and profound convictions as to the decisive point of time through which he was living moved Paul to project an overarching structure to human history, which – he was certain – was unfolding according to divine plan. For Paul, this overarching structure is clearly foretold in the Hebrew Bible, with which he was intimately familiar, initially in the Greek translation widely used by diaspora Jews. Whether he extracted this structure from his biblical sources or projected this structure onto them is very much the same insoluble question that is regularly asked of the teachings of the Pharisees/rabbis and their readings of the Hebrew Bible. In any case, Paul himself was convinced that the structure of universal history was securely embedded in Scripture and readily decipherable. Although the Pauline scheme put Jesus and his adherents at the pivotal point of the overarching trajectory of human history, the Israelite/ Jewish people had played a very significant role in it as well.

In Paul's view, God intended human history to unfold in stages. During these stages, differing relationships between God and humanity were to evolve, and alternative human communities were to occupy center stage. The differing divine–human relationships were to involve the transition from law to faith, and the alternative human communities were to be law-abiding Israel and faith-inspired gentiles, although these two disparate groupings were intimately linked and would ultimately fuse totally and creatively at the end of time. This overall structure had enormous meaning for the maturing Jesus movement; it had equally important – although less salutary – implications for Jews and Christian constructions of their present, past, and future.

Moses and the period of wilderness wandering dominate the first five books of the Hebrew Bible. It seems fair to say that Moses and the period of wilderness wandering likewise dominate subsequent Jewish reflection on the trajectory of human history, for which the formative period in the Jewish saga – exodus from Egypt, wilderness wandering, theophany at Sinai, and entry into the land promised by God to Abraham – serves as the pivotal point. For traditional Jews, Moses was the ideal leader figure, whose monumental achievement was leading his people out of bondage and into freedom; he was the progenitor of the prophets and the very greatest of them; he was Moshe *rabbenu*, "our rabbi Moses," the initial purveyor of rabbinic law and its ultimate authority. In striking contrast, Moses' role in the Jewish and human past is muted in the Pauline epistles, as he is superseded by an earlier and far less fully drawn biblical figure – the patriarch Abraham. To the extent that Moses and Sinai appear in the Pauline epistles, they are portrayed in a fairly negative light. It is rather Abraham who serves as the first decisive turning point in divine–human history.

In Paul's view, the biblical account of Abraham introduces the two crucial styles in the divine–human relationship – faith and law – and the two human groupings that God intended to attract to his service. Abraham, in Paul's view, shows God's focus on the centrality of faith in the divine– human relationship and – secondarily, because it is secondary – the role of law in that same relationship. The two forms of relating to the divinity are adumbrated in the Abraham saga and are portents of the eventual movement in human history from the era of the law, dominated by Moses and his Israelite/Jewish successors, to the era of faith, initiated by Jesus and his message of salvation for all humanity.

Abraham plays a dominant role in both Galatians and Romans, the two epistles in which Paul addresses most fully the overarching trajectory of human history and – in the process – the present, past, and future of the Jews. Abraham's importance in Galatians and Romans derives from the two related themes that are central to Paul's thinking and writing – the role of faith in the achievement of salvation and the extension of divine concern and blessing beyond the Jewish community to the larger gentile world. On both these critical issues, Abraham provided essential grounding for the position Paul sought to explicate and defend.

In Galatians, Abraham as the paradigm of faith is cited only briefly: "Look at Abraham: he put his faith in God, and that faith was reckoned to him as righteousness. You may take it, then, that it is those who have faith who are Abraham's sons."[7] This is a reference to Abraham's encounter with God depicted in Genesis 15. This encounter begins with God promising Abraham protection and great reward. Abraham inquires as to the nature of this reward, noting that he is childless and his legacy will therefore eventually pass to the overseer of his household. God assures Abraham that this will not happen, that he will produce his own descendants, who will be his heirs. God takes Abraham outdoors, points to the innumerable stars of the heavens, and assures Abraham that his offspring will be as many as these stars. At the close of this give-and-take, the narrative concludes: "Abram put his faith in the Lord, who reckoned it to him as righteousness."[8] For Paul, Abraham by accepting God's assurance wholeheartedly, serves as the paradigm of faith, and the positive divine reaction to his faith reported by the biblical narrative proves its preeminence.

The same claim is advanced in Romans, but at much greater length and with much fuller argumentation. Paul begins as follows:

If Abraham was justified by anything he did, then he has grounds for pride. But not in the eyes of God! For what does Scripture say? "Abram put his faith in the Lord, who reckoned it to him as righteousness."

Now, if someone does a piece of work, his wages are not "reckoned" to be a gift; they are paid as his due. But if someone without any work to his credit simply puts his faith in him who acquits the wrongdoer, then his faith is indeed "reckoned as righteousness."[9]

Here Paul makes explicit what was only implicit in the earlier Galatians. In Paul's view, the language of Genesis, when closely considered, indicates that Abraham's faith – noted prominently in the narrator's summary statement – was the critical element in God's acknowledging Abraham's righteousness.

In Romans, Paul takes the argument one step further.

We have just been saying: "Abraham's faith was reckoned as righteousness." In what circumstances was it so reckoned? Was he circumcised at the time, or not? He was not yet circumcised, but uncircumcised; he received circumcision later as the sign and hallmark of the righteousness that faith had given him when he was still uncircumcised.[10]

The passage cited by Paul in both Galatians and Romans is found in Genesis 15, while the commandment of circumcision comes somewhat later, in Genesis 17. Paul projects this sequencing as instructive, indicating that Abraham won God's blessing through his faith alone and that this blessing was later simply ratified through the imposition of the sign of circumcision.

Paul's insistence on faith as the key to salvation was thematically linked to his view of the mission entrusted to him directly by Jesus, his selection as apostle to the gentiles. For Paul, this extension of divine mercy beyond the confines of the Jewish community – intimately connected to his sense of faith as the key to salvation – is once again proven through a focus on Abraham and the divine promises made to him. Abraham is promised, according to Paul, that he will be the father of the nations – that is to say, gentiles – who serve God through faith. In the Galatians' formulation:

And Scripture, foreseeing that God would justify the gentiles through faith, declared the gospel to Abraham beforehand: "In you all nations shall find blessing."[11] Thus it is those with faith who share the blessings with the faithful Abraham.[12]

This divine promise to Abraham appears at two highly charged points in the Abraham narrative. In Chapter 12 of Genesis, Abraham appears precipitously out of nowhere. As Abram, he is enjoined by God to "leave his land, his homeland and his father's home for a place that I [God] will show you." God's purpose in ordering this transition was to confer great blessing on Abraham and through him on subsequent generations.

> I will make of you a great nation,
> And I will bless you;
> I will make your name great,
> And you shall be a blessing.
> I shall bless those who bless you
> And curse him that curses you;
> And all the families of the earth
> Shall bless themselves by you.[13]

This promise to Abraham is recalled at yet another important point in the Genesis narrative. As noted, Abraham was for many decades childless, a fact that was deeply distressing in light of the early promise of establishing a permanent legacy. This issue comes to a head in Chapter 18 of Genesis, when God sent three messengers to announce to Abraham and his wife that within a year a child would be born to them and thus the earlier promise would now be fulfilled. The three emissaries who delivered the divine message to Abraham then set out on their second mission, that of destroying the sinful cities of Sodom and Gomorrah.

God as it were ruminates on the need to inform Abraham of what is to transpire.

Now the Lord had said: "Shall I hide from Abraham what I am about to do, since Abraham is to become a great and populous nation and all the nations of the earth are to bless themselves by him? For I have singled him out, that he may instruct his children and his posterity to keep the way of the Lord by doing what is just and right, in order that the Lord may bring about for Abraham what he has promised him.[14]

Paul seems to understand this passage as suggesting that, since God was going to destroy the two cities, it was necessary to inform Abraham, who was to be the progenitor simultaneously of the Israelite/Jewish people and of all faithful humanity, of what he was about to do.

Paul provides an interesting additional perspective on this promise in Romans. In this later epistle, Paul shifts the grounding of the divine promise to the gentiles from the two episodes just now noted and introduces a third divine assurance: "For he [Abraham] is the father of us all, as Scripture says: 'I have appointed you to be the father of many nations.'"[15] This citation comes from yet another major episode in the saga of the patriarch – God's changing the name of this key figure from Abram to Abraham.

As for me, this is my covenant with you: You shall be the father of a multitude of nations. And you shall no longer be called Abram, but your name shall be Abraham, for I make you the father of a multitude of nations. I will make you exceedingly fertile and make nations of you; and kings will come forth from you.[16]

Thus, the very name Abraham – the name by which he was known and revered subsequently – reflects God's intention to make the first of the patriarchs the progenitor of many peoples, rather than simply the ancestor of the Jews. The appearance of Jesus and his commissioning of Paul as apostle to the gentiles constitutes fulfillment of this promise, so long

deferred. God's intention to spread his blessings throughout all humanity and the primacy of faith thus come together neatly for Paul into a
justification for the unique mission with which he felt himself entrusted.

Paul extends and sharpens his argument as to the significance of
Abraham by introducing the matriarch Sarah as well. The continuation
of this episode in Genesis 17 adds yet another key image in Paul's rewriting of the Jewish historical narrative. After the promise of a child and the
changing of Abraham's name, God extends the pattern of change and its
implications to Abraham's wife as well.

And God said to Abraham: "As for your wife Sarai, you shall not call her Sarai,
but her name will be Sarah. I will bless her; indeed, I will give you a son by her.
I will bless her so that she shall give rise to nations; rulers of peoples will issue
from her." 17

Sarah as well enjoyed name change, with – according to Paul – the promise of becoming the ancestress of many peoples.

The critical issue for Paul was the precise lineage descended from
Sarah, the true wife of the patriarch Abraham. Abraham himself was
projected, according to Paul, as the ancestor of many peoples, and this
could be readily and comfortably understood, since Abraham had more
than one wife and sired more than one child. Sarah – the true wife –
had only one son, and it was critical for Paul to identify the offspring
descended from that one son. For subsequent Israelite and Jewish tradition, the son promised by God and born of Sarah was Isaac, whose
offspring were Jacob and the tribes of Israel, which evolved eventually
into the Jewish people. Paul was surely aware of this lengthy and well-
established Jewish view.

For Paul, however, matters were far more complicated, leading to
alternative conclusions. Close reading of the biblical narrative suggested to Paul that Sarah – the true wife of Abraham – was intended
to share the bounty of propagating many peoples. Paul's conclusion
seems to be grounded in the juxtaposition of the two key verses: "I will
bless her; indeed, I will give you a son by her. I will bless her so that
she shall give rise to nations; rulers of peoples will issue from her." The
one son – Isaac – was in Paul's view intended to "give rise to nations,"
meaning that Isaac was to be the father of the nations, that is the faithful gentiles.

What this further means is that Abraham's other son, born to the serving maiden Hagar, was obviously to be the father of the Israelite people. Paul connects this conclusion to his generalized insistence that faith

preceded and was superior to the law. Thus, in Galatians Paul sketches the following portrait of Jewish origins:

It is written there that Abraham had two sons, the one by a slave, the other by a free-born woman. The slave's son was born in the ordinary course of nature, but the free woman's through God's promise. This is an allegory: The two women stand for two covenants. The one covenant comes from Mount Sinai, that is Hagar, and her children are born into slavery. Sinai is a mountain in Arabia and represents Jerusalem of today, for she and her children are in slavery. But the heavenly Jerusalem is the free woman; she is our mother.[18]

Paul reprises this theme in Romans and expands upon it. He begins with Abraham and Sarah once again.

"It is through the line of Isaac's descendants that your name will be traced."[19] That is to say, it is not the children of Abraham by natural descent who are children of God; it is the children born through God's promise who are reckoned as Abraham's descendants. For the promise runs: "In due season I will come and Sarah shall have a son."[20]

Allegorically, those who are committed to the true religiosity of faith deserve to be called the children of Abraham; those who remain committed to the prior and inferior religiosity of law are thus the children of Hagar.[21]

In Romans, Paul reinforces this argument with a second patriarchal image, that of Jacob and Esau. He begins by noting that "Rebecca's children had one and the same father." That is to say, in the case of Isaac's children there was not – as had been true for Abraham – one father and two mothers. Yet, according to Paul, here too divine promise created a critical distinction.

Yet even before they [the two sons] were born, when they had as yet done nothing, whether good or ill, in order that the purpose of God, which is a matter of his choice, might stand firm, based not on human deeds, but on the call of God, she was told: "The elder shall be servant to the younger." That accords with the text of scripture: "Jacob I loved and Esau I hated."[22]

Once more, Paul sees the contention between the followers of Jesus through faith and the Jews who follow God's dictates through the law as adumbrated in the patriarchal narrative, with the divine preference for the former clearly articulated by the biblical record.

To be sure, just as Jewish tradition – of which Paul was well aware – posited Israelite descent from Isaac, so too did it insist that Jacob was the forebearer of the tribes, out of which the later Israelite and Judean kingdoms and thus eventually the Jewish community within which Paul had grown up emerged. In the case of the Jacob–Esau dichotomy, there is an added irony. For Jews over the ages, Jacob was the father of the Jewish people, and his laudable attributes of humility and studiousness were conferred upon his Jewish offspring. In contrast, Esau was projected as the father of Christianity and Christendom, with his bellicose propensities inherited by his eventual Christian heirs. This contrasting and conflicted imagery had great impact in both camps.

In Paul's treatment of both the Abraham–Sarah–Hagar story and the Isaac–Rebecca episode, the two central Pauline themes coalesce. The Jews are the offspring of the natural son, who is the lesser figure, and live in servitude to the law, the lesser religious posture; through Christ, gentiles imbued with faith are the children of the divine promise and thus enjoy divinely conferred freedom and God's approbation. Paul utilizes his close reading of the patriarchal narrative to create a disparaging history of the Israelite/Jewish people, which at the same time adumbrates Paul's central criticism of the Jews of his own day as well. Paul's unusual reading of the biblical narrative was destined to exert enormous impact on subsequent Christian constructions of Jewish history.

Viewed overall, this portrait of Jewish origins and history seems overwhelmingly negative, and this is the way it has regularly been read. Jews are allegorically the offspring of Abraham's concubine and are committed to the slavery of the law; they are the descendants of Esau and were fated to serve their younger sibling Jacob and the followers of Jesus. It must, however, be emphasized that this negativity is perspectival and comparative. It lies in the contrasts that Paul draws between faithful gentiles, who are the descendants of Isaac and Jacob and are committed to the freedom provided by faith, and Jews, who are the descendants of Ishmael and Esau and live in servitude to the law. The negative imagery of Jewish origins stems from Jewish shortcomings as contrasted to the superiority of the faithful, primarily gentile followers of Christ, for whom Paul perceived himself to have been appointed as special emissary. When ranged against the faithful gentile followers of Jesus (although I have avoided labeling them Christians, which is what they would eventually come to call themselves), Jewish deficiencies are apparent and are highlighted by Paul.

There is, however, more to humanity than simply Jewish followers of the law and gentiles imbued with faith in the risen Christ. In fact, the bulk of humanity falls into a further camp, utterly unaware of either the law or faith. When compared with this enormous swath of humanity, Jewish descent from Abraham–Hagar–Ishmael and from Isaac–Rebecca–Esau, and Jewish commitment to what Paul projects as the ultimately outmoded religious centrality of the law appear in quite a different light. Ranged against the bulk of humanity, Jews constituted for a very long time the sole human community in a genuine relation with the one true God who created and rules the universe.

Indeed, for the lengthy era that stretched from Abraham to Jesus, the only two groups on the human scene were the somewhat deficient Jews and the utterly deficient gentile polytheists. It was only with the appearance of Jesus that a third option became manifest. Paul – living at the point in time when the third option emerged and profoundly committed to this third option – emphasizes for his immediate purposes the derogatory contrast between Jews who reject Jesus and the faith-inspired gentile followers of Christ; however, his construct implies considerable approbation for God's initial followers in the world. This is a theme that is secondary to Paul's thinking, focused as he was on his mission to the gentile followers of Christ; the contrast between Jews and polytheists – far more positive to the Jews – was nonetheless manifest in Paul's sense of the Jewish past and future and subsequently became a further element in much Christian thinking about the historical trajectory of the Jewish people.

Paul is quite articulate about his conflicted stances toward his former community. His ruminations at the beginning of Romans 9 have been widely cited:

My conscience assures me that I do not lie when I tell you that there is great grief and unceasing sorrow in my heart. I would even pray to be an outcast myself, cut off from Christ, if it would help my brothers, my kinsfolk by natural descent.[23]

Paul puts his concerns for the Jews, his "kinsfolk by natural descent," in personal terms, as an outgrowth of deep emotional ties with them, and this emphasis on Pauline emotion has regularly been absorbed by subsequent commentators. There is, however, more to the Pauline attitude than simply emotional loyalty to his former brethren.

Paul immediately proceeds in Romans 9 to a panegyric to the Jewish past, which appears to be at odds with the emphasis on the negative we have discerned thus far.

They are descendants of Israel, chosen to be God's sons; theirs is the glory of the divine presence, theirs the covenant, the law, the temple worship, and the promises. The patriarchs are theirs, and from them by natural descent came the Messiah.[24]

These far more positive reflections on the dignity of the Jewish past seem to conflict markedly with the Pauline observations cited earlier and are generally understood as a psychological complication on Paul's part, which they may well have been, at least in part. At the same time, there is a less psychological element as well, and that involves the unfolding of historical stages just now noted. For the lengthy time period between Abraham and Jesus, the Jews – shortcomings notwithstanding – were the sole bearers of the divine covenant in the world. Paul's encomium to the Jews reflects in part an awareness of this aspect of the Jewish historical journey.

Attention to Paul's extraordinary condemnation of the broad gentile world, unleashed earlier in Romans, is illuminating. The castigation is comprehensive, encompassing all facets of human existence. It begins with the thinking of the gentile world, which is – according to Paul – fallacious at its core. God's power has, from the beginning of time, been "visible to the eye of reason," but is suppressed and rejected assiduously. "Hence all their thinking has ended in futility, and their misguided minds are plunged in darkness. They boast of their wisdom, but they have made fools of themselves, exchanging the glory of the immortal God for an image shaped like a mortal man, even for images like birds, beasts, and reptiles."[25] A comparison of this castigation with the strictures advanced by Paul against the Jews highlights the far greater deficiencies of the pagan gentiles.

Paul then proceeds to moral condemnation of the Greco-Roman world. After noting once more the pagan tendency to offer "reverence to created things instead of the Creator," he proceeds to condemn the sexual mores of the larger ambiance in which he grew up, decrying female and male homosexuality. From here, he proceeds to more wide-ranging condemnation of pagan ways.

Thus, because they have not seen fit to acknowledge God, he has given them up to their own depraved ways of thinking, and this leads them to break all rules of conduct. They are filled with every kind of wickedness, villainy, greed, and malice; they are one mass of envy, murder, rivalry, treachery, and malevolence; gossips and scandalmongers; and blasphemers, insolent, arrogant, and boastful; they invent new kinds of vice: they show no respect to parents, they are without sense or fidelity, without natural affection or pity.[26]

By no means a pretty picture, this portrait of pagans shows them in a far less favorable light than the Jews upon whom Paul is normally focused. Again, it must be emphasized that between Abraham and Jesus the human alternatives were the somewhat deficient Jews and the utterly deficient polytheists. To the extent that Paul allowed himself to contemplate that contrast more fully, the Jews emerged in his thinking in a far more positive light.[27]

With the appearance of Jesus, divinely foreordained for the salvation of humanity in its entirety, the simple bifurcation of humanity into the Jewish bearers of God's message and pagan resisters of divine truth and guidance was undone. Human society now included three discernible elements: pagans still mired in their intellectual obtuseness and moral depravity; Jews whose shortcomings became apparent with the potential now available for a more profound religiosity grounded in faith; and the followers of Jesus – Jewish and gentile alike – who embodied the highest form of religious expression and who could be retrospectively seen to constitute the true heirs to Abraham–Sarah–Isaac and Isaac–Rebecca–Jacob. Paul's attention was intensely focused upon the present-day tensions between the second and third of these groups, indeed on the special needs of the gentile followers of Jesus against Jesus' Jewish adherents and what he perceived to be the erroneous demands placed by some in the Jesus movement on Paul's faithful gentiles. This focus should not, however, be permitted to obscure the broader Pauline picture of a three-part humanity, in which Jews were projected as inferior to the adherents of Jesus, while at the same time far superior to pagan gentiles.[28]

The advent of Jesus and the potential he introduced for the highest form of religiosity were preordained gifts of God. Why God chose to confer this gift at the particular time and place that he did constitutes a divine decision that – like all divine decisions – is ultimately inscrutable. In any case, this critical turning point in cosmic history was an enormous boon to humanity; it had, however, as a by product exposure of the inherent shortcomings of Jewish religiosity, as reflected in the Jewish propensities Paul had sketched and in a shift of the divine blessing from the law-obsessed Jews to the faith-filled adherents of Christ. The shortcomings of the law and the preference expressed by most Jews for servitude to the law over the freedom of faith now came to the fore.

As noted, Paul's derogatory comments on the earlier phases of the Jewish history were, above all else, prefigurations of what was to happen with the advent of the new era in human history, during which the highest form of religious expression suddenly became an option. Jewish resistance to this option was roundly condemned by Paul and was in fact projected backward into the past as an inherent predisposition decreed by God for this laudable, yet ultimately deficient people. All Paul's criticisms of his contemporary Jewish brethren flow from the onset of this new era and the tendency of most Jews to reject its promise. Viewed from the perspective of the appearance of Jesus and the salvation he represented, Jewish failure and gentile success now took center stage in Paul's thinking. Jews were no longer to be contrasted with gentile pagans immersed in their idolatry and immorality; they were now to be contrasted with those imbued with true faith, both Jewish and gentile.

Just as the advent of Jesus initiated the era of faith and supersession of the law, which God had always intended, so too did it actualize the falling away of the Jews, despite their significant service to the divine during the lengthy period between the promises made by God to Abraham and the ultimate fulfillment of these promises through Jesus. The imagery of descent from Hagar and Esau now took on, for the first time, important meaning. This descent was, according to Paul, now manifest in Jewish inferiority, indeed Jewish servitude to the offspring of the promise. According to Paul, such divine decisions, which result in the elevation of one family or group and demotion or even punishment of another, are arbitrary and impossible to understand, but such arbitrary decisions are ultimately the divine prerogative.

To be sure, implicit in Paul's view is the notion that Jews – while in a sense doomed to their preordained fate – bore at least a measure of guilt for their circumstances. Guardians of the legacy of revelation, Jews (as Paul well knew) read Scripture assiduously and pondered it endlessly. Their immersion in the record of revelation should have enabled them to decipher the truths that Paul discerned; regrettably, they did not. Failure to read Scripture properly was a serious Jewish shortcoming, although again this may simply have been divine design. In significant measure, this Jewish failure had elements of tragedy about it, which Paul – as we have already seen – deeply laments.

To the general critique of Jewish religiosity in the new era in which faith in God had become manifest as the true way to serve him, Paul added one further element that did not flow directly, but did flow obliquely from his reconstruction of patriarchal history as a prefiguration of what was to occur with the realization of the divine dispensation of faith-based religiosity and the extension of divine blessing beyond the Jewish community to the world. According to Paul, who knew this reality well, the Jews did more than simply reject the new dispensation; they actively persecuted the followers of Jesus. Paul mentions this regularly, noting recurrently that he himself had been a zealous participant in the persecution of Jesus' followers. His intense involvement in the persecution of the Jesus movement made him especially sensitive to this aspect of post-Jesus behavior, as did his own eventual suffering as a target of Jewish persecutory zeal.

To an extent, the persecutory tendency may be construed as an additional element in Jewish malfeasance. However, the patriarchal figures that Paul cites extensively once again prefigure this further aspect of the behavior of his Jewish contemporaries. The relationships between the half-brothers Ishmael and Isaac and the twin brothers Esau and Jacob were tension ridden. The contention over legacy drove a wedge between these siblings and engendered considerable hostility, especially on the part of the deposed siblings toward their younger brothers who were eventually accorded blessings and legacy. In this sense, Jewish hostility toward and persecution of Jesus and his followers – while certainly objectionable – was understandable, both as a normal human feature of sibling contention and, more specifically, as yet another element in the prefiguration of the eventual split between Jews and the recipients of the new divine dispensation.

Paul's criticism of his Jewish contemporaries was focused and intense. At the same time, he never lost his broader sense of human history, and that broader sense reasserts itself when Paul looks to the next stage of human history, which he felt was imminent. God had moved from selecting the Israelites/Jews for their limited but important mission to dispatching to the world Jesus and creating new options for deeper religious expression and new hope for broader swaths of the human community. Paul seems to have been convinced that, soon after this momentous gift to humanity, God would confer the even more remarkable blessing of full redemption – to those with the capacity to take advantage of the gift of Christ. At that point in time, Paul projected recompense for the important, albeit limited service that the Jews had performed through the long centuries between Abraham and Jesus. The service was real, and the reward was to be great.

We have already noted the anguish expressed by Paul over his Israelite brethren at the beginning of Romans 9. That anguish serves as the introduction to important Pauline reflections on God's overarching plan for human history. These reflections center in a striking way on the place of the Jews in the divine plan. At the outset, Paul reviews his sense of the movement from the Jews and their law-centeredness to the followers of Jesus, who understood the onset of the new era of faith that God had initiated by sending humanity his son. Paul again makes his case for the superiority of faith over law and of the faith-oriented followers of Jesus over the law-obsessed Jews.

Paul once more turns to Scripture in order to illuminate the movement from the Jews to faith-inspired gentiles. He first cites Moses: "I will
use a nation that is no nation to stir you to envy, and a foolish nation
to rouse your anger."[29] Paul then cites Isaiah, whom he identifies as yet
more daring.

"I was found," he [Isaiah] says, "by those who were not looking for me; I revealed
myself to those who never asked about me." But of Israel he says, "All day long
I have stretched out my hands to a disobedient and defiant people."[30]

Superficially, this seems like simply another formulation of the broad
Pauline thesis of Jewish failure and punishment, contrasted with gentile faithfulness and reward. This contrast is drawn extensively and stunningly throughout Isaiah 65 and reinforces the broader contentions of
Jewish deficiency and rejection seen throughout the Pauline corpus and
especially in Romans 9–10.

Yet, there is a curious disparity between the Deuteronomy and Isaiah
citations, which may possibly reflect some ambivalence on Paul's part.
The latter passage reflects a sense of divine wrath with sinful Israel, the
onset of a new era, and the establishment of a new Jerusalem. All these
images lend themselves nicely to the Pauline sense of historical change and
displacement we have observed. The earlier passage, however, focuses on
Israelite shortcoming, without projecting anything remotely resembling
the replacement of sinful Israel with a purer people. Indeed, the non-
Israelites cited by Moses are depicted in negative terms as a "no nation"
and a "foolish nation," hardly terminology of approbation. Israel, despite
all its faults, remains at the center of this harsh Mosaic diatribe. This
incongruity between the two passages may well reflect some Pauline
ambivalence; in any case, it serves as fitting prelude to Romans 11.

Romans 11 has been widely cited, especially in the recent literature
that has argued for a more nuanced and more positive Pauline view of
Judaism and Jews. Paul opens with a question that flows from the two
passages with which he ended the prior chapter: "I ask, then: Has God
rejected his people?" Noteworthy in this question is Paul's identification
of the Jews as God's people, which seems a bit different from identifying them as the offspring of the natural son, rather than the offspring of
the divinely promised son. Paul's answer is rapid and unequivocal: "Of
course not!" And he immediately proceeds to buttress this answer by
pointing to himself. "I am an Israelite myself, of the stock of Abraham,
of the tribe of Benjamin."[31] Clearly, Paul saw himself as by no means
rejected by God. He obviously perceived himself as an Israelite who made

the required leap from law to faith and as paradigmatic of a larger group that could – and would – make the same transition.

Paul spells out the meaning of pointing to himself, once again using biblical antecedents. These biblical texts point to the notion of a hetero-geneous Israel, made up of both the sinful and the righteous. The point is clear: "In just the same way at the present time, a remnant has come into being, chosen by the grace of God."[32] That remnant consists of Jews, like Paul himself, who had come to grasp the meaning of the transition from law to faith and who had recognized the role of Jesus in this monu-mental transition. The majority of Jews had failed to make this transi-tion, but this failure was consistent with earlier history, as recurrently the bulk of the Israelite/Jewish community fell short in its commitment to the divine. At no time, however, according to Paul, did these failures mean the wholesale rejection of the Jewish people. So too at the present moment, the majority of Jews fell short. There was, to be sure, a sav-ing remnant, but it was small. In this instance, it was gentiles – again to whom Paul perceived himself the messenger – who would lead the way. But these gentiles had to recognize the nature of their circumstances, and that is what Paul was most concerned with in Romans 11. In the process, he makes his last set of important comments on the trajectory of Jewish history, specifically the Jewish future.

God had – as a result of the obduracy of the Jews – passed their legacy on to the faithful gentiles, in fulfillment of the meaning of the patriarchal stories. Paul insists, however, that these stories and this dis-placement should not be misunderstood. God has by no means rejected the entirety of the Israelites/Jews. God's behavior in elevating the faith-ful gentiles has obvious meaning and purpose. "As an apostle to the gentiles, I make much of that ministry, yet always in the hope of stirring those of my own race to envy, and so saving some of them."[33] Important here is the emphasis on the saving of "some of them." Those Jews – like Paul himself – who might be moved by envy to ponder the secrets of history and to understand the momentousness of the new era ushered in by Jesus' advent become part of the new community of God's genuine adherents.

Thus, matters are somewhat more complex than they might have ini-tially seemed. Paul's reconstruction of Israelite history to show gentile descent from Sarah and Jacob and Jewish descent from Hagar and Esau turns out to have been a bit overstated and misleading. Neither the gen-tile world nor the Jewish world is monolithic. There are gentiles who remain outside the community of the faithful, and there are Jews who can and will become part of the community of the faithful. The implications of the patriarchal stories should not be exaggerated. They point to a shift from the centrality of the Israelites/Jews to the centrality of the followers of Jesus, but they do not imply the homogeneity of either group.

It is at this point that Paul introduces the famous image of the olive tree. The olive tree that is Israel has had numerous branches lopped off, as a result of disobedience. In their place, branches of the wild olive, that is gentiles, have been grafted onto the olive tree root. Addressing himself to the gentile believers to whom he has been sent, he reminds them: "Remember that you do not sustain the root; the root sustains you."[34] This image conflicts in considerable measure with the prior imagery we have examined. Here there is no notion whatsoever of the son of the true wife and the son of the serving woman and no younger brother supplanting the elder. Rather, here there is the image of a root that – shortcomings notwithstanding – continues to serve as the foundation for the true relationship to God. The Jews remain the root that sustains all the branches, original and grafted.

To be sure, this is part of an admonition addressed to gentiles warning against arrogance and hubris, whereas the earlier images were part of the message of encouragement to gentiles. As noted, one of the problems of the Pauline epistles is their reactive and partial nature. It seems that efforts to convince the gentiles of their role in the divine plan elicited imagery of gentile superiority to the Jews. In another context, the attempt to guard against gentile hubris necessitated an emphasis on the enduring significance of the Jews as the foundation for the divine relationship to the world. In terms of the Pauline legacy as regards the trajectory of Jewish history, this duality is confusing and creates the possibility of multiple readings on the part of later Christian thinkers.

Yet one more inconsistency surfaces in Romans 11. We have just now noted the Pauline sense of a heterogeneous Jewish (and indeed gentile) world. Jews who comprehend and accept the message of Jesus will be saved; the majority of Jews who do not will remain lopped off from the olive tree. This is clear and understandable, and Paul cites biblical proof-texts to substantiate his case. Yet at the close of this rich chapter, Paul shifts his stance:

This partial hardening has come on Israel only until the gentiles have been admitted in full strength; once that has happened, the whole of Israel will be saved, in accordance with Scripture: "From Zion shall come the Deliverer; he shall remove the wickedness from Jacob. And this is the covenant I will grant them, when I take away their sins."[35]

Here there is no negation of the role of the Jews and not even the notion of partial salvation of a saving remnant; here there is a continuation of the sense of the Jews as the root to all the branches. When the complex dynamic of salvation will have worked itself out, the Jews in their entirety will be saved. The patriarchs are invoked yet once again, but in an entirely new way:

Judged by their response to the gospel, they are God's enemies for your sake. But judged by his choice, they are dear to him for the sake of the patriarchs, for the gracious gifts of God and his calling are irrevocable.[36]

Notable here is a shift from partial salvation of the Jews to the salvation of the entirety of the Jewish people and a further shift from the Jews as the disadvantaged offspring of the patriarchs to the offspring whom God will recognize and reward.

At the close of this survey of Pauline positions on the trajectory of Jewish history, we might well feel more than a bit confused, since Paul seems to present a number of alternative views, at least as regards the Jewish past and future. Basic to Paul's views on human history are the diverse options for human relating to God. Paul focuses on two options – the law and faith, with firm insistence on the superiority of the latter. To be sure, there are broad swaths of humanity that have not attained even the level of the law. Paul is clear on this, but does not explore in great detail its implications. Thus, humanity has in fact historically been confronted with three religious possibilities: paganism, subservience to the law, and the freedom that comes with faith. These historical options are hierarchical in nature, with paganism at the low end of the hierarchy and service through faith at the highest end.

Related to these three options are three human communities. Again, Paul is focused heavily on two – the Jews who have remained subservient to the law and the faithful Jews and especially the faithful gentiles who have achieved freedom through their faith. Paul's focus on these two groups leads him to assert regularly the superiority of the latter over the former. In the process, Paul tends to underemphasize the large pagan element in human society. As a result, the superiority of the faithful gentiles to the legalistic Jews is foregrounded, while the superiority of the Jews to their pagan environment – which is certainly implied in his analysis of human religiosity – is regularly underplayed. Thus, the full hierarchy of human communities consists of pagans, law-committed Jews, and faith-imbued Jews and gentiles.

This overarching sense of the divine plan for humanity and of the full hierarchy of human communities leads to fairly clear and consistent criticism on Paul's part of his Jewish contemporaries. Living at the point in time when God had sent Christ and thus had made available the third and highest form of allegiance to the divine, Jews should have come to Paul's own conclusions and embraced this new option. Some Jews, including Jesus' own immediate circle and Paul himself, did so. To be sure, Jesus' immediate followers did not distance themselves sufficiently from subservience to the law, needlessly harassing Paul's gentile followers with demands for observance of the now-superseded legal obligations. As to the Jews of this period, however, the overwhelming majority of them were oblivious to the dawn of the new era and the option of a new and superior form of divine service. For this, they are clearly – in Paul's eyes – culpable, although God himself has caused much of their recalcitrance.

Jews who maintained their fidelity to the rule of law only were in fact failing to grasp the truths embedded by God in the Torah and the utterances of the prophets. As a former Pharisee, Paul was fully aware of the multiple and multifaceted readings that could emerge from immersion in Scripture. Yet his own view was that there was a blatantly obvious truth in Scripture that he grasped and that his Jewish contemporaries missed – the superiority of faith to law. For Paul, this was not a shadowy teaching that had to be ferreted out laboriously; it was perfectly plain and unmistakable. Thus, Paul's Jewish contemporaries are portrayed by him as unambiguously in the wrong as he contemplates them and their actions. Paul expresses no doubts as to the error of his Jewish contemporaries who have chosen to reject Jesus and his message.

Confusion sets in when we move from the Jewish present to the Jewish past and – even more so – the Jewish future. On the one hand, the shortcomings of Paul's Jewish contemporaries are projected deep into the past by Paul and portrayed as grounded in their much earlier history. Paul traces these shortcomings back into the earliest phase of Jewish history, the patriarchal period, suggesting that his Jewish contemporaries were predisposed by God to their eventual inferiority. The inferiority of law-based Judaism was, according to Paul, predetermined by God, although its shortcomings could not fully manifest themselves until the alternative of serving God through faith became a reality through the divine dispensation of Christ. Close examination of the Abraham saga and of the Isaac tale as well laid bare to Paul, in allegorical fashion, God's intention to make the law-obsessed Jews inferior to the faith-imbued adherents of

Jesus. Abraham, Sarah, Hagar, and their offspring are seen by Paul as pre-figuring the contemporary reality of the law-focused Jews and the faith-inspired followers of Christ; the same is true of Isaac, Rebecca, Esau, and Jacob.

At the same time, Paul's implicit acknowledgment of a trifurcated humanity means that for an extensive period of time Israelites and Jews constituted the most admirable element on the human scene, which included only pagans and followers of the law delivered at Sinai. Although Paul by no means emphasizes these implications, they constitute a reality nonetheless and suggest the distinguished role of Israelites/Jews on the historical scene. Beyond these implied positives in Israelite/Jewish history, Paul occasionally points explicitly to the virtues of the Israelites/Jews. Nowhere is this more the case than in his pondering the future trajectory of Jewish history. There he speaks glowingly of God's relationship to the Jews and of their valuable service to God, prior to the onset of the new era initiated by the advent of Christ.

Indeed, it is when Paul moves from the clear realities of the present to the soon-to-be realized full redemption that his view of the trajectory of Jewish history becomes most ambiguous and confusing. On the one hand, he maintains the sense of the superiority of the faith of the followers of Jesus and the inferiority of the Jewish commitment to Moses and the law. At the same time, there is emphasis on the heterogeneity of the Jewish world. Those Jews who – like Paul himself – absorb the true message of revelation and grasp the superiority of faith will of course be saved. Yet Paul eventually allows for the potential of salvation for the entire Jewish world, grounded in his conviction of the ongoing bond between God and the people that he had originally chosen. This last view undercuts his recurrent emphasis on the patriarchal allegories that foretold the miring of the Jews in their legalism and their failure to comprehend the superiority of faith in the divine scheme of things.

Paul's lack of consistency may well be lamentable. Nonetheless, the multiple perspectives he advanced and the rich and evocative imagery he created were fated to exert enormous impact on subsequent Christian thinking about the trajectory of Jewish history and further diversified Christian perspectives on the Jewish past, present, and future. In many ways Paul created a legacy that did incalculable harm to subsequent Jews; in yet other ways, he laid the foundations for many of the positive constructions of Jewish history that we shall encounter in the next two chapters.

Notes

1 There is an enormous and polarized recent literature on Paul. For a general introduction to Paul, see Raymond E. Brown, *An Introduction to the New Testament* (New York: Doubleday, 1996; Anchor Bible Reference Library), 407–680. For helpful reviews of the recent polarized literature, written from different perspectives, see John G. Gager, *Reinventing Paul* (Oxford: Oxford University Press, 2000), Francis Watson, *Paul. Judaism, and the Gentiles* (rev. ed., Grand Rapids: Eerdmans, 2007), and James D. G. Dunn, *The New Perspective on Paul* (rev. ed., Grand Rapids: Eerdmans, 2008). I have found Daniel Boyarin's *A Radical Jew: Paul and the Politics of Identity* (Berkeley: University of California Press, 1994) especially helpful. While all contemporary Paul scholars acknowledge his Jewish roots and style of thinking, Boyarin's mastery of rabbinic literature and thought puts him in a unique position to probe the Jewish depths of Pauline thought.

2 On these authentic letters, see Brown, *An Introduction to the New Testament*, 456–584.

3 This is especially true of Galatians, which is a major source for Paul's views of Judaism and Jews.

4 Gager, *Reinventing Paul*, summarizes the traditional view (the "old Paul") in chapter 1 and some of the newer view (the "new Paul") in chapter 2.

5 On these post-Holocaust concerns, see the Prologue and the Epilogue. This pejorative view of first-century Judaism is the first of the three pillars identified by Jules Isaac as the foundations for Christian teaching of contempt toward Judaism and Jews.

6 Boyarin, *A Radical Jew*, 52. His valuable review of the five new perspectives on Paul can be found on 42–52.

7 Galatians 3:6–7.

8 Genesis 15:6.

9 Romans 4:2–3.

10 Romans 4:9–11.

11 Genesis 12:3 and 18:18.

12 Galatians 3:8–9.

13 Genesis 12:2–3. The emphasis in this verse and the ones to be cited shortly on the greatness of the nation that will descend from Abraham may have resonated with special effect for Paul, the diaspora Jew. Growing up in an environment in which Jews constituted a rather small minority in an overwhelmingly larger gentile population may well have moved Paul to consider in a fresh light the meaning of these predictions of greatness.

14 Genesis 18:17–19.

15 Romans 4:17, citing Genesis 17:5.

16 Genesis 17:4–6.

17 Genesis 17:15–16.

18 Galatians 4:22–26.

19 Genesis 21:12.

20 Romans 9:7–9. The verse cited is Genesis 18:10.

21   This imagery plays throughout subsequent Christian thinking and was espe-
     cially invoked during the Middle Ages.
22   Romans 9:11–13. The verses cited are Genesis 25:23 and Malachi 1:2–3.
     Israel Jacob Yuval uses this episode as the title for his valuable study, *Two
     Nations in Your Womb; Perceptions of Jews and Christians in Late Antiquity
     and the Middle Ages*, trans. Barbara Harshav and Jonathan Chipman
     (Berkeley: University of California Press, 2006).
23   Romans 9:1–3.
24   Romans 9:4–5.
25   Romans 1:21–23.
26   Romans 1:28–31.
27   I hope that the pallid and limited nature of Pauline reflections on the
     Jewish past portrayed in the Acts of the Apostles is more obvious, now
     that we have seen the complexity of his thought reflected in his own
     writings.
28   I am well aware that this creates a sense of pagan–Jewish–Christian human-
     ity that seems to parallel in many ways the subsequent Muslim trifurcation
     of humanity into the realms of idolatry, of the peoples of the book, and of the
     Muslims. The parallel seems to me hardly accidental. To be sure, the trifurca-
     tion in Muslim thinking is far more explicit and has therefore drawn more
     attention. My argument is that Paul's focus on the Jewish-Christian tension
     has tended to obscure the more complex picture of humanity that is in fact
     at the core of his thinking.
29   Romans 10:19, citing Deut. 32:21.
30   Romans 10:20–21, citing Isaiah 65:1–2. Throughout this chapter, Isaiah cas-
     tigates Israel for its failures and promises divine retribution.
31   Romans 11:1.
32   Romans 11:5.
33   Romans 11:14.
34   Romans 11:18.
35   Romans 11:25–27, citing Isaiah 59:20–21 and 27:9.
36   Romans 11:28–29.

3

Eusebius

With Eusebius we pass into a new stage in Christian history and encounter a new kind of Christian intellectual leader. By the onset of the fourth century, Christian communities had become a major force in the Roman Empire. During the early years of Eusebius, who was born shortly after 260, persecution of Christians at the hands of the Roman authorities had come to a virtual halt, and Christian thinkers were using the new and more comfortable circumstances to create vigorously in a range of intellectual spheres. Eusebius's formative years, when his basic perspectives were being shaped, constituted a period of peaceful progress for the Church. To be sure, one last great paroxysm of persecution remained in the opening years of the fourth century, but that frightful episode ended with a Christian emperor on the throne and the Church poised to exercise a power never before possible. By the end of Eusebius's life, the Church in cooperation with Emperor Constantine had begun to define its theology in new ways, in order to eliminate the internal confusion and dissension that had abounded up to that point and to pave the way for augmented outreach to the pagans of the empire. The Church, as Eusebius expired in 339 at the end of a lengthy and active life, was a far cry from the Church into which he had been born. It had enhanced power, a more effective organizational structure, and even greater intellectual dynamism than at the beginning of Eusebius's lifetime.[1]

As the Church matured, so too did its opposition. Jewish objections to Christianity undoubtedly continued and deepened, although we have no direct evidence of these Jewish efforts. This lack of evidence suggests the minimal impact of the Jewish opposition on the increasingly powerful Church. From the pagan side, popular and primitive stereotyping of *opp. to Christ*

Christians gave way to much more serious engagement with Christianity and its truth claims. Toward the end of the third century, as Eusebius was entering his mature years, Porphyry – a serious student of philosophy and Christianity – composed a wide-ranging attack on Christianity in fifteen books. Porphyry's assault included refutations of Christian claims grounded in the Old Testament, independent analysis and critique of the Old Testament, trenchant criticisms of the New Testament, and reconsiderations of Christian history. The challenges posed by Porphyry and others like him were taken very seriously by the leadership of the Church. During the ensuing decades, a number of major intellectual leaders in the Christian community – including Eusebius – expended considerable effort to counter the serious arguments leveled by Porphyry.[2]

Fortunately for the Church, by this time it had produced thinkers with the scholarly expertise and the intellectual acuity to engage the sophisticated argumentation of Porphyry and other serious critics. A number of Christian academic centers had developed throughout the empire, in which libraries were created, schools were established for training young scholars, and major works were composed. One such center was in Caesarea, poised at the eastern end of the Mediterranean basin. Caesarea – founded on the remains of an old Phoenician city and built into a major metropolitan center by Herod the Great – had come to serve as the Roman administrative center for Palestine during the early Christian centuries. As a result, it attracted a large and heterogeneous population, including Jews, Samaritans, Christians, and pagans, who were thrust into significant contact with one another. Caesarea's location on the eastern shore of the Mediterranean Sea and its resultant economic, strategic, and administrative importance made it an increasingly vital urban enclave in the eastern half of the empire. Not surprisingly, it evolved into a major center of Christian life and creativity as well.[3]

Christ support

The key figure in the emergence of Caesarea as a major intellectual center for the evolving Church was Origen. Born in Egypt in 185/186, Origen was blessed with a wealthy and supportive Christian family, which was ruined as a result of the execution of the father by the Roman authorities for the Christian views he held. The support of a wealthy Christian widow enabled Origen to continue his education. For a period of time, Origen became a teacher of grammar and founded a school, eventually abandoning it for the life of an ascetic. In the mid-230s, he settled in Caesarea and established a Christian school there, composing important works that won him renown and setting the circumstances for a thriving intellectual center that would eventually house Eusebius.[4]

Origen's fame was grounded in his biblical studies and his theological speculation. In his biblical studies, he eventually produced the *Hexapla*, the Hebrew Bible presented in six columns – the Hebrew text, a transliteration of the Hebrew into Greek, and then four columns of diverse Greek translations. This scholarly vehicle set the stage for much more sophisticated Christian study of the Hebrew Bible and was widely utilized throughout the eastern half of the Roman Empire. Beyond the creation of this powerful aid to biblical scholarship, Origen immersed himself in the analysis of the biblical text, always insisting on its spiritual meaning. Origen's rich background in Greco-Roman philosophy set the backdrop for important theological speculation, for which he was widely admired – albeit often criticized as well.

The fame of Origen and his school attracted to Caesarea a devout and wealthy Christian named Pamphilus, who seems to have built on the foundation of the book collection of Origen an imposing library, which would further the efforts to make Caesarea a Christian intellectual center in the eastern Mediterranean. Pamphilus served as mentor to the young Eusebius and eventually adopted him. They subsequently worked together on expanding the library and on continuing the heritage of Origen, with Eusebius outliving and outstripping his mentor. Pamphilus's support for the Caesarea library and his direct support for the young Eusebius made the remarkable achievements of the latter possible.

Unlike Origen and Pamphilus, Eusebius served in an active leadership capacity in the evolving Church. He became bishop of Caesarea in 313 and served in this role until his death in 339. As bishop of Caesarea, he was both an administrative and an intellectual leader in the Church. At the important council of Nicaea, convened by Emperor Constantine in 325, Bishop Eusebius was accorded a place of honor next to the emperor himself, testimony to the high esteem in which he was held in his middle sixties. This esteem reflects both his administrative importance and the significance of his intellectual contributions. Eusebius's wide-ranging intellectual contributions included historical scholarship, the writing of a new kind of history, biblical scholarship, and apologetic and polemical writings anchored in his biblical scholarship. The combination of serious scholarship and works designed to strengthen the Church grounded in serious scholarship made Eusebius the special intellectual leader he became. Both his historical writings and his apologetic/polemical works resonated throughout the Christian world and became classics for subsequent generations of Christian thinkers.[5]

Eusebius's historical scholarship involved the compilation of historical tables that listed side by side the great societal groupings in history. Only fragments of this important work survive in the Greek, with lengthier portions extant in Jerome's Latin translation and in an Armenian translation. In response to the allegation that Christianity was a *novum*, a reprehensible innovation of no merit whatsoever, Eusebius's *Chronicon* places Christianity in a web of history that goes far beyond the Hebrew-Judaic and Greco-Roman spheres, carving out for it a role in the history of the entire world as it was then known. This historical scholarship on Eusebius's part created a solid foundation for his *History of the Church*, which constitutes a path-breaking and major statement of Church history, which we shall examine in short order.

In much the same kind of combination, Eusebius was a serious Bible scholar, whose biblical studies paved the way for sophisticated works of Christian apologetics. Eusebius's biblical scholarship was grounded in the prior work of Origen. Origen's *Hexapla* created the foundation for a new stage of Hebrew Bible study for many Christian thinkers in the fourth century, and Eusebius was one of them. He composed extended commentaries on Isaiah and Psalms, which are rich in textual insight. At the same time, the choice of these two books of the Hebrew Bible, which abound in citations that were meaningful to Christian apologetics, was no accident. Eusebius's biblical scholarship set the stage in turn for his great apologetic works – the *Praeparatio Evangelica* and the *Demonstratio Evangelica*. We shall in turn examine both these works at some length for the light they shed on Eusebius's view of the trajectory of Jewish history.

Eusebius insists at the outset of his *History of the Church* that he is creating something new. He asks his readers to pardon the deficiencies of his work and grounds his request in the fact that he is setting out on an innovative path. "I am the first to venture on such a project and to set out on what is indeed a lonely and untrodden path, but I pray that I may have God to guide me and the power of the Lord to assist me."[6] The innovative project that Eusebius intends to pursue is a narrative history of the Church. He notes that earlier Christian thinkers had written about the events of their own time, and he intends to use their materials, "plucking like flowers in literary pastures the helpful contributions of earlier writers."[7] These earlier contributions will, however, no longer be discrete items; they will be embedded in a continuous narrative flow. Eusebius makes explicit mention of his earlier historical scholarship, the

Chronicon. He identifies that work as a "summary of this material," but indicates that he will now proceed further. "In this new work, I am anxious to deal with it [the available material] in the fullest detail."[8] There is of course much more involved in the movement from the *Chronicon* to the *History of the Church*. In the latter, Eusebius is overtly composing a historically grounded apology for Christianity, as he viewed it.

Even before indicating the innovation in his *History of the Church*, Eusebius spells out the issues upon which he will focus. Both the content and the sequencing of these issues are important. He identifies five over-arching themes:

(1) Eusebius intends to begin by clarifying the leadership of the Church over the three centuries of its existence. In his terms, this includes "the lines of succession from the holy apostles...; the out-standing leaders and heroes of that story [the story of the Church] in the most famous Christian communities; the men of each generation who by preaching and writing were ambassadors of the divine word.

(2) The names and dates of those who through a passion for innovation have wandered as far as possible from the truth, proclaiming themselves the founts of knowledge, falsely so called, while mercilessly like savage wolves making havoc of Christ's flock.

(3) The calamities that immediately after their conspiracy against our Savior overwhelmed the entire Jewish race.

(4) The widespread, bitter, and recurrent campaigns launched by unbelievers against the divine message.

(5) The heroism with which – when occasion demanded – men faced torture and death to maintain the fight in its [the divine message's] defense. And the martyrdoms of later days down to my own times."

Eusebius indicates that his narrative will conclude on a happy note: "And at the end of it all, the kind and gracious deliverance accorded by our Savior."[9] Writing the final edition of his history subsequent to Constantine's emergence as sole ruler of the Roman Empire, Eusebius sees in this emergence the hand of God rewarding the genuine leaders of the Church and – especially – its martyrs.

This is a fascinating set of topics for Eusebius's narrative history of the Church. These five topics obviously break down into positive and negative. The positive figures include the genuine leaders of the Church and its martyrs; the negative figures include heretics, Jews, and persecuting

Roman authorities. It is striking that the Jews are no longer projected as the primary negative figures by Eusebius, as they were in the Gospels. Times and circumstances changed from first-century Palestine to the fourth-century Roman Empire. The dangers emanating from Jews have receded markedly, and they have been supplemented in Eusebius's catalogue of enemies by others, specifically heretics and persecuting Roman authorities.

The negative figures accorded the "honor" of being mentioned first and thus projected as key current enemies are the heretics, who in Eusebius's view do terrible damage internally to the Christian faithful.[10] The heretics are accorded pride of place in his list, ostensibly as the most harmful of the enemies of the Church, because they are internal enemies and because they continue to threaten it in serious ways. Eusebius completed the final edition of his history just after the Council of Nicaea, at which Church leadership and the newly supportive emperor met in order to begin to formulate Church doctrine in a way that would distinguish clearly and unequivocally between orthodoxy and heresy. With this definition now available, heretics of both present and past could be readily identified and their harmfulness assessed and combated. The story of the heretics is detailed by Eusebius largely in order to make certain that, under the new and happy circumstances enjoyed by the Church, they could be readily recognized for what they are, and the dangers emanating from them could be reduced or eliminated.

The remaining two negative groupings – the Jews and the persecuting Roman authorities – are both enemies from the past. The hostile Roman authorities were serious foes of the Church. The persecutions they initiated were on occasion horrific, but these persecutions had a paradoxically positive impact. Roman oppression inspired Christian martyrs, who in turn moved God to generate the new and sympathetic regime of Constantine. In this sense, the enmity of the Roman authorities serves a pedagogic purpose. It alerts readers to the workings of history, more specifically to the rewards that flow from Christian willingness for martyrdom, which was triggered by the reprehensible but ultimately useful waves of Roman persecution. Historical reward and punishment, controlled by God, is manifest through the enmity of the Roman authorities, the resultant heroism of the Christian martyrs, and the divine reward bestowed upon the Church of these loyal martyrs.

The Jews as well are no longer enemies of current significance. Their enmity was expressed in days of old, against Jesus and his followers. Jewish enmity was an expression of much the same human tendencies observable in Roman enmity – a commitment to the status quo and a failure to acknowledge new and profound religious truths. Jewish persecution of Jesus was grounded – for Eusebius and most Christian thinkers – in precisely these normal and destructive human tendencies. Once again, the Jewish enmity – like the Roman enmity – was confined to a specific time period and no longer constitutes a danger to the Church. Like Roman enmity, the past and no longer significant Jewish enmity serves a pedagogic function, illustrating once again divine reward and punishment. While the enmity of the Roman authorities and the related heroism of the Christian martyrs highlight divine reward, the enmity of the Jews alerts the reader to the operation of divine punishment in history. What is so striking about Jewish enmity in Eusebius's view was the rapidity and decisiveness of drastic divine punishment, which Eusebius will depict in excruciating detail. Drawing on a wide range of sources, Eusebius describes fully a range of Jewish suffering, all of which was triggered by God's anger over Jewish maltreatment of Jesus and his followers. Eusebius's combination of Roman oppression of the Church and Jewish persecution of Jesus serves to provide examples of both divine reward and divine punishment at work in history.

With his description of the Bar Kokhba rebellion and its suppression in 135, Jews disappear from Eusebius's history. For Eusebius, Jews have fulfilled their pedagogic function with the close of a string of misfortunes that are depicted as divine punishment. What makes this removal of post-135 Jews from the *History of the Church* so striking is that we know that Eusebius lived in Caesarea, which housed a considerable Jewish community in his days, as well as before and after. In fact, Eusebius indicates in his biblical commentaries instances of checking with Jewish scholars for their sense of key Hebrew terms and expressions.[11] Eusebius's familiarity with Caesarea's Jews and Jewish authorities should have alerted him to the reality of ongoing Jewish existence and creativity. His suppression of contemporary Jews reflects clearly the tendentious nature of his history. Organized around the theme of Christian successes and predicated on the assumption that the fates of the Church, anti-Christian Roman authorities, and the Jews all reflect clearly God's control of history, Eusebius introduced historical figures and episodes that reinforced his fundamental assumptions and eliminated those that did not.

What counted for Eusebius in Jewish affairs was not the Jewish present; it was the Jewish past or – more accurately – aspects of the Jewish past.[12] Two features of the Jewish past predominated for Eusebius – Jewish antiquity and Jewish suffering. Let us begin with the former. For

Eusebius, one of the most penetrating criticisms of Christianity involved the prevailing sense in many circles that it was a newly founded religious movement and that its recent origins betray a lack of genuine value. This new religious movement deserved and for a long time received no acknowledgment by the authorities and no respect from serious and thoughtful intellectuals. Eusebius's chronological tables constituted part of his effort to refute the allegation of newness. In his *History of the Church*, Eusebius combated the charge of innovation yet more forcefully. The greater detail of the *History* enabled Eusebius to make his case for the antiquity of Christianity more fully and more forcefully.

Immediately after his introductory remarks, in which he argues the innovativeness of his project and identifies the topics he intends to highlight, Eusebius indicates sensibly and seemingly innocuously that he will begin with a discussion of Christ. "Any man who intends to commit to writing the record of the Church's history is bound to go right back to Christ himself, whose name we are privileged to share, and to start with the beginning of a dispensation more divine than the world realizes."[13] Eusebius proceeds to argue the dual nature of Christ as both divine and human. He opens his argument with Christ's divine nature. "By this means, both the antiquity and the divine character of Christian origins will be demonstrated to those who imagine them to be recent and outlandish, appearing yesterday for the first time."[14] Here, Eusebius lays bare his concern with the anti-Christian allegation of recent origins and mounts his first argument against that allegation. Christians take their name from Christ, whose divine aspect predates everything and *ipso facto* predates every human society and religion. Christianity is hardly a new religious vision; to the contrary, it is the oldest religious vision imaginable, rooted in the deity who represents the hoariest antiquity conceivable.

After making an extended case for the divine nature of Christ, a case rooted in a sequence of stories from the Old Testament, Eusebius advances a second and more terrestrial argument for the ancient origins of Christianity. This more terrestrial case begins with the question of why Christ, as ancient as he is, "was not preached long ago, as he is now, to all men and to every nation."[15] The answer to this question lies, according to Eusebius, with the nature of early humanity. The sinfulness of the first man resulted in his banishment from his original heavenly state. Adam's descendants were far worse than he had been. "City and state, arts and sciences meant nothing to them; laws and statutes, mortality and philosophy were not even names; they lived a nomadic life in the desert like wild and savage creatures; nature's gift of reason and the germs of thought and culture in the human soul were destroyed by the immensity of their deliberate wickedness."[16] These desperate circumstances precluded preaching to these proto-humans the message of the already existent Christ.

Under these daunting circumstances, the best that could be achieved was occasional illumination of a small number of special individuals. "The first-begotten and first-created Wisdom of God, the pre-existent Word himself, in his measureless love for mankind showed himself – now by a vision of angels, now in person – as God's saving power to one or two of God's beloved servants of old, but always, always in human form, since in no other way could he appear to them."[17] While Eusebius does not expand on these instances of occasional divine appearance to special early humans, he is clearly pointing to some of the pre-patriarchal biblical figures such as Enoch and Noah, who populate the biblical narrative and enjoy a special relationship to God.

From these sporadic instances of divine appearance emerged, according to Eusebius, a people fated to play a crucial role in the history of humanity.

When these [the occasional figures illuminated by divine grace] in turn had sown the seeds of true religion in numbers of men, a whole nation, sprung from the ancient Hebrews and devoted to true religion, arose in the world. On these – a mass of men still tied and bound by ancient habits – he bestowed through the prophet Moses images and symbols of a mystical Sabbath and of circumcision and instruction in other spiritual principles, but without actual, open initiation. Their Law became famous and like a fragrant breeze penetrated to every corner of the world. From the Jews, the movement spread and soon the characters of most heathen races began to grow gentler, thanks to the lawgivers and thinkers in every land. Savage and cruel brutality changed to mildness, so that profound peace, friendship, and easy intercourse were enjoyed.[18]

This is a remarkable statement of the virtues and importance of the early Jewish people. While Eusebius generally speaks of this "nation" as Hebrews, in this important passage he speaks of these people as "sprung from the ancient Hebrews" and overtly identifies them as Jews. There is more here than the usual Jewish and Christian encomium to the Israelites/Jews as the first human community to recognize the one true God. According to Eusebius, the Jews did much more. Through their Law, they began a process of educating and humanizing a wide range of societies, in effect preparing humanity for the eventual advent of Jesus. Eusebius's greater awareness of the totality of humanity – reflected in his chronological tables – moved him to enhance the significance of the Israelite/Jewish contribution to human history. While he will subsequently focus heavily

[margin note: Jews prepared world for Jesus]

on past Jewish shortcoming, early on Eusebius highlights the remarkable Jewish impact on the history of the entire world.

The early Jewish contribution went beyond recognizing the divine and humanizing societies far and wide. Moses and the prophets who succeeded him also laid the groundwork for the advent of Jesus in other ways. According to Eusebius, Moses and his fellow-prophets foretold clearly the appearance of the preexistent Christ in human form.

That same teacher of virtue, the Father's minister in all that is good, the divine and heavenly Word of God in a human body that in all essentials shared our own nature, appeared in the early years of the Roman Empire. What he did and what he suffered accorded with the prophecies, which foretold that a man who was God would live in the world as a worker of miracles and would be revealed to all nations as a teacher of the worship that is due the Father. They foretold also the miracle of his birth, the new teaching, and the marvels of his works, and furthermore the manner of his death, his resurrection from the dead, and last of all his restoration to heaven by the power of God.[19]

The Jews brought God into the world, civilized societies of all kinds, and even predicted the next stage in the unfolding of the divine–human drama. Eusebius's accolades for the early Israelites/Jews – congruent with the Pauline teachings we have examined – are unusually extravagant.

The major leaders of Israelite society were singled out by anointing. Since the term Messiah in its Hebrew form (*mashiah*) means "the anointed," Eusebius suggests that the fundamental institutions of Israelite/Judean society were precursors of the ultimate "Anointed One" that would eventually appear. "Thus, it was not only those honored with the high priesthood, anointed with prepared oil for the symbol's sake, who were distinguished among the Hebrews with the name of Christ [i.e., *Mashiah*/Messiah], but the kings too. For they, at the bidding of God, received the chrism from prophets and were thus made Christ in image, in that they too bore in themselves the patterns of the kingly, sovereign authority of the one true Christ, the divine Word that rules over all. Again, some of the prophets themselves by chrism became Christs in pattern, as the records show, so that they all stand in relation to the true Christ, the divine and heavenly Word, who is the sole high priest of the universe, the sole king of all creation, and of prophets the sole arch-prophet of the Father."[20] In its fundamental pattern of cultic and political organization, the ancient Israelite institutions were steeped in and reflected the true faith of Christ, the religion of the ages; these basic Israelite institutions prefigured the leadership elements that would be fully realized in Christ himself.

Eusebius does not want matters misunderstood and proceeds quickly to distinguish between Christ and the early Israelite foreshadowings of him. The prefiguration is only that – it must not be confused with the ultimate reality of Christ's eventual leadership. The key point is that both metaphysically and terrestrially Christianity is the very oldest of religious faiths. The Church may seem like a recent creation, and the name Christian is indeed new, "nevertheless our life and mode of conduct, together with our religious principles, have not been recently invented by us, but from almost the beginning of man were built on the natural concepts of those whom God loved in the distant past, as I shall proceed to show."[21] The roots of Christianity lie in the genuine and ancient religiosity of the Hebrews, "whom God loved." These Hebrews/Jews knew Christ and the faith he promulgated, predicted the eventual advent of Christ, and foreshadowed key elements in his leadership.

When Eusebius turns to the advent of Christ in human form, he becomes immediately a careful, detail-oriented scholar. He begins by specifying the time of this advent by citing two interfacing incidents culled from a variety of reliable sources, most prominently Josephus, cited regularly by Eusebius in the early books of his history. These two incidents are the Roman registration ordered by Quirinius and the related uprising led by Judas the Galilean. The Gospel accounts of the birth of Jesus are thus reinforced for Eusebius by the external evidence provided by Josephus on Quirinius and Judas and can be fully trusted.

After reinforcing the historical reality of the birth of Jesus, Eusebius proceeds to the first of the many instances of fulfillment of biblical prophecy by his advent. The biblical prediction fulfilled according to Eusebius is Jacob's prophecy concerning his son Judah in Genesis 49:10, which speaks of Judah enjoying leadership among the brethren until some given time in the future. Eusebius understands this to mean Judah's exercise of leadership in Jewish society until the advent of Jesus, to whom such leadership properly belongs as the true Christ. He then introduces the historical figure of Herod, whom he identifies as "the first foreigner to be king of the Jewish nation."[22] Eusebius proceeds to depict accurately the succession of Jewish leaders from Moses and Joshua down through the ages to the point of the birth of Jesus. In his view, this lengthy span of Jewish leadership, lasting well over a millennium, came to an end with the accession to power of Herod, whose non-Jewish ancestry Eusebius describes in detail. Thus, with the historical circumstances of his birth Jesus began the process of fulfillment of prior prophecies of his advent.

These prior prophecies linked Christ's advent with a change for the worse in the fate of the Jews.

Herod serves yet a second useful purpose in Eusebius's history. Not only does his accession to power fulfill Jacob's prophecy and thus substantiate the messianic mission of Jesus, but also his cruel efforts to destroy the newborn baby and the punishments inflicted by God for these efforts serve to introduce the theme of human sin and divine punishment, which will loom large in Eusebius's treatment of the first- and second-century Jews. Eusebius expands on the story in Matthew that Herod attempted to slaughter the male babies in Bethlehem in order to eliminate the threat to his power introduced by the birth of a messianic redeemer. This then leads Eusebius to depict the aftermath of these cruel and misguided efforts. "It is worthwhile to recall the price paid by Herod for his crime against Christ and the other babies. Instantly, without the shortest delay, divine justice overtook him while still alive, giving him a foretaste of what awaited him in the next world."[23] Eusebius then quotes Josephus at considerable length on the illness and suffering endured by Herod and on his painful demise. This sorry tale indicates God's imposition of justice upon those who attempt to harm Christ and serves as a useful prelude to what Eusebius will detail with regard to the Jews.

One of the most interesting aspects of the *History of the Church* involves what Eusebius chooses to omit or downplay. With respect to the Jews, the very first interesting omission is the failure to introduce the details of the Crucifixion and the Jewish role in it. Although Eusebius directs considerable attention to the timing of Pilate's appointment by the Roman government as a way of substantiating the Gospel accounts of the Crucifixion, he omits any depiction of the Jewish role in it. It is possible of course that he simply assumed widespread knowledge of the extensive Gospel accounts. It is only in connection with the briefest possible reference to the stoning of Stephen that Eusebius mentions Jewish involvement in persecution of Jesus and his followers. After indicating the filling of the place of Judas among the apostles and the appointment of the seven deacons, he continues: "These [the seven deacons] were headed by Stephen, who was the first after the Lord – almost as soon as he was ordained, as if this was the real purpose of his advancement – to be put to death, stoned by the Lord's murderers."[24] Again, the lack of detail on the stoning of Stephen may reflect a sense that this episode was so well known as to require no elaboration. Although Eusebius may have simply assumed widespread familiarity with the details of the Crucifixion and of the stoning of Stephen, his omission of these details serves to soften somewhat the focus on Jewish guilt.

Almost immediately, Eusebius depicts – again rather briefly – further persecution of the Church by the Jews. "Stephen's martyrdom was followed by the first and greatest persecution by the Jews themselves of the Jerusalem Church. All the disciples except the twelve alone were dispersed about Judea and Samaria. Some, as the inspired record says, traveled as far as Phoenicia, Cyprus, and Antioch; but they could not yet venture to share the message of the faith with gentiles and proclaimed it to Jews alone."[25] The issue of conversion of the gentiles, raised in this passage, quickly comes to the fore, as Eusebius reports – again in remarkably brief terms – Paul's vision that set him on his course as apostle to the gentiles. No clarification of this momentous shift is provided by Eusebius. Put differently, the radical change in the historical role of the Jews is left utterly unexplained.

With this major alteration in the fortunes of the Church and the corresponding change in the fortunes of the Jews, Eusebius turns his attention to the Jews as a reflection of divine justice at work in the world. Like Herod, the Jews – whose guilty actions are not detailed, although arguably fully understood by Eusebius's readers – begin to appear as the sufferers of divine retribution, with much of the extensive detail drawn from two Jewish authors – Philo and Josephus. Eusebius lavishes considerable praise on Philo: "In Gaius's reign, Philo became widely known as one of the greatest scholars, not only among our people, but also among those brought up as pagans. By descent a Hebrew, he could hold his own with any of the occupants of official positions in Alexandria. The constant and conscientious labor that he bestowed on theological and traditional studies is plain for all to see."[26] Philo – well known to and esteemed by both Christians and pagans – serves as the major source for the first set of calamities that beset the Jews.

Eusebius quotes a brief rendition of this persecution by Josephus, but focuses on the far lengthier treatment provided by Philo. "Philo himself, in his historical work *The Mission*, gives us a detailed and precise account of his actions at the time. I shall omit the greater part, quoting only those points that will make abundantly clear to my readers the calamities that befell the Jews so promptly and after so short an interval in consequence of their crimes against Christ."[27] Eusebius, in reporting this sequence of events, opens with two episodes that already took place during the reign of Tiberius and then indicates that these incidents were only a prelude to the more extended persecution suffered under Caligula. To be sure, Caligula's bizarre behavior involved suffering for many elements in Roman society; however, "among the many victims of his numerous outrages the whole Jewish race suffered to a peculiar and extreme degree."[28]

Eusebius insists that this suffering was of course related to the Crucifixion. "His [Philo's] statements are confirmed by Josephus, who similarly points out that the calamities that overtook the whole nation began with the time of Pilate and the crimes against the Savior."[29] As further proof of the role of the Crucifixion in eliciting divine punishment, Eusebius also claims that Pilate himself – despite his exoneration in the Gospel accounts – likewise suffered, "forced to become his own executioner and to punish himself with his own hand. Divine justice, it seems, was not slow to overtake him."[30] Eusebius indicates that he has gleaned this fact from the Greeks, but does not cite a specific source. In any case, divine retribution was – according to Eusebius – delivered rapidly and broadly in the wake of the Crucifixion, with the Jews as the major sufferers.

The anti-Jewish measure introduced by the Roman authorities initiated, according to Eusebius, a vicious cycle that eventuated in the destruction of Jerusalem and the Temple in the year 70. "This same writer [Josephus] shows that in Jerusalem itself a great many other revolts broke out, making it clear that from then on the city and all Judea were in the grip of faction, war, and an endless succession of criminal plots, until the final hour overtook them – the siege under Vespasian. Such was the penalty laid upon the Jews by divine justice for their crimes against Christ."[31] While it might seem that there was a hiatus between the Crucifixion and the Roman conquest of Jerusalem in the year 70, Eusebius claims that in fact the divine punishment was initiated immediately, with the Roman anti-Jewish measures that were enacted at the time of Jesus' crucifixion. These measures, with the pain they inflicted on the Jews and the subsequent turmoil they created in Jewish society, constituted a process of punishment that began in the days of Jesus himself and reached their conclusion under Vespasian. Along the way, there were major incidents that highlighted the process of punishment, such as the tumult in Jerusalem that resulted in the death of 30,000 pilgrims and profound suffering for its Jews.[32]

A specific factor produced the protracted nature of this process of divine punishment, and that was the continued existence of the Church in the city of Jerusalem. Prior to the onset of the final destruction of the city, God warned these faithful to depart. "The members of the Jerusalem Church, by means of an oracle given by revelation to acceptable persons

there, were ordered to leave the city before the war began and to settle
in a town in Peraea called Pella. To Pella those who believed in Christ
migrated from Jerusalem; and, as if holy men had utterly abandoned the
royal metropolis of the Jews and the entire Jewish land, the judgment of
God overtook them [the Jews] for their abominable crimes against Christ
and his apostles, completely blotting out that generation from among
men."[33] Divine justice dictated punishment for the Jews, but in a way
that would inflict no harm on the Christian faithful who had remained in
Jerusalem. The combination of divine justice and divine mercy is reflected
in this double concern.

Eusebius lavishes extended attention on the calamity of the unsuccessful rebellion against Rome of 66–70 and the disasters attendant upon it.
His major source is Josephus, who for rather different reasons focused
attention on the calamity. For Josephus, the horrors of the war and its
conclusion had to be emphasized in order to warn potential Jewish militants against resuming their anti-Roman efforts. For Eusebius, these same
horrors had to be highlighted as God's punishment of the Jews, proving
simultaneously the reality of divine justice in human history and the truth
of Christ and Christianity. For Eusebius, the destruction of Jerusalem and
its temple constituted major evidence of the nature and role of Christ that
he had depicted at the very beginning of his history.

For a sense of the emotional tone of Eusebius's description of Jewish
suffering, let us note the following:

The calamities which at that time overwhelmed the whole nation in every part
of the world; the process by which the inhabitants of Judea were driven to the
limits of disaster; the thousands and thousands of men of every age who together
with women and children perished by the sword, by starvation, and by countless
other forms of death; the number of Jewish cities besieged and the horrors they
endured; especially the terrible and worse than terrible sights that met the eyes of
those who sought refuge in Jerusalem itself as an impregnable fortress; the character of the whole war and the detailed events in all its stages; the last scene of all
when the abomination of desolation announced by the prophets was set up in the
very temple of God, once world renowned, when it underwent utter destruction
and final dissolution by fire – all this anyone who wishes can gather in precise
detail from the pages of Josephus's history.[34]

This anguished description of Jewish suffering was not inspired by
sympathy for the Jewish plight. Rather, it was intended to drive home the
sense of Christ as the preexistent divine reality that took on human form,
Jewish error in failing to acknowledge this cosmic development, Jewish
crime in bringing about Jesus' crucifixion, and extreme divine punishment. Eusebius reinforces this combination of crime and punishment by

immediately noting that Jerusalem was filled with Jewish pilgrims celebrating the Passover holiday. He cites their number as three million, "shut up in Jerusalem as if in a prison." For Eusebius, "it was indeed proper that in the very week in which they had brought the savior and benefactor of mankind, God's Christ, to his Passion, they should be shut up as if in a prison and suffer the destruction that came upon them by the judgment of God."[35]

Although Eusebius sends his readers to Josephus for details on the tragedy/punishment that struck the Jewish people, he in fact embeds long sections from Josephus in his narrative. All these citations emphasize the horrors of the war against Rome and deepen the sense of Jewish suffering/divine punishment. Not surprisingly, Eusebius adds yet one further element, and that is Jesus' predictions of these future events. Now there is Old Testament prediction at work and Jesus' predictions as well. Divine foreknowledge of what was to transpire did not exculpate the Jewish malefactors or eliminate the punishments they had to endure as a result. The Jews had sinned with regard to Jesus and had to pay the price for that sinfulness.

Although there were – as we have seen – prior stages in the punishment of the Jews, the war of 66–70 and the destruction it inflicted represented the crescendo of the accelerating divine punishments. This did not mean, however, that the process of punishment ended in the year 70. "While our Savior's teaching and his Church were flourishing and progressing further every day, the Jewish tragedy was moving through a series of disasters, toward its climax."[36] What Eusebius means by this "climax," we shall address shortly. This series of post-70 disasters begins for Eusebius with the violence that erupted in Egypt in the mid-110s. According to Eusebius, Jews in Egypt once again broke out in rebellion, this time against their Greek fellow-citizens. "Another rebellion broke out and destroyed vast numbers of Jews. In Alexandria and the rest of Egypt and in Cyrene as well, as if inflamed by some terrible spirit of revolt they rushed into a faction fight against their Greek fellow-citizens, raised the temperature to fever heat, and in the following summers started a full-scale war."[37] Although these outbursts in Egypt are in fact quite complex, Eusebius simplifies them into the pattern he has established of Jewish militancy and propensity to violence.[38]

The yet more significant outburst of Jewish violence and resultant suffering/punishment took place in the 130s, with the second Jewish rebellion against Roman rule. This second rebellion had no Josephus to chronicle it and is thus far less well known in its details. Nonetheless, it was clearly a major uprising, necessitated again massive Roman resources to suppress it, and involved heavy casualties and destruction, which Eusebius highlights. "When the Jewish revolt again grew to formidable dimensions, Rufus, governor of Judea, on receiving military reinforcements from the emperor, took merciless advantage of their crazy folly and marched against them, destroying at one stroke unlimited numbers of men, women, and children alike and – as the laws of war permitted – confiscating all their land."[39]

Eusebius concludes this description of what he projects as the last in the series of divine punishments for the Crucifixion by highlighting a crowning indignity, which again serves the purpose of drawing attention simultaneously to Jewish sinfulness and Christian truth. Eusebius ends his brief account of the second rebellion by focusing on Roman prohibition of Jewish entry into Jerusalem, citing a law of Hadrian that "insured that not even from a distance might Jews have a view of their ancestral soil."[40] He proceeds to indicate the resettlement of Jerusalem with a new non-Jewish population and the renaming of the city. As a result of the resettlement, a new gentile Christian population became part of the city and eventuated in the reorganization of a Jerusalem Church, this time a gentile Christian Church, with a first bishop named Mark at its head. In this way, the cycle of divine punishment was – for Eusebius – completed, with Jerusalem at the center. In Jerusalem, the Jews committed their crime, and the transformation of Jerusalem into the gentile city of Aelia – with a new gentile Christian Church – represents the final proof of the sinfulness of the Jews, the truth of Christianity, and the operation of divine justice in the human sphere.

This closing stage of punishment explains – I would suggest – Eusebius's sense of a drama drawing to a climax. This final indignity – Jewish banishment from Jerusalem and the reestablishment of the Church therein – brings the cycle of punishment to a close. It is for this reason, then, that fourth-century Jews do not appear in Eusebius's history. Their saga and significance had, in his view, ended. Although he lived, taught, and wrote in Caesarea, with its Jewish population, and although he himself interacted with Jewish scholars, the meaningful story of the Jews from his perspective had come to a close. Interestingly, Eusebius offers no speculation as to the future of the Jews. Were they simply removed from the divine–human relationship altogether? Were they eventually to be reconciled with God, in the way projected by Paul? All this lies beyond Eusebius's field of interest. For him, the significance of the story of the Jews lies in their early and creative past, their subsequent sinfulness, and their immediate punishment.

Thus, Eusebius's *History of the Church* says nothing of Jewish present and future, focusing only on the Jewish past. For Eusebius, the Jewish past has enormous meaning, in fact a double meaning. On the one hand, the early history of the Jews serves to rebut the damaging allegation that Christianity is an innovation. The early Jews recognized God, humanized savage humanity, and offered prophetic prediction of subsequent events in the history of the Church. Eusebius does not dwell at all on the transition of the Jews from important precursors of Christ and Christianity to their enemies. Their fate as enemies of Christ and Christianity offers great insight into God's imposition of punishment for sin and buttresses the truth of Jesus and the Church he founded. The suffering of the Jews illustrates convincingly for Eusebius the dynamic of human sin and divine punishment; it also proves that Jewish opposition to Jesus was wrong, indeed criminal.

In this sense, then, Eusebius truly composed a *History of the Church*. His history is focused single-mindedly on the Church. To the extent that the Jews served the purposes of the Church, aspects of their history were depicted in detail; beyond that, there was no interest on Eusebius's part in the Jews. For this reason, only the Jewish past appears in the *History of the Church*. Jewish present and future – irrelevant to Church concerns as Eusebius perceived them – were omitted.

The second major front on which Eusebius waged battle against the pagan world was the apologetic. In this arena, he composed a massive work intended to rebuff the criticisms leveled by this pagan world against Christianity and to demonstrate copiously and clearly what he perceived to be the indisputable truths of the Christian faith. Eusebius himself envisioned this massive work as a two-volume effort. He projected the first volume as preparation for the ultimate task of proving the truth of Christianity and devoted it to responses to pagan critiques of Christianity. With this preparatory work in place, the second volume was to proceed to the constructive, to Eusebius's extensive proofs of the truth of Christianity. Following Eusebius himself, the first volume came to be called *Preparation for the Gospel* and the second volume *Demonstration of the Gospel*. The two volumes were viewed and presented by Eusebius himself, however, as one unified work, which he projected as the two-part *Demonstration of the Gospel*.[41] The depth and detail with which Eusebius treats these issues is striking – a tribute partly to the intervening maturation of pagan criticism and Christian response and partly to the scholarship and creativity of Eusebius himself.

Just as Eusebius drew on his serious historical scholarship in compiling the *Chronicon* as the grounding for his *History of the Church*, so too did his immersion in biblical studies serve the purposes of his apologetic composition. Eusebius's biblical studies – to which he was deeply devoted – were closely related to his apologetic concerns and laid much of the foundation for his two-volume *Demonstration of the Gospel*. As both a historian and an apologist, Euseius was successful in combining his scholarly interests with his apologetic writings intended to make the case for Christianity in both historical and theological terms. It is the seriousness of Eusebius's biblical studies that provides the basis for the depth and detail that is so striking in his massive two-volume work of apology.

To be sure, these two enterprises – Eusebius's *History of the Church* and his two-volume *Demonstration of the Gospel* – should not be totally dissociated one from the other. For Eusebius, the historical dimension of religion is crucial, and he advances Christianity's historical achievements as one of the definitive proofs of its truth. This is of course the major argument in Eusebius's *History*, and – although it is less central to the two-volume *Demonstration of the Gospel* – it is there nonetheless. Early on, when speaking of his intention to cite Scripture and to prove "by mathematical demonstrations the unerring truthfulness of those who from the beginning preached to us the work of godliness,"[42] he proceeds to add the importance of the historical sphere within which divine truths are concretized. "Nevertheless, all words are superfluous when the works are more manifest and plain than the words – works which the divine and heavenly power of our Savior distinctly exhibits even now, while preaching good tidings of the divine to all men."[43]

Eusebius's concern with history manifests itself in yet a second way in his apologetic composition. Besides the truth of religion being made manifest in the historical fate of religious communities (which in the *History* meant that Christian truth was manifest from Christian successes and Jewish error was manifest from Jewish suffering), religions have a history *qua* religions, and Eusebius treats the history of a wide range of religious faiths and communities in his two-volume *Demonstration of the Gospel*. Egyptian religion, Greek religion, Roman religion, Hebrew/Jewish religion, and Christian religion are all examined historically, and for Eusebius the histories of these diverse religious communities provide important evidence for assessing their truth claims. The two-volume *Demonstration of the Gospel* is quite different from the *History of the Church* in objectives, structure, and argumentation, but Eusebius the theologian and apologist remains committed to consideration of history throughout.

Eusebius spells out clearly the objectives for his *Preparation for the Gospel*, and these objectives are essentially defensive. Well aware of the increasingly sophisticated arguments leveled against Christianity, he intends to rebut them. The first argument with which he plans to deal involves the claim that Christians are deniers of the traditional religious faiths of civilized societies. In this anti-Christian view, "how can men fail to be in every way impious and atheistical, who have apostatized from these very ancestral gods by whom every nation and every state is sustained? Or what good can they reasonably hope for, who have set themselves at enmity and at war against their preservers and have thrust away their benefactors? For what else are they doing than fighting against the gods?"[44]

Abandoning the long-established gods and customs of all known societies is a major charge against Christianity, but the alternative for which Christians have opted makes this purported sinfulness and apostasy yet more distressing to their critics. "To what kind of punishment would they not justly be subjected, who – deserting the customs of their forefathers – have become zealots for the foreign mythologies of the Jews, who are of evil report among all men?"[45] Abandoning ancestral religion is despicable in and of itself; abandoning ancestral religion for an unthinkable alternative makes matters far worse. Here Judaism and Jews enter the Eusebian picture in a new and different way. It is the Jewish present (absent in the *History of the Church*) that intrudes at this point. Critics of Christianity allege that Christians follow the historical and contemporary path of the Jews, who are – it is widely agreed – "the impious enemies of all nations."[46] Abandoning Greco-Roman religious commitments is heinous enough; subverting them in the name of Judaism makes the shift all the more reprehensible. The negative views of Judaism and Jews abroad in society at large thus become part of the burden that Eusebius bears as he prepares to defend Christianity by rebutting anti-Christian allegations.

In fact, the issue of Judaism and the Jews has not yet been exhausted in this effort to define the objectives of the *Preparation for the Gospel*, for there is a third objective also. Eusebius suggests a third criticism, which is that Christians – while attracted to Judaism and the Jews – in fact break with them as well. He describes non-Christians admonishing Christians for their propensity "not even to adhere to the God who is honored among the Jews according to their customary rites, but to cut out for themselves a new kind of track in a pathless desert, that keeps neither the ways of the Greeks nor those of the Jews."[47] Christians reject their Greco-Roman legacy; they opt instead for the mythologies of the Jews, who constitute a despised people; and then they in fact do not follow the Jewish faith system either. This is a triply damning indictment of Christians by pagan contemporaries.

Eusebius notes that this last criticism resonates among the Jews as well. "Sons of the Hebrews would find fault with us as well, that being strangers and aliens we misuse their books, which do not belong to us at all, and because in an impudent and shameless way – as they would say – we thrust ourselves in and try violently to thrust out the true family and kindred from their own ancestral rights."[48] Eusebius is of course far more concerned with the pagan criticisms than with the Jewish criticisms, but once again contemporary Jews – so strikingly absent from the *History of the Church* – make an early and significant appearance in the *Preparation for the Gospel*, which will extend into the second volume of the work as well. Eusebius must construct a complicated case for Judaism, in order to defuse the criticism of abandonment of Greco-Roman civilization in favor of a despised alternative; he must at the same time construct a critique of Judaism that justifies Christian deviation from its tenets and practices. This is a truly complex undertaking.

Countering the claim that Christians abandon the traditional gods and culture of Greco-Roman civilization is a relatively simple matter for Eusebius, although his treatment is hardly simplistic. He begins by analyzing the fundamental nature of religions and religious societies. He argues that all religions have three dimensions to them; they have a historical/mythological core; they have a scientific/philosophical aspect; and they involve the political life of society as well. In Books I through III of the *Preparation for the Gospel*, Eusebius dissects a number of pagan religious systems – Egyptian, Greek, and Roman – and argues the deficiencies of their historical/mythological foundations and of their scientific/philosophical views. The argument is protracted and very learned, with Eusebius's scholarly proclivities once again highlighted. In Books IV through VI, Eusebius deals with the political dimension of these same pagan religious traditions, again leveling potent criticisms.[49] The overall argument then is that Christians should not be castigated for abandoning the prevailing culture; rather, they should be congratulated for recognizing the deficiencies of this prevailing culture. As Eusebius himself puts it in summary fashion: "It has been proved that our abandonment of the false theology of Greeks and barbarians alike has not been made without reason, but with well-judged and prudent consideration."[50]

Eusebius opens the third section of the *Preparation for the* Gospel –
Books VII through IX – by indicating overtly the transition he was making. "Next as to the Hebrews and their philosophy and religion which we
have preferred above all our ancestral systems, it is time to describe their
mode of life. For since it has been proved that our abandonment of the
false theology of Greeks and barbarians alike has not been made without reason, but with well-judged and prudent consideration, it is now
time to solve the second question [i.e., to rebut the second anti-Christian
allegation] by stating the cause of our claiming a share in the Hebrew
doctrine."[51] The next section of the *Preparation for the Gospel* will be
devoted to the advantages of the Hebrew/Jewish system over that of the
Greco-Roman world.

Immediately, Eusebius intensifies his case in a strikingly unexpected
way. "When therefore we have the necessary leisure, we shall prove
that our borrowing what was profitable from barbarians [i.e., the Jews]
brings no blame on us. For we shall show that the Greeks and even
their renowned philosophers had plagiarized all their philosophic lore
and all that was otherwise of common benefit and profitable for their
social needs from barbarians, but that nothing at all has yet been found
among any of the nations like the boon that has been provided for
us from the Hebrews."[52] Eusebius intends to make a powerful double
case. First, he will argue that borrowing from the Jews – projected as
a criticism by anti-Christian thinkers – makes perfect sense, given the
nobility and utility of Hebrew/Jewish thinking. Second, he will show
that in fact the great thinkers of Greco-Roman civilization themselves
borrowed their most important insights from this same Hebrew/Jewish
tradition. This is high praise indeed for the often maligned Jews and
their traditions.

After recapitulating briefly the shortcomings of humanity he had
detailed in Books I through VI, Eusebius plunges into a full description
of the contrasting greatness of the Hebrews. In his view, the Hebrews
"were the first and sole people who from the very foundation of social
life devoted their thought to rational speculation. Having set themselves
to study reverently the physical laws of the universe, first as to the elements of bodies – earth, water, air, and fire – of which they perceived that
the universe consisted – the sun also and moon and stars, they considered
them not gods, but the works of God.... With these thoughts then and
such as these, the fathers of the Hebrew religion, with purified mind and
clear-sighted eyes of the soul, learned from the grandeur and beauty of
his creatures to worship God, the Creator of all."[53] High praise indeed.

Following in the footsteps of Paul, Eusebius insists that these early Hebrews did all this and found favor in God's eyes without the laws that would eventually be revealed to Moses and promulgated by him. There might well be a temptation to create some kind of disjuncture between the early Hebrews and the later Jews. Such a disjuncture, however, is untenable. Eusebius defines the two terms and his definition involves temporality only. The Hebrews are the descendants of the very early figure Eber, although Jews take their name from the somewhat later patriarchal figure Judah, one of the sons of Jacob. Ultimately, there is a direct line of continuity between the two. The basic argument that Eusebius is addressing at this point in his apologetic is the anti-Christian claim that Christians have abandoned Greco-Roman culture and religion for the reprehensible faith of the Jews. The glowing depiction of the Hebrews is Eusebius's response, which argues that the Hebrew/Jewish faith is in fact the opposite of reprehensible and is superior in every way to the Greco-Roman culture that Christians have abandoned.

Utilizing his identification of the three elements in religion – a historical/mythological core; a scientific/philosophical aspect; and a grasp of politics, Eusebius proceeds to make the case for the Mosaic history as an effective historical foundation for Judaism and for the philosophic sophistication of the Hebrews/Jews. At the beginning of Book VIII, he moves to the third element in all religions – the political – and argues the virtues of the system of law and governance introduced by Moses. With this, Eusebius has – by the early part of Book VIII – completed his case for the grandeur, indeed the superiority of the Hebrew/Jewish system. The anti-Christian criticisms grounded in the sense that Christians abandon a higher civilization for a much lower civilization has been doubly combated: Greco-Roman civilization is by no means a superior civilization, and Judaism is by no means an inferior civilization. Both elements in this criticism are misguided.

At this point, Eusebius strikes off in the new direction that he has already announced. As noted, Eusebius indicated his intention to do more than simply reject the allegation that Christians abandon superior Greco-Roman civilization for inferior Jewish civilization. He announced that he was going to show that the most sophisticated elements in Greco-Roman civilization were borrowed from the Hebrews/Jews. It is to this further claim he proceeds early in Book VIII, after treating rather briefly the political superiority of the Jewish tradition. The first step in this new thrust was to prove that the Greco-Roman world had access to Hebrew/Jewish thinking. Eusebius proves this access by citing through the rest of

Book VIII and the entirety of Book IX an extensive sequence of sources for Greek knowledge of Judaism. To an extent, these sources are Jewish, for example Philo and Josephus; to an extent, they are non-Jewish. Out of this combination emerges Eusebius's case for considerable Greek knowledge of Jewish tradition.

In the ensuing three books, Eusebius makes the case that the Greeks, armed with considerable knowledge of Jewish thinking, adapted that thinking for their own purposes. Perhaps a better way to put this is that Greeks plagiarized Jewish thinking in their most impressive works of philosophy and politics. In Books XI and XII, the focus is upon Plato, whom Eusebius obviously considers the greatest of the Greek thinkers and who is depicted as utterly beholden to the prior thinking of the Jews. Eusebius makes his case in detail, citing Platonic doctrine at great length and adducing Jewish precedents.

The final three books of the *Preparation for the Gospel* focus on Plato and his indebtedness of the Hebrew/Jewish tradition. The closing book is the most striking of all. There, Eusebius introduces Aristotle and attacks his thinking. In effect, Eusebius argues that, on a series of key philosophic issues, the Hebrew/Platonic perspectives are correct, while the Aristotelian perspectives are erroneous. This is the concluding praise offered by Eusebius for the unerring insight and truth of the Hebrew/Jewish tradition. Eusebius has offered the most vigorous rebuttal imaginable to the widespread Greco-Roman negativity toward Judaism and the Jews.

In his *Preparation for the Gospels*, Eusebius mounted major arguments against two of the three anti-Christian allegations that he identifies. What remained is the charge that, while claiming Hebraic/Jewish grounding for Christianity, Christians in fact deviate markedly from the teachings and traditions of the Jews. To this third anti-Christian allegation, Eusebius devotes himself rather briefly at the beginning of the second volume of his apology. Adopting part – but by no means all – of Paul's thinking on the deficiencies of Judaism, he focuses on the divine intention that all societies eventually worship the true God, noting that the Jewish system was oriented toward Jews alone. God had always intended a more universal message, and this is clearly proven from the words of the prophets. "Of course it is clear to you that it was hard enough to follow Moses' rule of life for those who lived around Jerusalem or only inhabited Judea and that it was quite out of the question for the other nations to fulfill it. Hence of course our Lord and Savior, Jesus the son of God, said to his disciples after his resurrection: 'Go and make disciples of all the nations' and added: 'teaching them to observe all things, whatsoever I have commanded you.' "[54] Jesus conveyed a message intended for all of humanity and within the reach of all men and women.

The Jewish system, by limiting Judaism to a small audience of Jewish believers, in fact controverts the teachings of its own authoritative prophetic authorities. In this respect, then, Christians who fulfill the teachings of Jesus are – Eusebius claims – true to the prophets in ways that Jews are not. This is criticism, but it is by no means devastating criticism. The remarkable praise lavished by Eusebius on the early stages of Hebrew/Jewish history is far more impressive than this fairly tepid critique of Jews.

In the remainder of the second volume of his apologetic work, Eusebius turns constructive. In ten books, he argues that the prophets predicted the subsequent fate of Christians and Jews, with remarkable success for the former and disaster for the latter (a reprise of the central thrust of the *History of the Church*). From this starting point, he proceeds to address a large number of Christian theological beliefs and to adduce sequences of biblical verses that undergird these beliefs. The realization of biblical prophecies in the life of Jesus and in his Church is for Eusebius incontrovertible proof of the truth of the Christian belief system.

Eusebius addressed his readers in two alternative formats – the historical and the apologetic, with considerable overlap between the conclusions of his history and his apologies. Jews occupy a major place in both compositions, serving the cause of Christianity in a variety of ways. Eusebius's interest in both his works involves rebuttal of anti-Christian canards, on the one hand, and reinforcement of Christian truths, on the other. He is concerned largely with the Jewish past, although he also points to aspects of the Jewish present as well. The early Jewish past has a remarkably positive aspect to it in both the *History of the Church* and the *Demonstration of the Gospel*. For Eusebius, the Hebrews and their Jewish successors introduced God to a savage humanity, in an unparalleled contribution to human history. All that is good and noble in human history can be traced to the influence of the Hebrews/Jews. In the *Demonstration of the Gospel*, Eusebius makes the yet more audacious claim that all that is praiseworthy in Greco-Roman civilization can be traced to the teachings of the Hebrews/Jews, from which the genuine insights of the Greeks and Romans derive.

Jewish history works for Eusebius in a second and opposite fashion. The errors of the Jews – to which Eusebius devotes considerably less

[handwritten marginal note: Jews are proof of sin & divine punishment]

attention than their truths – led eventually to their persecution of Jesus and his followers, which constituted a monumental crime and called forth immediate and wide-ranging divine punishment. The punishment process began almost simultaneously with the crime itself, reached a crescendo with the destruction of Jerusalem and its temple in the year 70, and continued thereafter, climaxing in the Roman suppression of the second Jewish rebellion in the year 135 and denial to Jews of any contact with Jerusalem. For Eusebius, the tribulations suffered by the Jews serve a double purpose. In a general way, they should convince any objective observer of the operation of the sin–punishment scheme in history. No combination of human sin and divine punishment could be clearer than that offered by the dolorous fate of the Jews. More specifically, Jewish fate at the same time offers proof for the truth of Jesus and his mission. The reality of divine punishment visited upon the Jews, when read backward, implies a drastic sin. The fact that the Jewish role in the Crucifixion was precisely that drastic sin serves to indicate the special place of Jesus in cosmic history. Jewish fate serves as an important index of Christian truth.

Although the focus of Eusebius's interest is the Jewish past, this past leads in the direction of the Jewish present as well. Eusebius faced the difficult task of ennobling the Jewish past, while castigating the Jewish present. To an extent, the Jews of the past did not fully understand or abide by the elevated religious insights and ideals taught to them by their inspired leaders. This failure on the part of the Jewish populace eventually led to catastrophic error in reacting to the divinely predicted and divinely dispatched Messiah. Present-day Jews continue to live with this shortcoming. Beyond this careful denunciation of contemporary Jews is Eusebius's insistence on their circumstances as a defeated and dispersed people, which again serves important Christian purposes. Interestingly, this assessment of defeat and dispersion included no acknowledgment of the reality of a vibrant Jewish community in the very city that Eusebius served as bishop. It was the historical paradigm he projected, not immediate historical realities that absorbed Eusebius. Interestingly, Eusebius expends no energy on ruminating on the Jewish future. Paul did; Eusebius did not.

Above all else, it was the movement of the Church into the larger Greco-Roman ambiance, the drive to win over converts from the pagan populations, the resistance of these pagans to aspects of Christianity, and the usefulness of Judaism and the Jews in meeting this resistance that conditioned Eusebius's complicated ruminations on the Jews.

These ruminations – focused heavily on the Jewish past – identified both virtues and vices in the Jewish past, and both the achievements and the shortcomings very much served Christian purposes, to be sure in complex ways. The rather simplistic sense of direct conflict between Jews and followers of Jesus that is central to the Gospels softened noticeably in Paul. Eusebius, writing under different circumstances than Paul, much advanced the process of complicating the trajectory of Jewish history. The complications introduced by Eusebius deepened the sense of the extremely positive features of the Jewish past, while simultaneously highlighting Jewish failures by emphasizing the dire post-Jesus fate of the Jews.

Notes

1   The literature on Eusebius is vast. For the purposes of this chapter, I have found the following most valuable: Timothy David Barnes, *Eusebius and Constantine* (Cambridge, MA: Harvard University Press, 1981); Jorg Ulrich, *Euseb von Caesarea und die Juden* (Berlin: De Gruyter, 1998); and many of the essays in Harold W. Attridge and Gohei Hata, eds., *Eusebius, Christianity, and Judaism* (Leiden: Brill, 1992).

2   On Porphyry's anti-Christian strictures, see R. Joseph Hoffman, *Porphyry's Against the Christians: The Literary Remains* (Amherst, NY: Prometheus Press, 1994).

3   On Caesarea in late antiquity, see Lee I. Levine, *Caesarea under Roman Rule* (Leiden: Brill, 1975), especially chapters 4 through 7.

4   On Origen, see Henri Crouzel, *Origen* (Sana Francisco: Harper & Row, 1989), and William Lawrence Petersen and Charles Kannengiesser, eds. *Origen of Alexandria: His World and His Legacy* (Notre Dame: University of Notre Dame Press, 1988). On Origen and the Jews, see N. R. M. De Lange, *Origen and the Jews: Studies in Jewish-Christian Relations in Third-Century Palestine* (Cambridge: Cambridge University Press, 1976).

5   Again, see the works cited in n. 1.

6   There are a number of English translations available of the *History of the Church*, which attests to its importance and popularity. I have chosen to cite from the translation of G. A. Williamson because of its clarity and its accessibility – Eusebius, *The History of the Church*, trans. G. A. Williamson, rev. Andrew Louth (London: Penguin Books, 1989: *Penguin Classics*), 2.

7   Ibid.

8   Ibid.

9   Ibid., 1.

10 Both the Hebrew Bible and the New Testament emphasize the overriding importance of internal enemies.

11 Levine, *Caesarea under Roman Rule*, 80–84, and Michael J. Hollerich, *Eusebius of Caesarea's* Commentary on Isaiah (Oxford: Clarendon Press, 1999), 147–148

12 This contrasts markedly with the Gospels, which – as we have seen – are so closely focused on the Jewish present. As noted in the previous chapter, Paul already began the shift toward the awareness of the total trajectory of Jewish history.

13 Eusebius, *History of the Church*, 2.

14 Ibid., 3.

15 Ibid., 7.

16 Ibid.

17 Ibid., 8.

18 Ibid.

19 Ibid., 8–9.

20 Ibid., 11.

21 Ibid., 14–15.

22 Ibid., 18.

23 Ibid., 23.

24 Ibid., 35.

25 Ibid., 37.

26 Ibid., 40.

27 Ibid., 41.

28 Ibid., 42.

29 Ibid.

30 Ibid., 43.

31 Ibid.

32 Ibid., 55.

33 Ibid., 68.

34 Ibid., 68–69.

35 Ibid., 69.

36 Ibid., 105.

37 Ibid.

38 For a recent review of these incidents, see Miriam Pucci Ben Zeev, "The Uprisings in the Jewish Diaspora, 116–117," in *The Cambridge History of Judaism, vol. IV: The Late Roman-Rabbinic Period*, ed. Steven T. Katz (Cambridge: Cambridge University Press, 2006), 93–104.

39 Eusebius, *History of the Church*, 107.

40 Ibid., 108.

41 The first of the two volumes, usually identified as the *Preparation for the Gospel*, is available in its entirety in a French translation; only the first nine books are available in English translation – Eusebius, *Preparation for the Gospel*, trans. Edwin Hamilton Gifford (Oxford: Clarendon Press, 1903). The second of the two volumes, usually identified as *Demonstration of the Gospel*, is available as Eusebius, *The Proof of the Gospel*, trans. W. J. Ferrar (London: SPCK, 1920). When referring to the two-volume work in its entirety, I shall use the designation "the two-volume *Demonstration of the Gospel.*" When focusing specifically on one of the two volumes, I shall use the simple titles *Preparation for the Gospel* or *Demonstration of the Gospel*.

42 Eusebius, *Preparation for the Gospel*, 8.

43 Ibid.

44 Ibid., 5.
45 Ibid., 6.
46 Ibid.
47 Ibid.
48 Ibid.
49 Note the lumping of three books by Eusebius. This pattern will be maintained throughout the *Preparation for the Gospel.*
50 Ibid., 321.
51 Ibid.
52 Ibid.
53 Ibid., 324.
54 Eusebius, *Demonstration of the Gospel,* 19–20.

4

Augustine

Eusebius brimmed with confidence about the future direction of the Church. He was convinced that Constantine represented a decisive turning point in Christian history, both in terms of external imperial threats to the Church and its internal unity. According to Eusebius, with Constantine the emperors of Rome were transformed from persecutors to adherents and supporters, who would not only end prior governmental persecution but also assist in achieving requisite doctrinal uniformity. This high level of confidence is a useful warning against readings of the future advanced by intelligent and learned observers, especially by intelligent and learned historians. Eusebius could hardly have been more misguided. It took centuries for the imperial authorities to solidify their support for the Church. During the fourth century alone, subsequent to the death of Eusebius in 339, emperors with a variety of points of view on Christianity came to power. The most dangerous of all – from the perspective of the Church – was Julian, who ruled from 360 to 363. Born into a Christian family, Julian rejected his Christian upbringing and committed himself to restoring traditional Roman polytheism to its former position of power in the empire. His sudden death on the battlefield averted what might have evolved into a truly serious setback for the Church.[1]

The situation internally was equally problematic. While Eusebius projected hopes that Constantine's support for the Church would obviate the disparate and conflicting theological perspectives that had been rife in the Church for so long (recall Eusebius's own listing of the "heretics," i.e., those with whom he disagreed, as the most pernicious of the Church's foes), in fact the multiplicity of views that had plagued the Church only increased throughout the remaining decades of the fourth

.century. The range of these views was broad, with preachers and schol-ars of all stripes attracting large and committed followings. The Church of Augustine's early years was – if anything – more fractious than the Church of Eusebius's day.[2]

Augustine was born in 354, only fifteen years after the death of Eusebius and shortly before the ascension of Julian to the imperial throne. All through his long and active life, he was witness to the vicis-situdes of power within the Roman Empire. As he matured, there was an accelerating rift between the eastern and western segments of the empire, with the western half – in which he lived – increasingly beset by threats from the "barbarian" populations living on the peripheries of the empire. In 410, the Visigoths sacked the imperial city of Rome, occasioning *inter alia* his writing the *City of God* as a defense against the pagan claim that Christianity had disastrously weakened Roman political and military power. In 430, the year of his death, his own town of Hippo was besieged by the Vandals, a further sign of erosion of governmental power in the western half of the empire.

Augustine's life was influenced yet more deeply by the internal con-flicts within the Christian fold. As a young man, Augustine was subject to a variety of Christian views and influences. Particularly attractive to him were the Manicheans, who insisted that the battle between the forces of good and evil constituted the core of cosmic history and human experi-ence. For Augustine – consumed with his own sense of personal shortcom-ing and guilt and the desire for intellectual consistency – these Manichean views held great emotional appeal and at the same time offered satisfying intellectual clarity. Subsequent to his conversion to the orthodox per-spectives of the Church, Augustine spent much of his enormous intel-lectual energy and power on battling the views of a range of alternative Christian positions, which he saw as both wrong and profoundly harm-ful. Indeed, the role that Augustine came to play as normative theologian for the Church over the ages was based in large measure on the vigor and clarity of his polemical writings. Many of these polemical tracts address the Manichean teachings with which he had wrestled so intensely in his early years, but the Manicheans constituted only one of the many divisive positions he set out to rebut.

There is a striking progression in the data available for the lives of the two Church Fathers treated in this section of the book. Eusebius was an active figure in the Church and a prolific writer. He has left a wide range of works and diverse reactions from his contemporaries. Although the data available for reconstructing the life and thought of Eusebius are considerable, the data available for reconstructing the life and thought of Augustine are overwhelming. Like Eusebius, he was both a serious scholar and a "public intellectual" (to borrow modern terminology). His writings cover the widest possible range – biblical commentary, theological treatises, polemical works, and a curious history that many subsequent observers have seen as his crowning achievement. In addition, he left a voluminous correspondence that reveals a great deal about his era, his contemporaries, and himself. Finally, he penned a remarkable autobiographic memoir, which must be addressed with a good deal of caution, but which introduces readers to a remarkable period, life, and mind. Augustine is known in a depth rarely available for a premodern figure.[3]

As a result of these plentiful data, the literature on Augustine is voluminous. Over the past few decades, two overarching biographies have carved out a position of unusual recognition. The first, that of Peter Brown, was published in 1967.[4] Brown traces the progress of Augustine's life and career in five chronological segments. At the time of its initial publication, it was hailed as authoritative; it has been reprinted regularly, was issued in a new edition in 2000, and has been widely cited. Subsequently, James J. O'Donnell – editor of the most recent version of Augustine's *Confessions* – published in 2005 a second authoritative biography, this one organized somewhat differently.[5] O'Donnell's study, while moving to an extent chronologically, addresses Augustine topically as well. The combination of these two works and innumerable more specialized others provides a sense of Augustine that cannot be matched for any other figure in antiquity.

What then of Augustine and the Jews? Here the data are far less rich. Jewish life in the western half of the Roman Empire during the fourth and fifth centuries is not very well documented. Although we know that there was a vibrant Jewish community in Caesarea in Eusebius's lifetime, before him, and thereafter as well, we are uncertain as to the nature of the fourth- and fifth-century Jewish communities of the Italian peninsula and North Africa, the two settings in which Augustine lived and wrote. Jews do not appear in his *Confessions*, which might suggest their minimal significance in his environment. On the contrary, Jews do appear with some frequency in his letters; he composed a brief but interesting treatise addressed to the issue of the Jews; his *City of God* is extremely rich in reflections on the early history of the Jews; and his polemical *Answer to Faustus a Manichean* abounds in references to Judaism and Jews. Precisely what Jewish life looked like in Augustine's ambiance may not be clear, but his references to Jews are of vital importance, both for their reflection of the late fourth and early fifth centuries and for their impact on subsequent Church perspectives on Judaism and Jews. Modern scholars have come to speak of an "Augustinian synthesis" that set the parameters for Jewish life in the Christian West from late antiquity well down into the modern era.

As a result of the data provided in the writings of Augustine and the widely acknowledged importance of his views on Judaism and Jews, much recent scholarly attention has been lavished on him and these views. Two especially important works deserve mention. The first is Jeremy Cohen's *Living Letters of the Law: Ideas of the Jews in Medieval Christianity.*[6] In Cohen's valuable study, Augustine serves as something of an organizing principle. Cohen's Part One is entitled: "Augustinian Foundations," reflecting the sense just now noted that Augustine set the parameters for subsequent Christian perspectives on Judaism and Jews. Part Two of *Living Letters of the Law* is entitled: "The Augustinian Legacy in the Early Middle Ages, Adaptation, Reinterpretation, Resistance." Augustine disappears from the titles of Parts Three and Four of the Cohen study, but he dominates these sections as well. In Cohen's presentation, Augustine is the opening figure discussed, and his views are core to the entire survey of *Ideas of the Jews in Medieval Christianity.* This is not to say that all subsequent Christian leaders and thinkers accepted the views of Augustine; it does mean, however, that all these subsequent figures began with the Augustinian position, whether accepting it, modifying it, or ultimately rejecting it.

Cohen's analysis of the position of Augustine has opened new perspectives on the bishop of Hippo and his views on Judaism and Jews. At the outset of his treatment of Augustine, Cohen provides a rapid look at the lengthy life of his subject, noting changes that took place in the broad views of a deeply engaged intellectual, grappling seriously and regularly with the issues of his era. With this background, Cohen then proceeds to what he labels "the doctrine of witness," which he dissects both in terms of constituent elements and evolution. Cohen identifies six constituent elements in the Augustinian doctrine vis-à-vis Judaism and Jews:

- "The survival of the Jews, scattered in exile from their land and oppressed into servitude, testifies to their punishment for rejecting (and crucifying) Jesus and to the reward of faithful Christians by contrast."[7] We recall the centrality of this theme already in Eusebius's *History of the Church.*

- "Their blindness and disbelief also fulfill biblical predictions of their repudiation and replacement.
- Carrying and preserving the books of the Old Testament wherever they go, they offer proof to all people that Christians have not ~~forged~~ *faked* biblical prophecies concerning Jesus. ꒐
- The Jews provide such corroborating testimony not only in their books, but also in their continued compliance with biblical law.
- The words of Psalm 59:12, 'Slay them not, lest at any time they forget your law; scatter them in your might,' constitute a prophetic policy statement on the appropriate treatment of Jews in Christendom.
- Hand in hand with Jewish survival, the refutation of Judaism contributes directly to the vindication of Christianity."[8]

This distillation of Augustine's views on Judaism and Jews is invaluable, but Cohen provides yet more. He offers his readers a table of fifteen sources in which Augustine treats the issue of Judaism and Jews, arranges these sources chronologically, and indicates which of the six themes appears in each source.[9] As a guide to Augustine's thinking on Judaism and Jews, this table is of inestimable value. It enables readers to discern chronological development in Augustine's thinking and/or to chart the appearances of any one of the six themes.

Cohen concludes his study by emphasizing the impact of Augustine's retreat from the Manichean dismissal of the physical on his thinking about Jews and Judaism. As we have seen, Paul distinguished between the physicality of the Jews in their religious thinking and the contrasting spirituality of Christians. Precisely how far to take this contrast was an ongoing issue for subsequent Christians. Those who took this contrast to an extreme – like the Manicheans – tended to project Jewish physicality as a decisive and irreversible failing of the Jews and in some cases ended by rejecting Jewish Scripture altogether. Augustine, in breaking with the Manicheans and undertaking protracted polemical confrontation against them, was led ineluctably to a more moderate position on the physical nature of Jewish religion, meaning a more moderate view of Judaism and Jews altogether.

Finally, throughout his treatment of Augustine Cohen insists on the ambiguity and ambivalence of the Augustinian position on Judaism and Jews. In fact, this focus on ambiguity and ambivalence precedes Cohen's treatment of Augustine. Prior to addressing Augustine, Cohen provides a brief but extremely useful introductory statement on Augustine's predecessors, starting with the New Testament and emphasizing the role of

Paul. After adducing the key Pauline texts and their seeming contradictions (which we have noted), he concludes:

Struggling to find consistency in Paul's attitudes regarding the Jews, modern Christian writers continue to debate the ramifications of these texts. Some have discerned a Pauline stratum at the base of Christian anti-Semitism; others have found his idea virtually free of hostility toward Judaism, which they instead attribute to Paul's interpreters. For our purposes, Paul's undeniable ambivalence retains a primary importance, as does his retention of Israel and Israel's relationship to Scripture within the divine economy of salvation.[10]

Cohen highlights this ambivalence throughout his investigation, and it will be important to keep it in mind in the course of this study as well. In fact, we have already seen evidence of this ambivalence in the Synoptic Gospels, Paul, and Eusebius and have suggested that this ambivalence is grounded at least in part in the conflicting aims of Christian use of Jewish history, which is designed to provide a foundation for Christian truth while at the same time explaining how the Jewish heirs of ancient Israel erred and the Christian heirs of ancient Israel have comprehended correctly the true legacy of the Israelite corpus.

More recently, Paula Fredriksen has published a book-length study of Augustine and the Jews, significantly subtitled *A Christian Defense of Jews and Judaism.*[11] Fredriksen does not set out to cover the vast chronological range of *Living Letters of the Law.* What was the opening chapter of the Cohen study is the entire substance of *Augustine and the Jews.* The result is narrower boundaries and greater detail. The entire first section of *Augustine and the Jews* is devoted to depicting the world in which Augustine lived and functioned. It is a superb introduction to the openness, richness, and diversity that was characteristic of the Roman Empire of late antiquity. Of particular importance for our purposes is Fredriksen's emphasis on a world in which Christians, Jews, and pagans regularly interacted with one another. This meant of course that each group might use another for the purposes of constructing a case against a third. In this way, the Jews – who were the smallest of the three groups – could emerge as a regular feature in the polemics between the two larger communities. We have already noted that Jews recurrently served Eusebius as important elements in anti-pagan argumentation – sometimes defensively in apologetics and sometimes offensively in polemics. The same tendencies are clearly reflected in the six central themes identified by Cohen in his study of Augustine.

Part Two of the Fredriksen study is devoted to Augustine's personal evolution. As noted already, the richness of the Augustinian data – both his own writings and the writings of others to and about him – provide a solid evidentiary base for identifying the major lines of development in his lengthy and convoluted life. Fredriksen entitles this section of her book "The Prodigal Son," a heading that focuses attention on the religious vicissitudes of Augustine's life. This section of the study opens with Augustine's flirtations with heresy, especially his Manichean period, and closes with Augustine as "The Biblical Theologian." This closing chapter to Part Two highlights the extent to which the thinker who once dismissed the biblical books for their lack of rhetorical polish came to immerse himself in these books, to master them, and to make them the foundations for his thinking. In the process, Augustine – like Eusebius before him – came to esteem the people of the Hebrew Bible, at least to a significant extent.

Part Three of *Augustine and the Jews* is devoted directly to the issue announced in the title. The first two chapters of this last section of the book focus on Augustine's polemic against the Manicheans, aired especially in his lengthy response to a former Manichean mentor named Faustus. For Fredriksen, Augustine's voluminous *Answer to Faustus a Manichean* is critical to understanding him in general, but is especially important for comprehending his stance on Judaism and Jews. This work dominates the first two chapters of Part Three of Fredriksen's study. The arguments leveled against Faustus involved, above all else, a moderate position on Paul's criticism of Jewish physicality and a heightened commitment to the importance of the Hebrew Bible.

The closing two chapters of *Augustine and the Jews* are devoted to two key biblical images central to Augustine's thinking about Judaism and Jews. These two chapters are entitled "The Mark of Cain" and "'Slay Them Not ...'" Again, for Fredriksen as for many others, Augustine was a profound and deeply committed Bible scholar, and these two images played a key role in his distilling central Christian perspectives on Judaism and Jews. Fredriksen analyzes carefully the development and the meaning of these images for Augustine, eventually emphasizing their positive and protective implications. In this sense, these two closing chapters make the argument for the subtitle of the book, which is *A Christian Defense of Jews and Judaism*. The protective implications of Genesis 4 and Psalms 59:12 lie at the heart of this defense of Jews and Judaism, according to Fredriksen. Given the Augustinian impact on the thinking of subsequent western Christendom, these two passages as interpreted by Augustine thus came to play a key role in the subsequent history of the Jews in the Western world.

Like Cohen, Fredriksen likewise leaves us with some important methodological observations. The first has to do with the chronology of Augustine's writing and thus the evolution of Augustinian thinking. Fredriksen notes that the sequence of Augustine's literary corpus is fairly well established, thanks largely to the *Retractions* he composed very late in life, which provides the basis for dating his major literary works. On the contrary, the traditional dating of Augustine's letters and sermons is very much in flux, given the importance of some striking new finds. This methodological issue is surely crucial for the kind of analysis conducted by Fredriksen. However, since such analysis of the evolution of Augustine's thinking is well beyond the intention of this study, we will be unaffected by this important issue.

Fredriksen's second methodological caveat has to do with the rhetorical techniques of which Augustine was a master. A former teacher of rhetoric, Augustine was intimately familiar with the well-established techniques of argumentation that had reached a very high level in the Greco-Roman world of late antiquity. For Fredriksen, failure to attend to the use of these techniques can only lead to misinterpretation. "Theological argument in late antiquity, when conducted at the level that we examine it here, occurred in and through highly constructed rhetoric. The author of *Against Faustus* was one of the most brilliant ecclesiastical rhetoricians of his period, or of any other.... We will search our sources in vain, or we will misinterpret them, if we read them to discern how their authors 'really felt' or what they 'really thought' about a given topic or person or group of people."[12] This observation, taken in conjunction with the observations of Jeremy Cohen and the conclusions we have already reached on some of the pre-Augustinian writings as to the fundamental ambivalence of Christianity and Christians vis-à-vis Judaism and Jews, will serve as a warning against excessive concretization of findings regarding Augustine's constructions of Jewish present, past, and future.

Because Fredriksen focuses heavily on two biblical passages – Genesis 4 and Psalms 59:12 – I would add a third methodological consideration as well. Both biblical images are potent and highly ambiguous in their own right. Fredriksen accurately notes the protective element in the mark of Cain. In the face of Cain's fears of being murdered during the course of his wanderings, God provides a sign that will protect him. Thus, the ultimate outcome of the sign is protective. However, it cannot be forgotten by anyone who invokes the mark of Cain that the biblical figure provided with this mark is a fratricide and that the mark is intended to protect him in the course of the wanderings to which he has been consigned as punishment. Thus, invocation of the mark of Cain by Augustine or anyone else is inherently ambiguous and ambivalent. In the Christian context, the invocation of Cain has added resonance, reminding Christians of the Jewish role in the crucifixion of their fellow-Jew, Jesus. Thus, the sign provides protection to be sure, but involves profound condemnation at the same time.

This same ambiguity and ambivalence pervades Psalm 59. The author of the psalm is a figure surrounded by enemies who seek to murder him. The heading suggests David as this figure, "when Saul sent men to watch his house in order to put him to death."[13] Whoever the author might have been, he describes his circumstances movingly in the opening verses of the psalm.

> Save me from my enemies, O my God;
> Secure me against my assailants.
> Save me from evildoers;
> Deliver me from murderers.
> For see, they lie in wait for me;
> Fierce men plot against me
> For no offense of mine,
> For no transgression, O Lord;
> For no guilt of mine
> Do they rush to array themselves against me.[14]

For any reader, the request that these figures not be killed would necessarily be seen against the backdrop of these opening verses, which suggest that those whom the psalmist wishes to save from death are utterly reprehensible. Once again, these verses have special resonance for Christian readers, upon whom the imagery of a guiltless victim being done to death by despicable enemies could conjure up only one guiltless victim and one set of despicable enemies. Thus, both sets of protective biblical images are themselves deeply ambivalent, urging protection for people deserving of drastic divine punishment.

Given the multiplicity of Augustinian sources that include references to Judaism and Jews, how might our present investigation of constructions of Jewish past, present, and future best proceed? I have opted to divide the Augustinian sources into three groupings. The first will be materials that might reflect actual direct engagement with Jews, namely, Augustine's polemic/sermon concerning the Jews and Judaism. I will look especially for references to the Jewish present in these materials, although discussion of the Jewish past and future will of course be relevant as well. The second source I shall address is Augustine's monumental *City of God*. Composed largely in rebuttal to pagan argumentation, although certainly meaningful to an orthodox Christian readership as well, the *City of God* is extremely rich in observations on the Jewish past.

The final source considered will be Augustine's *In Answer to Faustus a Manichean*. Both Cohen and Fredriksen emphasize the importance of this source for understanding Augustine in general and his position on Judaism and Jews in particular. For the present study, the polemic against Manichaeism breaks new ground. To this point, we have engaged materials that either related directly to Jews as opponents or to pagans as third parties for whom invocation of the Jews might be useful. Eusebius's *History of the Church* and *Demonstration of the Gospel* surely fall into the latter category. Now, for the first time, we shall encounter a Christian text composed for "heretics," in which Judaism and Jews play a useful role. In the *Answer to Faustus a Manichean*, Augustine focuses on the Jewish past, adducing it as an important element in his polemic. Thus, the tripartite division involves largely the audience engaged by the Augustinian writings, although the potential audience is always fluid to a significant extent. Not surprisingly, it is likely that the most extensive Augustinian observations – like those of Eusebius – will have to do with the Jewish past, with lesser attention accorded to Jewish present and Jewish future.

Augustine's treatise *In Answer to the Jews* was written late in life and reflects his mature thinking. It raises all the problematic issues normally encountered in polemical/apologetic works. The intended audience for such works is always difficult to assess. Are they addressed to the opposing side in an effort to convince adherents of the other side to convert, or are they intended to buttress the faith of the author's community by exposing the alleged shortcomings of the alternative group? In the case of Augustine's *In Answer to the Jews*, the problem is exacerbated by the rhetorical skills emphasized by Fredriksen. As a highly skilled writer, Augustine makes it unusually difficult to be certain of his intended audience.

Augustine opens and closes his work with extensive reference to Paul, who was of decisive significance to Augustine at the key turning point in his life. In the section of his *Confessions* in which he depicts movingly his acceptance of the Church, after protracted and painful struggle, the epistles of Paul played a decisive role. At the crisis moment in his process of conversion, when he thought he heard a child's voice urging him to "take it and read," he rushed from the garden where he had been weeping into the adjacent house and picked up a book, which contained the Pauline epistles. He opened the book at random, and read from Romans 13:13: "Let us behave with decency as befits the day: No drunken orgies, no debauchery or vice, no quarrels or jealousies. Let Christ Jesus himself be the armor you wear; give your unspiritual nature no opportunity to satisfy your desires." The appropriateness of this verse to his circumstances completed the process of his transformation, in which he saw the hand of God at work.[15] It is thus hardly surprising that on most issues – including Judaism and Jews – Augustine was deeply influenced by Paul.

Augustine's view of the Jewish present, past, and future is profoundly Pauline. He emphasizes at both the beginning and end of *In Answer to the Jews* Paul's image of the olive tree. This immediately introduces the notion of an early and distinguished Jewish role in the covenantal relationship with God, the disruption of this relationship "on account of their [the Jews'] unbelief,"[16] the grafting of wild olive branches onto the olive tree in place of the Jews, and the future regrafting of the Jewish branches back onto the tree. This image is obviously intended to reinforce the gentile Christian community that Augustine led in its sense of religious rectitude, although one of Augustine's major concern – like Paul's – is the potential for dangerous pride. At the same time, this image also includes the conviction of eventual repentance on the part of Jews and their reintegration into the covenant.

Proper faith, according to Paul and Augustine, is not a permanent achievement. The Jews lost their way and thus their place in the covenant; Christians should not indulge themselves in pride over this failure and loss, since they too are faced with the ongoing challenge of maintaining proper faith. Christians who fall into error will lose their place in the divine-human covenant, as did the Jews. Conversely, Jews who recognize their errors and repent will return to their honored position. As someone who had struggled heroically to find his own way, Augustine was keenly sensitive to the ongoing battle for proper religious faith. He saw the positive potential of this struggle – sinners like himself and the Jews always have the potential for reaching true faith and gaining divine blessing. At the same time, Christians – who enjoy membership in the true faith community – always face the danger of misunderstanding their faith and losing their way, as in the past the Jews had done. Thus, ongoing sympathy toward the Jews and continued preaching to them is a Christian obligation. Fulfillment of this obligation involves full

[handwritten margin note: faith of the covenant can be lost – look at the Jews!]

invocation of the Pauline perspective on Jewish past, present, and future – past Jewish greatness, subsequent and current error, eventual return. The key to effective Christian preaching lies in acknowledging the past period of Jewish greatness, that is to say the biblical legacy bequeathed to contemporary Jews by ancient Israel. The Jews are blessed with this legacy, although they err in comprehending it. This biblical legacy must be fully grasped by Christians and utilized in addressing the Jews. In their outreach to Jews, sympathetic Christians must also acquaint themselves with the central thrusts of contemporary Jewish resistance. In order to counter this resistance, Christians must begin by identifying it and then rebutting it. The reward for this effort will be advancing the eventual reconciliation of Jews with their God, of which Paul was convinced. Although the ultimate reconciliation lies in the hands of God, Christians bear the responsibility for doing their part in the present to begin the process. To be sure, identifying biblical sources of Christian truth and rebutting Jewish objections simultaneously serve the Christian community as well, strengthening Christian belief and eliminating potential doubts. It is for this reason that it becomes so difficult – perhaps even impossible – to assess the audience for a treatise like *In Answer to the Jews*, since it aspires to offer utility to both Jews and Christians.

[handwritten margin note: Jews will be reconciled eventually but Christians must help]

Augustine begins his treatise by invoking the Pauline imagery of Jewish past, present, and future, indicating that Jews – when confronted with this Pauline imagery – perhaps not surprisingly reject it. "When these Scriptural words are quoted to the Jews, they scorn the Gospel and the Apostle."[17] Augustine's anticipation that Jews might accept the Pauline perspective seems a bit strange at first blush. Why should Jews react positively to Christian Scripture, which they do not acknowledge? However, because of his understanding of Paul as a learned Jew – assigned a special task as apostle to the gentiles but nonetheless still faithful to his Jewish identity, Augustine can make the unusual suggestion of beginning with Paul, whom Jews will immediately reject.

For Augustine, the grounds for this rejection are crucial. He argues that "they [the Jews] do not understand what they read."[18] What he means is that, if Jews were to understand their own Scripture properly (as their coreligionist Paul did), they would realize that the truths proclaimed in the Gospels and Paul are in fact the truths taught in the Hebrew Bible. The key to addressing fourth-century Jews lies in the greatness of the Jewish past, that is in the legacy of biblical Israel, which Paul understood accurately and which these Jews must be brought to understand properly as well.

The very first biblical prophecy cited by Augustine involves the spread of Israelite truth in its Christian version throughout the world. "Certainly, if they understood what the prophet – whom they read – is foretelling: 'I have given you to be light of the gentiles, that you may be my salvation to the farthest part of the earth,' they would not be so blind and so sick as not to recognize in Jesus Christ both light and salvation."[19] Augustine, born and raised far from the Land of Israel and fully cognizant of the spread of Christianity far and wide, sees this as the most obvious reality that was predicted by the prophets of Israel and fulfilled by gentile Christianity and thus a solid starting point for addressing Jews. Jews should be in a position to grasp the relationship between this prophetic prediction and contemporary reality. They read the prophetic literature assiduously; the reality should be readily grasped by any objective observer. Jewish failure to connect the prediction and its fulfillment leads to Augustine's introduction of imagery of blindness and sickness, for only such blindness and sickness can explain – for Augustine – the Jewish failure to grasp the obvious relationship between prophetic prediction of the spread of divine truth and the current successes of gentile Christianity.

Augustine cites yet another biblical prediction of the spread of divine truth, namely Psalms 19:5: "Their voice carries throughout the earth; their words to the end of the world." Here too Augustine sees an unequivocal prediction of the spread of divine truth, with which Jews are intimately familiar and which they ought to connect with the emergence and spread of gentile Christianity. "Consequently, testimonies are to be selected from sacred Scripture, which has great authority among the Jews. If they do not want to be cured by means of this advantage offered them, they can at least be convicted by its evident truth."[20] Augustine seems to urge Christians to confront Jews with what he views as simple and obvious empirical truth in hopes of breaking Jewish resistance. Eschewing complex theological issues like the role and nature of Jesus, he chooses to focus at the outset on the successful spread of the Christian message, which – he believed – could not be denied.

Augustine begins with the combination of biblical prediction and contemporary reality, which should readily convince Jews of Christian truth. Since it does not, he proceeds quickly to identify the points of Jewish resistance. "First of all, however, this error of theirs must be refuted – that the books of the Old Testament do not concern us at all, because we observe the new sacraments and no longer preserve the old. For they say to us: 'What is the reading of the law and prophets doing among you who do not want to follow the precepts contained in them?' "[21] This is

1st concern

a concern we have already encountered in Eusebius. For Augustine, this issue makes perfect sense as the next step in the progression of his argument. Since he began with the correspondence between prophetic prediction and the fourth-century reality of the spread of gentile Christianity, Jewish objections that Christians are not related to the biblical corpus and its predictions must be combated. Making the Christian argument to the Jews requires refutation of this Jewish claim. However, at the same time, one cannot help but feel that this is an apologetic statement intended equally for Christian readers. In any case, Augustine has a ready answer for this Jewish objection, and his answer points to the past, but also very much to the Jewish and Christian present. For Augustine – again as for Paul – a new era had dawned with the advent of Jesus, an era in which the physical gave way to the spiritual and physical fulfillment of the precepts of the Hebrew Bible gave way to their spiritualization.

Augustine identifies a number of such precepts and explicates their spiritualization. "It would take too long, however, to dispute these charges one by one – how we are circumcised by putting off the old man and not in despoiling our natural body; how their abstinence from certain foods of animals corresponds to our mortification in habits and morals; how we present our bodies as a living sacrifice, holy and pleasing to God before whom we intelligently pour forth our souls in holy desires, instead of blood; how we are cleansed from iniquity by the blood of Christ as the immaculate lamb.... It was necessary indeed that all things be fulfilled in him who came to fulfill, not destroy the law or the prophets."[22] Although Jews perceive Christians to be deviating from the demands of the law, they do not understand that Jesus did not destroy any aspect of the law; rather, he fulfilled the law by leading to its highest fulfillment, that is to say its spiritualization. This is fully Pauline and – at the same time – reminiscent of the Platonic sense of ascent from the material to the spiritual, which would be understandable and appealing to Greco-Roman thinking.

Thus, the Jewish present portrayed by Augustine is one in which the Jews are afflicted by an ongoing incapacity to rise above material fulfillment of the dictates of biblical law. Such material fulfillment of the law was appropriate to the pre-Jesus period of Jewish history, but a new period has dawned, in which the spiritual meaning of the law has superseded its physical observance. For Augustine, it was not sufficient to assert this sequencing, even to assert it in the name of Paul. Rather, in order for this assertion to be effective with Jews, it had to be grounded in the Hebrew Bible itself. Here, the biblical scholar in Augustine emerges.

He proceeds to identify three important psalms that – in his view – predict the change he is suggesting. The three are Psalms 44, 69, and 80, with the enigmatic Hebrew term *shoshanim* found in the heading of all three.[23] For Augustine, the root of the term is the Hebrew verb *sh-n-h*, which means to change. Augustine proceeds through each of the psalms and argues their Christological meaning. For Augustine, Christ is obviously indicated in these psalms, with the clear implication that he would initiate religious change. The change predicted in these psalms is the spiritualization of the material elements in the law, as Paul had argued.

There is yet a second Jewish objection that – Augustine urges – must be identified and rebutted. This second objection – like the first – has to do with the relationship of Christians and Christianity to the legacy of biblical Israel. This second Jewish objection focuses on the meaning of the term "Israel" in the biblical corpus. According to Augustine, Jews respond to the Christian citation of verses about Israel as follows: "When the Jews hear the following words from the psalm, they answer with their heads held high: 'We are they; the psalm is about us; it is said to us. We are Israel, the people of God; we recognized ourselves in the word of the speaker.' "[24] For Jews, the designation "Israel" is reserved for them, and Christians have no right to see themselves reflected in the term and in the promises associated with it.

For Augustine, rebutting this Jewish objection is as simple as countering the prior Jewish claim. In fact, the rebuttal follows along the very same lines. Once again, the Jewish objection is founded upon the now outmoded Jewish materialism to which Paul had pointed. "We know of course the spiritual Israel about which the apostle says: 'And whoever follows this rule – peace and mercy upon them, even upon the Israel of God.'[25] The Israel, however, about which the apostle says: 'Behold Israel according to the flesh'[26] we know to be the natural Israel. But the Jews do not grasp this meaning, and as a result they prove themselves indisputably natural."[27] Once again, the Jewish disability is the failure to see things in any other than limited physical terms.

As with the prior Jewish resistance, here too the rebuttal lies in objective reality that the Jews cannot deny – the objective reality of the spread of Christianity throughout the world. Turning as it were to Jews, Augustine asks: "And so you belong to that people whom the God of gods has called from the rising of the sun to the going down thereof?" His answer to this rhetorical question is obviously negative. Jews have not been called from the rising of the sun to its setting. Jewish circumstances are in fact the opposite. "Were you not brought from Egypt to the land of Canaan? Not from there were you called from the rising of the sun to its setting; rather, from there you were dispersed from the rising of the sun to its setting."[28] Augustine adds a sequence of verses that – in his view – cannot possibly be seen as predictive of the spread of Judaism, but can readily be applied to the rapidly expanding Church. According to Augustine, the term "Israel" in a spiritual sense can and must be applied to Christians, who have obviously fulfilled predictions made for the future of Israel.

What Augustine set out to do was to augment the Pauline case primarily in one way, which involved the fourth-century present – both Christian and Jewish. The obvious successes of Christianity and the equally obvious failures of the Jews constituted objective evidence for the accession of the former to the mantle of the latter. Fourth-century Jews were wrong in clinging to their no-longer-appropriate understanding of the biblical corpus. Christians believed that biblical prediction was fulfilled in Jesus, and Jews disagreed. For Augustine, solving this disagreement could be readily achieved by shifting the argument from Jesus to the Church and showing that biblical prediction had been fulfilled by the successes of the followers of Jesus. In Augustine's view, this was a claim to which Jews had no choice but to assent, since the predictions were clear, and the empirical evidence of Christian success was overwhelming.

In his monumental *City of God*, Augustine rewrote the history of Rome and of Christianity. Stung by the suggestion that the sack of Rome in 410 had been occasioned by its embrace of Christianity, Augustine devoted the first five books of the *City of God* to the history of Rome, with the argument that worship of the gods – instead of the one true God – lay at the core of the failed experience of that earthly city. Embedded within this lengthy history of Rome is a brief but intriguing comparison of the Roman experience with the saga of the Jews, which comes at the close of Book IV. This capsule history of the Jews is intended to highlight through contrast all the negatives associated with Rome. According to Augustine, "those earthly blessings – the sole object of breathless desire for those who can imagine nothing better – are dependent on the power of the one God, not on that of the many false gods, whom the Romans believed they ought to worship."[29] In order to prove his point, Augustine then offers the contrasting portrait of Israel, whose people worshipped the one true God and whom the one true God blessed.

Augustine highlights God's consistent intervention on behalf of the Israelites. He focuses heavily on the Egypt experience and the exodus, citing God's rapid increase of the Israelite population, the succoring of the young in the face of Egyptian persecution, the miraculous signs and wonders produced against the Egyptians, the parting of the Red Sea, the manna in the wilderness, and the provision of water for the thirsty wanderers. Subsequently, the Jews were successful in their wars and in their peacetime pursuits as well. All this was achieved through appeal to the one true God who rules the universe. "In fact, the Israelites received from the one true God all the blessings for which the Romans thought it necessary to pray to all the host of false gods, and they received them [these blessings] in a far happier manner."[30]

This telling contrast of Jews and Romans – useful for Augustine's immediate purposes – could not be allowed to stand unmitigated. There remained the Christian conviction of divine rejection of the Jews, which had to be introduced into the picture as well. Augustine's complication of the portrait of Jewish felicity follows along lines already noted. "If they [the Jews] had not sinned against God by turning aside to the worship of strange gods and of idols, seduced by impious superstition as if by magic arts, if they had not finally sinned by putting Christ to death, they would have continued in possession of the same realm, a realm exceeding others in happiness, if not in extent."[31] Augustine introduces positive elements in the Jewish past and then depicts the Jews as forfeiting their blessings through abandonment of the God whom they had been the first of humans to recognize.

In Books XVI through XVIII of the *City of God* Augustine provides a far lengthier account of the Jewish past. This account is rich and dense, drawing extensively upon the entire biblical corpus; it begins with Abraham and continues the story down through the time of Christ. The basic notion of Jewish virtue ultimately undone by Jewish sin remains in place, but Augustine complicates the picture considerably. The roots of this complexity can be noted already in the passage from Book IV of the *City of God* just now cited. There, the blessedness of the Jews is depicted in distinctly earthly terms. To recall Augustine's central point, if the Jews had not erred, "they would have continued in possession of the same realm [the land of Israel], a realm exceeding others in happiness, if not in extent." Although this statement serves the purpose of highlighting the distinction between the Jews and the Romans, it still leaves the Jews as distinguished citizens of the merely earthly city. Thus, the Jewish shortcomings were ultimately twofold. The first and more obvious was deviation from their original religious insights; the second and equally telling was their failure to achieve full understanding of these religious insights, their inability to comprehend the true spiritual nature of religious life and beatitude. Here of course Augustine was, in one sense, merely restating the Pauline sense of the Jews as physical or carnal Israel, which is prominent in his *In Answer to the Jews*. Given the majestic edifice constructed in the *City of God*, however, it is unfair to speak of a mere restatement of prior notions. Augustine amplifies many traditional notions by embedding them in the context of his analysis of the two cities.

The narrative history of biblical Israel and the overt prophecies contained therein must, according to Augustine, be understood on a number of levels. Augustine is explicit in Book XVII of the *City of God* about the nature and interpretation of biblical prophecy. For him, biblical prophecy operates at three different levels. They are in part intended to delineate the future of the physical people of Israel, which we have already seen to be the Jewish earthly city, felicitous but limited and ultimately unsuccessful; they at the same time are intended to clarify the fate of the spiritual people of Israel, that is to say the Church; finally, biblical prophecies on occasion can refer simultaneously to both. Augustine makes this important point early in Book XVII.

Now, the divine oracles given to Abraham, Isaac, and Jacob, and all the other prophetic signs or words found in previous sacred writings, refer partly to the nation physically derived from Abraham, but partly to those descendants of his in whom all nations are blessed as co-heirs of Christ through the new covenant, so as to obtain possession of eternal life and the kingdom of heaven. The same is true of the rest of the prophecies, from this period of the kings.[32] Thus the prophecies refer in part to the maidservant whose children are born into slavery, that is the earthly Jerusalem, who is in slavery, as are also her sons;[33] but in part they refer to the free City of God, the true Jerusalem, eternal in heaven, whose sons are men who live according to God's will in their pilgrimage on earth. There are, however, some prophecies that are understood as referring to both – literally to the bondmaid, symbolically to the free woman.[34]

Augustine proceeds immediately to indicate that these three referents can be identified in more than prophecies only. They are to be discerned in the biblical narrative as well. Speaking a bit further on of the third group of prophecies, those that have a double referent, Augustine goes on to say:

Now this class of prophecy, in which there is a compounding and commingling, as it were, of both references, is of the greatest importance in the ancient canonical books, which contain historical narratives; and it has exercised and still exercises the wits of those who examine the sacred literature. And so, when we read of prophecy and fulfillment in the story of Abraham's physical descendants, we also look for an allegorical meaning which is to be fulfilled in those descended from Abraham in respect of faith.[35]

In fact, Augustine makes this point with respect to the biblical narrative even earlier in Book XVII, prior to his establishment of the triple-referent system in all its fullness. At the very beginning of Book XVII, Augustine says the following:

The scriptural narrative itself gives an account of the succession of kings and their achievements and the events of their reigns; and yet a careful examination of the narrative, with the help of God's spirit, reveals it to be more concerned – or at least not less concerned – with foretelling the future than with recording the past.[36]

Thus, it is incumbent upon Augustine to parse the history of Israel in order to illuminate the evolution of the City of God. The history of Israel as recounted in Scripture can and must be seen as moving along parallel tracks. It is, on the one hand, the story of an especially successful earthly city (much more successful – according to Augustine – than Rome), eventually undone to be sure; it is, on the other hand, the saga of the heavenly city, realized in those special Jews and gentiles who plumbed the depths of the divine message.

Indeed, the lengthy passage cited, which describes the three levels of biblical prophecy, is suffused with complex readings of key biblical episodes, readings proffered by Augustine in the previous book of the *City of God*. Augustine refers early in the passage to "the nation physically derived from Abraham" and to "those descendants of his [Abraham's] in whom all nations are blessed as co-heirs of Christ through the new covenant, so as to obtain possession of eternal life and the kingdom of heaven."[37] This reference takes us back to Augustine's lengthy recounting of the life of Abraham, with whom "our knowledge of that City [the City of God] becomes clearer and we find more evident promises from God that we now see fulfilled in Christ."[38]

Augustine examines closely all the divine promises to Abraham, distinguishing sharply between those intended for the physical offspring of Abraham and those intended for his spiritual heirs. Critical in this regard is God's opening command/promise to Abraham: "Go forth from your native land and from your father's house to the land I will show you. I will make of you a great nation, and I will bless you; I will make your name great, and you shall be a blessing. I will bless those who bless you and curse him that curses you; and all the families of the earth shall bless themselves by you."[39] For Augustine, this rich command/promise addresses in fact both sets of heirs. The command to leave Mesopotamia and journey to Canaan is addressed to the physical Israel; the promise of universal blessing is addressed to the spiritual heirs of Abraham.[40]

A second critical motif in the Abraham story is likewise clearly adumbrated in the lengthy passage quoted earlier. Augustine refers, on the one hand, "to the maidservant whose children are born into slavery, that is the earthly Jerusalem, who is in slavery, as are also her sons" and, on the other, to "the free City of God, the true Jerusalem, eternal in heaven, whose sons are men who live according to God's will in their pilgrimage on earth." This distinction is taken by Augustine from Paul's interpretation of the two wives of Abraham, which we have already encountered. Augustine treats the Pauline reading of this episode as yet another instance of biblical symbolism that must be read on multiple levels, with a focus ultimately on the spiritual.

The biblical story is replete with rich promises to Abraham and Sarah. Abraham is to be made "the father of a multitude of nations." God says: "I will make you exceedingly fertile and make nations of you; and kings shall come forth from you."[41] Sarah also is given parallel promises. "I will bless her so that she gives rise to nations; rulers of peoples shall issue from her."[42] For Augustine, most of these promises involve the spiritual heirs of Abraham and Sarah. "Here are more explicit promises about the calling of the gentiles in Isaac, that is in the son of the promise, in whom grace, rather than nature, is symbolized, because he is promised as the son of an old man and a barren old woman." For Augustine, the overarching motif in this passage is newness.

Newness is the note struck in every detail; and the new covenant is presented, in a veiled manner, in the old. For what is the "Old Testament" but a concealed form of the new? And what is the "New Testament" but the revelation of the old?[43]

Thus, for Augustine – as for Paul – the Jews represent allegorically the continuity of Ishmael, the son of the bondswoman Hagar, while Christianity represents allegorically the legacy of Isaac, the son of the free woman Sarah.

Not at all surprisingly, this dual legacy is reprised in Augustine's treatment of Rebecca's twin children, Esau and Jacob, again a key Pauline theme. Pained by the struggles of the twins in her womb, Rebecca turned to God, who answered her in the following famous terms:

> Two nations are in your womb,
> Two separate peoples shall issue from your body;
> One people shall be mightier than the other,
> And the older shall serve the younger.[44]

For Jews, the meaning of this passage had long been clear. Jacob the younger was to be the progenitor of the Jewish people, while Esau the elder was to sire another people. The reality of Jacob's selection for the maintenance of the covenant was, for Jewish readers, clear from the continuation through his sons, who became in turn fathers of the twelve tribes of Israel.

For Augustine, on the contrary, matters were equally – albeit differently – clear.

As for the statement "The older shall serve the younger," hardly anyone of our people has taken it to mean anything else but that the older people of the Jews was destined to serve the younger people, the Christians.

Augustine does allow for another possible reading.

Now it is true that this prophecy might seem to have been fulfilled in the nation of the Idumeans, which was derived from the elder son (who had two names, being called Esau and also Edom, which is the source of "Idumeans"), for the Idumeans were later to be overcome by the people descended from the younger son, that is by the Israelites.

This possible reading is, however, not the profound reading.

But in fact it is more appropriate to believe that the prophetic statement, "One people shall be mightier than the other, and the older shall serve the younger," was intended to convey some more important meaning. And what can this meaning be except a prophecy that is now being clearly fulfilled in the Jews and the Christians?[45]

Here we see quite clearly Augustine's notion of a double meaning to one prophecy. On one level, the prophecy delivered to Rebecca did involve the physical heirs of Abraham overcoming the Idumeans; on another and deeper level, the prophecy foretold the victory of the spiritual heirs of Abraham over precisely those physical heirs.

I shall bring one last example of Augustine's reinterpretation of the biblical record, in order to show that his readings were not confined to the patriarchal period only. In Book XVI, Augustine followed the history of the City of God through the patriarchal period, down through the sojourn in Egypt and liberation therefrom, and finally into the Holy Land and its conquest. Book XVII moves into the period of the kings of Israel and Judah, with a focus on the prophets of this period and their prophecies. Early in Book XVII, Augustine discusses briefly the disruptions associated with the beginnings of the monarchy, specifically the replacement of Saul with David and of the house of Eli the priest with Samuel.

The City of God thus developed down to the period of the kings, to the time when Saul was rejected and David first ascended to the throne, so that his descendants thereafter reigned in the earthly Jerusalem in a succession that lasted a long time. This change was symbolic; it was an event that pointed prophetically to the future, and its significance must not be passed over in silence. It betokened the change that was to come in the future in respect of the two covenants, the old and the new, and the transformation of priesthood and monarchy by the new and eternal priest-king, who is Christ Jesus. For when Eli the priest had been rejected and Samuel was substituted for him in the service of God and performed the double function of priest and judge and when Saul was put aside and King David was established in the royal power, those events prophetically symbolized the change that I have mentioned.[46]

Again, both biblical prophecy and biblical events must be understood on multiple levels. The Samuel/David stories can be read on one level as significant for the history of physical Israel; they can be read yet more meaningfully as predictive of the history of spiritual Israel.

Augustine's history of the Jews, as reconstructed in the *City of God*, is rich and complex. It is the tale of a successful human community gone astray; it is, at the same time, the prefiguration of a more meaningful history than that of the Jews. It is partly the sad saga of a successful people that subsequently slipped into error; more importantly and more poignantly, it is the relatively meaningless history of yet another earthly kingdom doomed to be superseded by the true City of God. The Jews of the past were blessed figures, who must be respected; they were, at the same time, figures limited by the inherent religiosity of the period in which they were embedded. Once again, like his mentor Paul, Augustine paints a portrait of the Jewish past that is ambiguous and ambivalent. Jews are to be respected for their past and its contribution to human history; they are to be pitied for the shortcomings of this past; they are to be addressed regularly in an effort to move them to the higher level of religiosity represented in the city of God.

Augustine's anti-Manichean polemic introduces us to a new setting for the Christian constructions of Jewish history. We have thus far engaged such constructions in treatises ostensibly directed at Jews themselves – Augustine's *In Answer to the Jews*; we have also examined such constructions in works ostensibly directed at Christians – Eusebius's *History of the Church* – and in compositions ostensibly intended largely for pagan readers – Eusebius's *Demonstration of the Gospel* and Augustine's *City of God*. Now for the first time we encounter Christian grappling with Jewish history in a treatise devoted to combating Christian heresy.

Augustine was deeply committed to Manichean views in his youth. As a result, although he devoted himself to rebutting a wide range of non-Catholic positions, his commitment to providing guidance against the Manicheans was especially intense. The most important format he chose for the clarification of the errors of the Manicheans was his rebuttal of the writings of a major North African spokesman for the group named Faustus. Faustus had composed in the late 380s a work entitled *The Chapters*. In this work, he had confronted his Manichean protagonist with a series of questions raised from a Catholic perspective and then had provided Manichean responses to these questions. In this way, a guide to Manichean truth was fashioned. There is little organizational rhyme or reason in the sequencing of issues in *The Chapters* – the questions addressed to the Manichean spokesman are haphazard and often repetitive. Nonetheless, the responses provided by Faustus are important, advancing central Manichean views with vigor and clarity.

Augustine chose the thirty-two sections of this rather poorly organized work as the basis for making his major anti-Manichean statement. After an introductory book, Augustine composed thirty-two further books against the views of Faustus. He opens each book by citing Faustus's Catholic question and the Manichean response. The latter forms the foundation for Augustine's critique of the Manichean position and his justification of Catholic Christianity. Since one of the central issues in Manichean thinking involved the relationship between the Old and New Testaments and since Manicheans like Faustus rejected the Old Testament for a variety of reasons, Augustine's *Answer to Faustus a Manichean* forces Augustine yet again and from a somewhat different perspective to engage the Jewish past.

Because of the haphazard organization of Faustus's opus, it is necessary to approach Faustus and Augustine's rebuttals analytically. I shall divide the Manichean claims engaged by Augustine into four categories: the general barbarism of the Old Testament; Christian rejection of the laws of the Old Testament; the inescapable differences between the Old Testament and the New Testament; and the testimonies provided in the Old Testament to Christ. The first issue represents a Manichean reformulation of pagan critiques we have already encountered in Eusebius; the second issue was raised by both pagans and Jews, as we have seen in both Church Fathers; the closing two reflect specifically Christian concerns. Once again, this reinforces our sense of a complex environment, in which differing groups challenged one another, a setting in which the same claim could be mounted by more than one party and in which a group like the Jews might be used in multiple ways by the contending communities.

A word of warning to the reader: Although we will examine four different attacks on Catholic teaching mounted by Faustus, there will be no real variation in Augustine's rebuttal. His claim of the need to read the Old Testament properly, that is spiritually, is an argument we have already encountered. This will be the constant refrain in the Augustinian rebuttals of Faustus. Although the lack of variety may be somewhat tiresome, it illuminates for us how significant this perspective was for Augustine. It colored profoundly his stance on the errors of both the Jews and the Manicheans; it was thus of critical importance for his understanding of the Catholic faith to which he was committed.

We have already seen the broad claim that Judaism was a foreign and barbaric religious faith attributed by Eusebius to pagans. Now, we meet the same claim made by a Manichean. In the twenty-first of his *Chapters*, Faustus has the Catholic protagonist ask why Manicheans "blaspheme the Law and the prophets."[47] Faustus's reply is fairly lengthy, and in it he castigates both biblical narrative and biblical law. For a flavor of the castigation, let us focus on Moses: "Nor did we write that Moses committed murder, that he robbed the Egyptians, that he waged war, that he commanded and carried out many cruel acts, and that even he himself was not content with one marriage."[48] Faustus levels similar criticism against the earlier patriarchs and against the later prophets. In effect, he argues that the behaviors depicted in the narrative sections of the Old Testament are the reasons that Manicheans reject the biblical narratives.

Faustus's attack on biblical law is equally intense. According to Faustus, there is a fundamental set of human laws, upon which all societies have over the ages agreed. These include the prohibition of murder and adultery. However, Israelite law attenuated these universally accepted precepts through an admixture of nonsense. "The writers of the Hebrews burst in upon and mingled with it [the universally accepted law], like leprosy and mange, these abominable and shameful commandments of theirs, which refer to circumcision and sacrifice."[49] This is much like the pagan critique of Israelite law, except that Faustus – as a Manichean – is much better informed as to the content of this law and thus far more focused in his attack on it.

The fundamental error of Faustus, according to Augustine, was essentially the same error he had identified in the Jewish reading of the Hebrew Bible, that is the failure to read the biblical record properly. When read properly, that is spiritually, the seeming shortcomings of both the narratives and the law are proved to be spurious. Let us adduce his defense of biblical law. "The commandment made guilty people desire salvation, but the promise enacted symbols so that they would look toward a savior. In that way, by the coming of the New Testament, the grace given them would set those people free, and the truth realized would remove those symbols. For the law, which was given through Moses, became grace and truth through Jesus Christ."[50] There are two issues reflected here – the proper way of reading biblical texts and the progression of history reflected in the move from the era of the law to the era of grace. According to Augustine, Faustus – like the Jews – fails in understanding both. He reads the texts through a physical lens only, and he fails to perceive the essential combination of continuity and change that characterizes the movement from era to era. Augustine's response to the Manichean criticism of biblical narrative is essentially the same – Manicheans like Faustus fail to grasp the connection between the Old and New Testaments, between the era of law and the era of grace.

A second Manichean critique of the Catholic position involves the basic fact that Catholics honor the Hebrew Bible, while at the same time failing to observe its fundamental precepts. We have encountered this position attributed by Eusebius to both pagans and Jews. Here, the very same stance is adopted by Faustus. The Catholic question is: "Do you accept the Old Testament?" To this challenge, the Manichean reply proposed by Faustus is: "How do I, since I do not keep its commandments? In fact, I think that you [Catholics] do not either. For I despise circumcision as shameful, and, if I am not mistaken, you do too. I regard the Sabbath rest as needless; I believe you do too. I have no doubt that you too regard the sacrifices as idolatry."[51] Given what has been said already of Augustine's response to the Manichean outright dismissal of biblical narrative and history, the lines of his response to this new assault are clear.

The remaining two Manichean attacks are by now almost predictable, as are the Augustinian responses. In Book X, for example, Faustus argues the obvious incompatibility of the New Testament and the Old Testament, and Augustine responds along the lines already noted. In Book XII, Faustus contends that there are in fact no predictions of Jesus in the Old Testament, and Augustine responds strongly to what he perceives to be the repudiation of the New Testament itself. Unlike the two prior Manichean claims, these latter two attacks reflect intra-Christian issues, grounded in core Christian belief itself. The very same lines of response adduced by Augustine to the first two attacks are reinvoked here as well.

In taking the position he took on all these Manichean thrusts, Augustine necessarily focused once again on the Jewish past. As noted in our analysis of his polemical/apologetic treatise and the *City of God*, his position is one of deep respect, tempered by a sense of the limitations of the Israelites. The issue in the context of the large and heterogeneous Greco-Roman world is no longer simple right versus simple wrong. In this diversified environment, the Jews are far superior to their polytheistic neighbors and introduced major religious change into human society. Unfortunately, they could not make the required transition from the era of the law to the era of grace, but someday they will.

In relating to the past, present, and future of the Jews, Augustine was profoundly influenced by the Pauline legacy, in a double sense. He perceived of a Pauline tripartite division in the history of the Jews – a past period of greatness, a present period of error and sinfulness, and a future period of salvation. At the same time, for Augustine the key to understanding the unfolding of these three periods was Paul's distinction between the material and the spiritual. The period of the law necessarily required divine acceptance of the limitations of the Israelite people, which meant largely their focus on the material. This was a necessary stage in human history, and the contribution of the Israelites and Judeans to humanity was incalculable, limitations notwithstanding. To be sure, with the dawning of the period of grace, Jews should have been able to make the transition from the physical to the spiritual. Thus, the present-day incapacity of the Jews to rise above the material obstructs their way to truth, which is of course Christian truth. Those who understand properly biblical truth – like Paul – recognize that a day will come when the Jews will break through this barrier and join the new covenant people.

We have seen Augustine relating to the trajectory of Jewish history in a number of settings. In his direct polemical/apologetic treatise, he focuses on the Jewish present and its shortcomings. The failure of the Jews to comprehend the legacy of their great past lies in their inability to penetrate that legacy in its deepest, spiritual meaning. For Augustine, who rejected of necessity Eusebius's political triumphalism but maintained a sense of spiritual triumphalism, the clearest and most convincing proof of Christian truth lies in the spread of Christianity, which cannot be denied. Biblical prophecy predicted such a development; the development has taken place; Jews cannot deny either the prophecies or their fulfillment. To be sure, whether Jews acknowledge or continue to deny this obvious combination, Christians can be usefully reinforced in their convictions by the awareness of this undeniable combination.

Augustine's most detailed presentation of the Jewish past comes in *The City of God*. As he addressed the pagan world, the Jewish past served him – as it served Eusebius – as a critical element in countering the pagan claim that Christianity is new and hence intellectually shallow and politically illegitimate. For Augustine, as for Eusebius, the Israelites/Judeans go far back in time and have a distinguished lineage. Christianity is grounded in the Israelite legacy, and thus it is the very opposite of new and shallow. For Augustine, the Jewish past serves yet a second function. Moving like Eusebius from a defensive position to an attack on Greco-Roman civilization, Augustine uses early Jewish history as a foil to Roman history, arguing that the Israelite commitment to the one true God made them a blessed people far happier than their Roman contemporaries, again limitations notwithstanding.

In a manner not pursued by Eusebius, Augustine uses the Jewish past when confronting his Manichean opponents as well. The Manicheans attack Catholic reliance on and praise for the history and legacy of the Jewish people. Augustine invokes many of the same stances cited already to dispute this attack and to insist on the greatness of biblical Israel, despite the shortcomings that would become manifest with the passage of time. The transition from biblical Israel to its successor, the Church, and from the Old Testament to the New was seamless, so long as the proper perspective in understanding both periods and both bodies of literature is firmly in place. That proper perspective involves attention to the spiritual dimensions of life in general and to the need for a spiritual reading of the literary legacy of biblical Israel in particular.

For Augustine, Jewish past and present reflect a mixed picture. The Jewish past was great, but with limitations that would become increasingly obvious and problematic with the passage of time. The Jewish present is flawed, but it is rich in promise. Jews must continue to be addressed with sympathy and love, in the conviction that one day they will come to grasp the truth. The one sector of Jewish history for Augustine (as for Paul) that is unambiguously positive is the Jewish future. God has promised the eventual repentance–maturation–spiritualization for some of the Jewish people, which will regain for them the fullness of divine blessing.

The Gospels reflect the constricted and turbulent atmosphere of first-century Roman Palestine and the intense intra-Jewish rivalries fostered by that stifling environment. The Gospel focus is upon the realities of first-century Jewish life, especially the overall Jewish rejection of Jesus and responsibility for his crucifixion. The Jewish past is largely evoked to anchor first-century Jewish error in prior Jewish shortcomings, although there is necessary acknowledgment of past Jewish dignity, for example in the divine choice of the Jews as God's initial human partners, God's selection of the prophets of Israel and Judah as his messengers, and the divine choice of the house of David for leadership. The Jewish future is portrayed in even more cursory fashion in the Gospels, with the simple suggestion that the Jews had forever forfeited their cosmic role through their errors and had been replaced by the Church.

With Paul, the intense environment of first-century Palestine was left behind, and his movement into the vast Roman Empire allowed for extended vistas and horizons, both spatially and temporally. Paul sees the Jews in the context of a heterogeneous imperial population made up of a small number of Christians, a likewise small number of Jews, and huge multitudes of pagans. Awareness of this wide swath of humanity in and of itself created a more positive view of the Jews, projected as far superior to their pagan contemporaries. As a result of his enhanced spatial and ethnographic context, Paul presents a far broader perspective on the history of the Jews, engaging their past, present, and future at length. This shift in perspective results in the attenuation of some of the sharp Gospel negativity and a far more balanced portrait of Judaism and Jews, with recognition of complex combinations of virtues and vices, of achievements and failures.

What was true for Paul was even truer for Eusebius and Augustine. For both, the Jews were seen in the context of heterogeneous humanity. Seen comparatively, the virtues of the Jews were projected in far more positive terms. Present-day Jews were still seen as living in error for their failure to acknowledge what should have been obvious Christian truth. However, the Jews proved themselves extremely useful to the increasingly large and powerful Church in the richly diversified Roman world. They could be utilized in multiple ways in combating pagan anti-Christian polemics and advancing the case for Christian truth. Indeed, for Augustine, Judaism and the Jews could be marshaled effectively in the important arena of anti-heretical polemics as well. The Jewish past came to be portrayed in nuanced terms as a combination of greatness and shortcoming. Following Paul, Jews were projected by Augustine as fated to enjoy a happy future, in full recognition of the enormous contribution they had made to humanity.

The more complex perspectives of Paul, Eusebius, and Augustine became the foundations for subsequent Church doctrine and policy. As noted, historians of the Jews and the Church regularly speak of an Augustinian synthesis undergirding subsequent Jewish existence in Christendom. However, the more simplistic and more negative Gospel perspectives continued to dominate popular Christian thinking. The story of the crucifixion of Jesus was straightforward and dramatic, with clear-cut heroes and villains and with enormous emotional appeal. The tension between the narrow popular view and the broader and more elitist perspective represented by Paul, Eusebius, and Augustine emerged sharply from time to time, with the Church leadership attempting – sometime successfully and sometime not – to limit the negativity and harmful impact of the Gospel narrative.

In the second part of this book, we shall examine significant revision of the broader and more balanced intellectual perspectives bequeathed from late antiquity. A radically new environment in medieval Christian Europe produced pervasive hostility toward Judaism and Jews, regular outbursts of popular violence against Jews, and the development of strikingly negative popular imagery of Jews as hostile and harmful to Christianity and Christians. While the Church leadership by and large insisted on the more balanced legacy of Paul, Eusebius, and Augustine, we shall encounter and analyze medieval intellectual efforts that built upon and reinforced the popular antipathy, in the process effacing much of the balance that was the legacy of late antiquity and creating a new set of intellectual constructions of Judaism and Jews that was transmitted – along with the radical popular stereotypes and to an extent more effectively – to the modern West.

Notes

1   For an overview of the Julian episode, see Robert Browning, *The Emperor Julian* (Berkeley: University of California Press, 1976).
2   For a full description of the tumultuous world into which Augustine was born, see Paula Fredriksen, *Augustine and the Jews: A Christian Defense of Jews and Judaism* (New York: Doubleday, 2008), Part 1. Fredriksen devotes the first part of her study to the rich and complex context in which Augustine was situated.
3   Augustine's ongoing importance to the Church is reflected in the recent creation of the Augustinian Heritage Institute and the development of a new set of translations under the rubric *The Works of Augustine: A Translation for the 21st Century*. Augustine's memoir, which has appeal for a remarkably wide audience, is available in a multitude of translations.

4 Peter Brown, *Augustine of Hippo* (Berkeley: University of California Press, 1967).
5 James J. O'Donnell, *Augustine: A New Biography* (New York: Ecco, 2005).
6 Jeremy Cohen, *Living Letters of the Law: Ideas of the Jew in Medieval Christianity* (Berkeley: University of California Press, 1999).
7 Ibid., 35.
8 Ibid., 36.
9 Ibid., 41.
10 Ibid., 8–9.
11 Fredriksen, *Augustine and the Jews.*
12 Ibid., 260–261.
13 Psalms 59:1.
14 Psalms 59:2–4.
15 Saint Augustine, *Confessions*, trans. R. S. Pines (Harmondsworth: Penguin Books, 1961; *Penguin Classics*), 178. I have chosen this translation out of the many available, because it is so readily accessible.
16 Augustine, "In Answer to the Jews," trans. Sister Marie Ligouri, in *Saint Augustine: Treatises on Marriage and Other Subjects*, 387–414, ed. Roy J. Deferrari (Washington: Catholic University of America Press, 1955; *The Fathers of the Church: A New Translation*), 391.
17 Ibid., 392.
18 Ibid.
19 Ibid. The biblical verse is Isaiah 49:5.
20 Ibid., 392–393.
21 Ibid., 393.
22 Ibid., 394.
23 A rapid examination of the recent Bible translations indicates how difficult this term is, how contemporary translators wrestle with it, and how diverse their renderings are.
24 Augustine, "In Answer to the Jews," 402.
25 Galatians 6:16.
26 I Corinthians 10:18.
27 Augustine, "In Answer to the Jews," 402–403.
28 Ibid., 403.
29 St. Augustine, *City of God*, trans. Henry Bettenson (Harmondsworth: Penguin Books, 1972; *Penguin Classics*), IV:34, p. 177. Once again, this is a highly accessible translation.
30 Ibid., 178.
31 Ibid.
32 These prophecies are in fact the focus of Book XVII.
33 Recall this Pauline theme from Chapter 2.
34 Augustine, *City of God*, XVII:3, pp. 713–714.
35 Ibid., pp. 714–715.
36 Ibid. XVII:1, pp. 711–712.
37 Ibid., XVII:3, p. 713.
38 Ibid., XVI:12, 670.
39 Gen. 12:1.

40   For all the blessings and their referents, see Augustine, *City of God*, XVI:16–
     32; Augustine identifies the referent in each case, sometimes to physical
     Israel, sometimes to spiritual Israel.
41   Gen. 17:6.
42   Gen. 17:16.
43   Augustine, *City of God*, XVI:26, p. 687.
44   Gen. 25:23.
45   Augustine, *City of God*, XVI:35, p. 698.
46   Ibid., XVII:4, pp. 715–716. Augustine continues to parse the Saul-David
     story throughout XVII:7–8.
47   Augustine, *Answer to Faustus a Manichean*, trans. Roland Teske (Hyde Park
     NY: New City Press, 2007; *The Works of Augustine: A Translation for the
     21st Century*), Book XXII, p. 298.
48   Ibid., 300.
49   Ibid., 298.
50   Ibid., 301.
51   Ibid., Book VI, p. 93.

PART II

JEWISH HISTORY: MEDIEVAL CHRISTIAN CONSTRUCTIONS

5

The Crusading Epoch and Spirit

Peter the Venerable

We have already seen the impact of differing environments on Christian constructions of the Jewish present, past, and future. First-century Roman Palestine created one set of constructions; Paul's forays into Asia Minor resulted in strikingly different perspectives; the remarkable growth of the Church across the Roman Empire and its resultant needs fostered further changes in Christian stances toward the trajectory of Jewish history during the fourth and fifth centuries.

From time immemorial down through the end of the first Christian millennium, the worldwide Jewish population – while exhibiting significant shifts periodically – was centered in the broad band of territory that stretched from Mesopotamia westward across the Mediterranean Basin. Within this area, there was an occasional ebb and flow, with the largest Jewish population fluctuating between Palestine and Mesopotamia. By the end of the first Christian millennium, the major center of Jewish habitation had crystallized in Mesopotamia, with Baghdad hosting the world's largest Jewish urban enclave. Nonetheless, Jews had long been settled throughout this vast area, had developed over the millennia diversified economic outlets, had established comfortable relations with their non-Jewish neighbors, and were widely viewed as indigenous elements in society. Jewish life was relatively stable throughout this area of traditional Jewish settlement, and rarely did Jews venture in any numbers beyond its perimeters.

In a totally unanticipated way, a new venue for Jewish settlement emerged toward the end of the first Christian millennium, as a by-product of major changes in western Christendom. The changes took place in northern Europe, an area that had long languished as a retrograde

109

hinterland to the Mediterranean south, with its inhabitants viewed as backward and barbaric. For reasons that remain unclear, northern Europe began toward the end of the first millennium a process of vitalization that brought it to the forefront of the West, transforming Christian Europe in its entirety from the weakest of the three major religio-political blocs – the Islamic sphere, eastern Christendom, and western Christendom – into the strongest, a position it maintained throughout most of the modern centuries.

The vitalization of northern Europe fostered a major alteration of the prior pattern of worldwide Jewish population. As a result of this vitalization, the preexistent boundaries of Jewish settlement were breached. In the year 1000, the Jewish population of northern Europe was minuscule, constituting only the tiniest proportion of world Jewry. Five hundred years later, northern Europe housed a considerable segment of world Jewry and within a few centuries thereafter became home to a majority of the world's Jews.

The process of creation and expansion of this new Jewry involved migration, which was spurred to a large extent by the Jewish perception of the economic opportunities available in this rapidly developing sector of Europe. Migration from the Mediterranean Basin up into northern Europe was not all that arduous, if the economic prospects were deemed encouraging, and they by and large were. Jewish immigration was further enhanced by the encouragement and support of some of the most far-sighted political leaders of northern Europe. These political authorities recognized the need for capable and productive urban settlers, who might bring the fruits of the better-developed Mediterranean ambiance up into their domains.

The setting into which the Mediterranean Jews immigrated was radically different from the environments we have encountered and examined thus far. Gone was the heterogeneity of the Roman Empire of the days of Paul, with only a tiny Christian minority, or the days of Eusebius and Augustine with a sizeable but not dominant Christian minority. The northern Europe into which these Jews migrated was almost entirely Christian, although the level of full absorption of Christian teachings and values may be questioned. Questioning aside, the inhabitants of northern Europe saw themselves as living in a thoroughly Christian society, which was organized around a common religious vision, was served by an effectively organized Church, and was governed by secular authorities deeply committed to the fulfillment of Christian ideals. Thus, the Jewish immigrants constituted from the outset a small minority of dissidents in an otherwise religiously homogeneous environment. This was – to say the least – a difficult setting, one likely to arouse considerable majority antipathy and hostility. *for Jews*

By this time, the larger world surrounding northern Europe had become almost completely monotheistic, in the process giving rise to a much less tolerant view of others than had been the norm in earlier polytheistic days. For all three Western monotheisms, there was only one God and only one divinely created covenant with a chosen human community. That one chosen human community enjoyed the blessing of divinely revealed truth and carried the burden of spreading that one truth among all of humanity. While there might well be accommodations that permitted other monotheistic believers a modicum of respect and the right to safe existence, the ultimate objective – or at least hope – was a world in which all of humanity would share the one true faith. On occasion, this aspiration could lead to violence in an effort to force this truth on others. This underlying intolerance further exacerbated the problems of the young Jewry seeking a place in medieval northern Europe.

The Jews who settled in the reaches of northern Europe enjoyed the opportunities available in their new setting and seem to have made useful contributions to the burgeoning economy of northern Europe. At the same time, these Jews faced enormous obstacles, the first of which has already been noted – the status of singular dissidents in an otherwise homogeneous society. Complicating this initial obstacle was the newness of these immigrants. Although there is often lip service paid to newcomers in society, they very much tend to arouse the antipathy of the prior inhabitants in all human settings, and medieval northern Europe was no exception. Moreover, these new settlers brought with them their Jewishness and the negative popular imagery we have already examined. To be sure, the Roman Catholic Church had fully adopted the complex Augustinian perspectives on Judaism and Jews we have analyzed and sought to enforce the protective policies that derived from these perspectives. Again, however, the pervasive popular appeal of the Gospel narratives tended to dominate popular consciousness and sow further seeds of animosity toward the new Jewish settlers.

This initial threefold initial popular resistance to the new Jewish immigrants had important secondary effects as well. It precluded the development of normal economic diversification and thrust these Jews into lacunae in the economy that were often highly unpopular. The outstanding example of this dynamic involved the twelfth-century Church assault on Christian usury, the resultant opening of a new field of economic

endeavor for the Jews of northern Europe, and the hostilities this economic activity aroused. In the same way, popular antipathy forced the
Jews into extensive reliance on the support of the political authorities,
which meant ultimately that anti-governmental agitation generally
involved an anti-Jewish component as well.

These impediments to the acceptance of the Jews in northern Europe
were not sufficient to derail Jewish settlement and the steady expansion of
the Jewish population. They did, however, result in a high level of popular animosity, occasional explosions of popular violence, and the fashioning of a number of virulently negative popular stereotypes of these Jews
as hostile in the extreme toward their Christian host environment and
poised at all times to inflict great harm on that host environment. Once
again, the authorities of both church and state made strenuous efforts
to suppress the popular violence and to rebut the damaging allegations,
with partial success – but partial success only.[1]

What we shall now proceed to examine is the ways in which the popular hostility eventually found intellectual resonance in a series of damning
reexaminations of the broader trajectory of Jewish history. These new
constructions of Jewish history effaced most of the positive perspectives
on Judaism and Jews bequeathed from late antiquity and made a significant contribution to the anti-Jewish legacy passed on by medieval Europe
to the modern West.

Western Christendom began its process of vitalization in the late tenth
and early eleventh century, and this vitalization expressed itself almost
immediately in aggression against Muslim enclaves in Europe. Already by
the middle decades of the eleventh century, Christian warriors had begun
to conquer territories held by the Muslims on the Italian and Iberian
peninsulas. Although these Christian conquests were largely fueled by the
territorial ambitions of Christian magnates, there was a religious element
that reinforced these material desires, a sense of religiously inspired combat against the forces of Islam. Thus, for example, when the symbolic city
of Toledo was conquered by Christian armies in 1085, there was rejoicing
over the return of an important metropolis to Christian hands.

At the end of the eleventh century, the religious authorities of western
Christendom created an entirely new military venture, which has subsequently been designated crusading. As announced by Pope Urban II in
1095, the new movement was identified as a distinctly religious undertaking. The objective was no longer contiguous European territory to
be wrested from Muslim control. Rather, Christian warriors were to

set out under the banner of the Church to reconquer the sacred sites of Christianity in the Holy Land. The key symbol of the enterprise was to be the cross, and warriors undertaking the arduous effort were assured religious rewards, culminating in martyrdom for those who lost their lives in the undertaking. This aggressive initiative represented a considerable departure in Christian perspectives on military violence.

In its earliest history, the Church had suffered violence, with little concern over or potential for inflicting it. Indeed, it was the capacity to suffer Roman imperial violence with remarkable resolve that profoundly impressed many pagans and contributed in a major way to their conversion to Christianity. In the wake of the revolution initiated by Constantine, the Church had to relate to a host of new issues, among them recourse to military violence. As the rulers of the Roman Empire became Christian, the issue of military violence could not be avoided, as there was at the very least a need for self-defense in the face of external threat. Once again, Augustine emerged as a key synthesizer, adumbrating a doctrine of just warfare that emphasized its defensive and protective aspects. Christian societies had a right, indeed a duty, to protect their members from external treat. Although military violence might well be lamentable, it was a lamentable necessity.

The papal call to the crusade was no longer founded on the need to protect Christendom from its enemies, although there was some effort to advance arguments from protective necessity, including concern for pilgrims to the sacred sites and aid to beleaguered Byzantine fellow-Christians. However, the aggressive nature of crusading and the admixture of religious symbolism and rewards signaled a new stage in the Church's stance toward the legitimacy of military violence. In the process, the warrior class – an important group in rapidly developing western Christendom – came to enjoy a new prestige and new religious importance.

In order to understand the implications of this new sense of battle with the monotheistic forces of Islam and the innovative valorization of military violence in service to this struggle, we shall analyze first a number of views of Judaism and Jews that emerged during the early crusading period. At the outset, we shall note some radical popular perceptions of Jews sparked by the call to religious war against Islam. We shall then study the repudiation of these radical views by two giants of the twelfth-century Church – Bernard of Clairvaux and Peter the Venerable. While these two Church leaders both roundly rejected the call to anti-Jewish violence advocated by the popular crusading bands, they nonetheless disagreed seriously in their assessment of Judaism and Jews, especially in their views on twelfth-century Jews and their relationship to the Jewish past. After identifying their alternative positions on Jews in the context of crusading, we shall examine the more purely negative view of Peter the Venerable, as articulated in his major anti-Jewish treatise. Peter the Venerable will serve as a fitting introduction to the accelerating negativity of the intellectuals of medieval western Christendom toward its Jews and their history.

The details of Urban II's call to the crusade at Clermont in 1095 are uncertain. Nonetheless, two conclusions have been widely drawn. The first is that the call was profoundly inspirational, galvanizing a wide range of listeners into a frenzied response. Listeners are portrayed as tearing their cloaks into crosses as a sign of acceptance of the papal challenge. This enthusiasm for the enterprise spread rapidly in many directions. Given the newness of the crusading ideal, the inevitable lack of clarity in such a new ideal, and the intense exhilaration this new ideal generated, it was almost inevitable that a wide range of interpretations of the papal message would quickly evolve. Some of these interpretations exploited the religious motifs as rationales for the terrestrial aspirations on the part of Christian warriors. On a more spiritual level, some preachers saw in the call to the crusade the onset of the end of days, with all the changes such imagery implied.[2] The papacy and the established leadership of the Church, which had set the campaign in motion, strove desperately to control it, but with only limited success. Preaching of all kinds proliferated, and unruly bands of popular crusaders – ill equipped for serious military engagement – sprang up across western Christendom.

A second widely shared conclusion is that – whatever Pope Urban II did say – he did not address the issue of the Jews. The enemy identified by the pope was Islam, specifically those Muslims holding the holy city of Jerusalem and its major shrine. Judaism and Jews were unlikely to have been mentioned at all. To be sure, the call to battle against Muslims holding and purportedly abusing the sacred sites of Christendom in the Holy Land, especially the Holy Sepulcher, bore the potential for fastening the attention of Christians attracted to crusading on Jews in a number of ways. Most directly, the notion of attacking the enemies of Christianity might easily have been understood to imply some kind of action against Jews, who were – as we have seen – identified in the Gospels as Jesus' sole and implacable enemies. Moreover, the attention paid to Jerusalem and the Holy Sepulcher also bore the potential for a focus on the Jews, whose ancestors had, according to all the Gospel accounts, persecuted Jesus in Jerusalem and had been responsible for his death there, thus creating in effect the religious shrine that the Muslims were now being accused of sullying. Quite clearly, the pope would not have raised such associations; at the same time, he and his advisors were unlikely to have foreseen the emergence of such associations and to have warned against them. All students of the early stages of the First Crusade agree that the Jews did not figure at all in the Clermont call to the crusade.

Given the newness of crusading and the intense emotionality of its appeal, it is hardly surprising that in a few of the many spontaneously organized crusading circles the ill-defined papal initiative was deflected against the Jews of western Christendom. The crusading militias that succeeded in conquering Jerusalem in 1099 show no evidence of this deflection; across southern Europe there are no signs of significant anti-Jewish violence; and in the northwestern areas of Europe, evidence of anti-Jewish sentiment is limited to the exploitation of Jewish anxieties for the financial support of the enterprise. In this last instance, a Hebrew narrative suggests that the large popular band that coalesced around the charismatic French preacher Peter the Hermit carried with it a message from French Jews to their Rhineland coreligionists urging material assistance to Peter, in return for which he would ensure Jewish safety from crusader depredations. This narrative informs us that the advice of the French Jews was heeded and was successful, with the Jews of Trier spared harm at the hands of Peter's followers.[3]

In the Rhineland, however, popular understanding of the new and nebulously defined religious initiative resulted in major violence against a number of important Jewish settlements. The rationale for these assaults lay in a popularly articulated inference, which transformed the Jews into more heinous enemies of Christianity than the Muslims. According to the argument, the Muslims were being attacked simply because they denied Jesus, while Jews were more reprehensible in that they occasioned his death. This slogan is attested in both Jewish and Christian sources on the First Crusade. The oldest of the Hebrew narratives that depict the 1096 Christian assaults and Jewish responses presents the popular German crusaders proclaiming the following: "Behold we travel to a distant land to do battle with the kings of that land. We take our lives in our hands in order to kill and subjugate all those kingdoms that do not believe in the Crucified. How much more [should we kill and subjugate] the Jews, who killed and crucified him."[4]

This argument was of course never advanced by the pope or his court, but it reflects the malleability of the as yet ill-defined crusading ideal. This passage shows a variety of misunderstandings/misinterpretations of the papal call. Pope Urban II did not call for a campaign to "kill and subjugate" all non-Christian kingdoms, but popular crusaders reinterpreted or misinterpreted his message in these terms, perhaps reflecting the millenarian expectations aroused by the enterprise.[5] Likewise, he surely did not suggest that killing Jews was part of this plan, but it is not difficult to envision popular preachers recalling Gospel accounts of Jewish enmity and drawing such anti-Jewish implications from the papal announcement. Here then, perceptions of the Jewish past – to be sure, extreme and simplistic – had serious impact. This impact reflects once more the power of the Gospel narratives of the Crucifixion and their capacity to eclipse the more nuanced views we have seen in the Gospels in their totality and in Paul and the Church Fathers. Although such radical interpretations of the crusade and its implications vis-à-vis Jews were not widespread, they lay at the core of the significant anti-Jewish violence in the Rhineland during the spring months of 1096.[6]

As the Second Crusade was being organized in the 1140s, its leadership was well aware of the deflection of the crusading ideal against Jews in 1096. The great spiritual leader of the Second Crusade was Bernard of Clairvaux, who sent letters throughout western Christendom urging Christian warriors to commit themselves to the sacred undertaking. As the organization of the crusade proceeded, Bernard heard rumors that the earlier Rhineland rationales for anti-Jewish violence were resurfacing, and he was determined to quash the potential for repetition of the 1096 bloodshed. Thus, he appended a closing paragraph to his crusade epistle, in which he made an extensive case against anti-Jewish violence, presenting an array of arguments. While his observations are conveyed in one fairly brief paragraph, Bernard presents in rapid succession a rich sequence of observations on the Jewish present, past, and future.

Let us begin with Bernard's perceptions of the twelfth-century Jewish present, which include important perspectives on Jews, their circumstances, and their attitudes. His initial observation on the present of his Jewish contemporaries focuses on their dispersion and subjugation. This dispersion and subjugation constitute fulfillment of biblical prediction. "The same psalm [which he quoted shortly before, that is Psalm 59, which had played such an important role in the thinking of Augustine] adds: 'Only let your power disperse them.' And so it is, dispersed they are. Under Christian princes they endure a hard captivity."[7] Jewish dispersion and captivity had been predicted and has eventuated. Indeed, Jews are, according to Bernard, "dispersed all over the world." It is difficult to know whether this is a theological comment on his part or whether he was in fact aware of the reality of Jewish settlement all across Christian and Muslim lands.

Bernard makes an important related observation on Jewish dispersion and captivity, which highlights the response of the Jews to their difficult circumstances. Bernard contrasts the pagans, that is Muslims, who have – he claims – "begun to attack us," necessitating armed Christian response. In Bernard's view, however, twelfth-century Jews are docile, accepting of their dolorous fate. Thus, "it is an act of Christian piety both to vanquish the proud and also to spare the subjected." For Bernard, twelfth-century Muslims fall into the former category and twelfth-century Jews into the latter category. Thus, Christian piety requires that Jews be spared harm from crusading. This is by no means Bernard's only argument against crusading anti-Jewish violence, but it reflects an important perspective on twelfth-century European Jewry.

A strange digression in this letter reveals a third aspect of twelfth-century Jewish life as seen by Bernard. Addressing the Jewish future and eventual salvation for Jews, he indicates that Jews killed in the course of crusading would be denied such salvation, which constitutes yet another reason why Jews should not be attacked. Speaking of those Jews who die before ultimate redemption and their loss of the potential for salvation, Bernard ruminates for a moment on others similarly denied salvation, abandoning briefly the issue at hand. Bernard's association involves the following: "I will not mention those Christian moneylenders, if they can be called Christian, who – when there are no Jews – act, I grieve to say, in a manner worse than any Jews." In this curious digression, Bernard adds another group that will be denied salvation, in the process providing a further perspective on twelfth-century Jews, who – he suggests – have immersed themselves heavily in moneylending.

[handwritten margin note: if there are no Jews, Christs have to be worried if they'll go to hell]

The translation offered here does not quite capture the force of Bernard's observation. A more literal translation would be that these Christian moneylenders "Jew in a worse manner," suggesting the equation of Jews and moneylending. To be sure, Bernard does not offer an evaluation of this new phenomenon. Although he castigates Christian moneylending, which contravenes Church law, he does not take a stand on Jewish moneylending – he simply highlights it.

Thus, Bernard's perspectives on the Jewish present are complex. Jews are dispersed and subjugated, as a result of their historic sin; on a positive note, these Jews at least have the good grace to accept their subjugation and thus pose no harm to their Christian neighbors. In a casual aside, he also notes the new economic specialization in moneylending, which is well documented in many other mid-twelfth century sources. Bernard is not at all clear on his view of Jewish moneylending, which he simply introduces in his strange digression.

At the center of Bernard's reflections on the Jewish past lie the Crucifixion and the Jewish role in it. Jews remind Christians "always of what our Lord suffered." This is the utilitarian reason for the dispersion of the Jews. They are dispersed, partly as a punishment for their crime, but also as a useful reminder to Christians of the crucified Christ. In this sense, Bernard shares the same focus on Jewish past sinfulness with those popular crusaders who killed Jews in 1096. However, he comes to the diametrically opposed conclusion that Jews must not be harmed for a number of reasons, partly because – following Augustine – he knows that God so commanded in Psalm 59, partly because of future salvation of the Jews, partly because the dispersed Jews serve as an effective reminder of Jesus and his suffering, and partly because there are countervailing aspects of the Jewish past.

[handwritten margin note: reasons not to kill them]

Toward the end of his letter, Bernard insists – as noted – that Christian piety requires that those who docilely accept their subjugation must be spared, and he claims that twelfth-century Jews accept their subjugation. For Bernard, nonviolence toward all those who accept their subjugation is a standard requirement of Christian behavior. With respect to the Jews, the force of this requirement is much augmented. It is especially meaningful with respect to "those from whom we have a law and a promise and whose flesh was shared by Christ, whose name be forever blessed." Like Paul and the Church Fathers whom we have examined, Bernard is fully cognizant of egregious Jewish wrongdoing in the past, but that wrongdoing is balanced to an extent by the earlier history of biblical Israel, when the Israelites provided the world with divine law and the divine promise. Even at the point of their critical sinfulness, Jews were bound to Jesus by the bond of physical brotherhood. Once again and in ways that the simplistic slogan of the 1096 crusaders could not possibly capture, the past of the Jews is multifaceted, involving both the negative and the positive.

Bernard's view of the Jewish future is Pauline, of the especially optimistic variety. According to Bernard, "we are told by the Apostle that, when the time is ripe, all Israel shall be saved." As we have seen, Paul's optimism over the Jewish future was expressed in multiple ways. All followers of the Pauline view agreed to his optimism as to the Jewish future, but in differing degrees. For some, eventual salvation of the Jews would include those Jews who came to acknowledge the truth of Christianity, which meant in effect a portion of the Jewish people. For Bernard, "all Israel shall be saved," which means that at the time of universal redemption all Jews would come to recognize the Christian truths they had long resisted. Although Bernard's views of Jewish present and past were multi-faceted, combining negatives and positives, his view of the Jewish future has only one dimension; it is focused on the positive only.

Bernard constructed a rich case for Jewish safety grounded in many considerations. In opposing the overly zealous Christian warriors who might be tempted to attack Jews, Bernard built a multidimensional argument intended to be overwhelmingly persuasive. Perhaps the strongest of his many arguments is divine *fiat*. God had decreed in Psalm 59 that Jews not be harmed, despite their guilt for the Crucifixion. Whatever their motivation, such divine orders must be scrupulously observed, and thus Jews must not be attacked and harmed. To be sure, in the case of this order God revealed at least some of his thinking. Jews must remain alive in their state of dispersal and subjugation as a constant reminder to Christians among whom they live of the suffering of Jesus on the Cross. This sense of the purposes that Jews serve reinforces the divine order, although such an order requires no reinforcement.

In fact, there are additional considerations as well, which further buttress Bernard's conclusions. Although the past of the Jews was marred by their role in the Crucifixion, there were positive aspects of the Jewish past as well. The Jews introduced the one true God into human history and brought his law and promises into human society. This is the position advanced by the two Church Fathers we have examined, and Bernard reprised this position. In addition, Christians should recall that Jesus himself was a member of the Jewish people, which has earned respect over the ages for Jews, their shortcomings notwithstanding. Finally, considerations of the Jewish future again point in the direction of Jewish safety, for Paul had insisted that at the time of ultimate redemption Jews would be saved. This promise for the future necessitates the ongoing existence of Jews, which serves as the final element in Bernard's complex case against killing Jews.

The stance of Bernard's great contemporary, Peter the Venerable, offers one significant parallel to Bernard and – at the same time – a number of striking contrasts. For our purposes, it suggests how malleable the elements in Christian constructions of the Jewish present, past, and future were. As a result of alternative empirical assessment of contemporary Jewish life and alternative arrangement of the elements in the pre-medieval legacy, disparate conclusions could be reached. Peter shared Bernard's opposition to the killing of Jews, but there is little else he shared. The starting point for Peter's divergence from Bernard's position was his disagreement with Bernard's assessment of twelfth-century Jews. For Bernard, these Jews had accepted their subjugation and were living docilely in Christian society; for Peter they were as consumed by enmity toward Christianity as their ancestors had been toward the founder of the Christian faith. From this starting point, Peter came to disagree on the practical level as to treatment of Jews during the crusading period and fashioned a portrait of the Jewish past that was consistently negative and damning.

The differences between the two great abbots were shaped to an extent by the objectives of the letters in which they expressed their views on crusading and the Jews. As noted, Bernard formulated his views on crusading and the Jews as an addendum to the wide-ranging set of letters he addressed to the knights of Europe, urging them to undertake the crusade. Learning of the revival of illegitimate anti-Jewish sentiment, he added a closing section in which he made his case for Jewish safety. Bernard's letter was addressed to a broad audience of crusaders and was crafted in such a way as to argue the case for the security of illegitimately endangered Jews. Peter's letter, on the contrary, had but one specific addressee, King Louis VII of France; it focuses on crusading and the Jewish place within the campaign. The letter in its entirety was devoted to the Jews and urged both physical safety for them and the imposition of financial obligations toward the sacred enterprise upon them as well.

Peter begins his letter neutrally enough by praising the crusading effort. His introduction of the Jews is striking, especially when viewed against the backdrop of the 1096 crusading slogan we have cited and the position articulated by Bernard of Clairvaux.

> But what value in pursing and attacking the enemies of the Christian faith in remote and distant lands, while the Jews – wretched blasphemers far worse than the Saracens – not far away but in our midst so freely and audaciously blaspheme, abuse, and trample on Christ and the Christian sacraments with impunity? In what way does the zeal for God consume the sons of God, if the Jews – the worst enemy of Christ and Christians – thus escape utterly unaffected?[8]

Notable here immediately is Peter's closeness to the popular crusading slogan we have examined. Peter repeats the fundamental contention of the popular slogan. For him as for the 1096 crusaders, it is absurd that Christian warriors travel to a "remote and distant land" to fight a lesser enemy, while a more heinous enemy lurks at home unscathed. That Peter's formulation is so close to that of the murderous Rhineland crusaders suggests that what we have identified as radical views of the crusade were widely disseminated in northern European society and came to be shared by a figure as distinguished as Peter the Venerable.

The reality of crusaders traveling long distances, while Jewish communities remain comfortably ensconced in western Christendom, is obvious and requires no comment on the part of Peter. Precisely the ways in which the Jews are an enemy worse than the Muslims must be clarified, and here Peter breaks with the 1096 crusaders. These latter – it will be recalled – contrasted the Muslims who simply deny Christ with the Jews who crucified him. Not so Peter. Let us note his formulation of the difference between Muslims and Jews.

The Saracens are to be detested – although they believe like us that Christ was born of a virgin and agree with us on many matters concerning him – because they deny that he is God and the son of God, which is more important, and deny his death and resurrection, in which the totality of our salvation lies. Thus, how much more are the Jews to be despised and hated, who – believing nothing concerning Christ and the Christian faith – reject, blaspheme, and deride that virgin birth and all the sacraments of human salvation.[9]

The differences between the 1096 popular crusading perception of Jews and Peter's perceptions are striking. While Peter agrees with the popular crusading slogan in his preference for Muslims over Jews (his deeper hatred of Jews might be more accurate), his reasoning is quite different. For Peter, Muslims are less reprehensible because they acknowledge certain Christian truths, for example the Virgin Birth. They are nonetheless enemies, because they deny other central Christian dogma, for example Christ's divinity and his resurrection. Jews are worse than Muslims, but not because of their historic role in the Crucifixion; they are more reprehensible than Muslims – in part – because they deny all Christian beliefs, failing to acknowledge, as Muslims do, at least some Christian doctrine.

More important yet is the nature of Muslim and Jewish opposition to Christianity. Although the First Crusade was launched ostensibly because of Muslim abuse of the sacred sites of Christianity, Peter faults the Muslims with failure only to believe in key Christian beliefs; crusading rationales notwithstanding, he does not ascribe to Muslims active attacks on Christian belief and practice. In his view, Jews are aggressive in their opposition to all the tenets of Christianity and its practices; not only do they reject these beliefs and practices – they also "blaspheme and deride" them and "freely and audaciously blaspheme, abuse, and trample on Christ and the Christian sacraments with impunity." For Peter the Venerable, the problem with the Jews lies not in the distant past in Jerusalem, but rather in twelfth-century western Christendom and their abusive behavior toward Christianity, its doctrines, and its *sancta*.

Just as Peter parts ways with the slogans of 1096, so too does he disagree markedly with Bernard of Clairvaux. Bernard insisted on safety for Jews because – among other considerations – he believed that twelfth-century Jews lived docilely under Christian rule, while Muslims allegedly had taken up arms against Christianity and Christians. Peter reverses Bernard's perception. The true contemporary enemies are the Jews, in part because of the totality of their rejection of Christian belief, but more importantly because of their ongoing aggressive behavior, their unceasing blasphemy of Christ and Christianity. From these alternative starting points, the two powerful abbots and thinkers came to alternative pragmatic conclusions. For Bernard, Jews lay outside the crusading enterprise altogether; for Peter, Psalm 59 still precluded anti-Jewish violence, but alleged anti-Christian behaviors by Jews nonetheless made them part of the sacred effort undertaken against the enemies of Christianity.

Peter accepted the Augustinian reading of Psalm 59 and the resultant prohibition of anti-Jewish violence. However, his construction of the Jewish past differs from Bernard's, at least in tone. Whereas Bernard treated only minimally historic Jewish sin and adduced evidence of past Jewish nobility, Peter focuses on the negative only, with repeated evidence of past Jewish enmity and crime.

I do not say these things so that I might sharpen the royal or Christian sword against the necks of these execrable [Jews], since I bear in mind that it is said concerning them in the divine psalm, with the prophet saying the following in the spirit of God: "God will show me victorious over my enemies. Do not kill them, lest my people be unmindful." Indeed, God does not wish that they be killed or destroyed entirely; rather, for the purpose of greater torment and ignominy [he wishes that] they be preserved for a life worse than death.... [Peter introduces the Cain image and then continues] Thus did the just severity of God enact concerning the damned and damnable Jews from that time of the passion and death of Christ, and so shall be done through the end of the present world order. Since they spilled the blood of Christ – their brother in the flesh – they are enslaved, afflicted, anxious, suffering, and wanderers of the earth, until according to the prophet the miserable remnants of this people, when the full of the nations is realized, will be converted to God.[10]

There is nothing in this statement with which Bernard would have disagreed in principle; the tone, however, is altogether different. Bernard,
committed to restraining the animus of crusaders, sought to minimize the
negative features of the Jewish past and to balance these negative features
with the positive; Peter, seeking to arouse the king to anti-Jewish action,
emphasized relentlessly the central negative aspects of the Jewish past.

These two differing projections of Jewish present, past, and future (Peter is
far less generous in his depiction of eventual salvation for the Jews) led to alternative action proposals. Bernard's action proposal was simple. Consideration
of Jewish past, present, and future requires a policy of crusading nonviolence
vis-à-vis Jews. Peter's action proposal was more complex. Given that war had
been declared against Islam, action was called for against the Jews, for Peter
so obviously more hateful than the Muslims. This crusade-related anti-Jewish
action could not involve violence, which had been expressly forbidden by
Psalm 59. The precise form of this action was for Peter determined by Jewish
economic activity and its anti-Christian results.

Peter – like Bernard – was aware of a limited Jewish economic posture
in twelfth-century western Christendom. These perceptions seem reasonably accurate. In northern Europe, where Jewish presence was new, the
Jewish immigrants had responded to the limits placed on their economic
activity by popular resistance and had exploited lacunae in the economy
in order to carve out for themselves useful economic niches.[11] Bernard
fairly accurately perceives the major niche as involving moneylending,
which – as we have seen – he does not seem to judge negatively. Peter
focuses on the limited activity of buying stolen goods. Although Jews
may have done so, this could hardly be the sustaining element in Jewish
economic activity. In any case, for Peter this activity allowed Jews opportunity to vent their hatred of Christianity and pointed toward crusade-
related actions that could be legitimately taken against the Jewish enemy.

Following is Peter's depiction of Jewish economic activity and its anti-
Christian outcomes. In the process of depicting these activities, Peter
expands on his general claim of ongoing Jewish blasphemy, abuse, and
trampling on Christ and the Christian sacraments.

He [the thief] hands over the vessels of Christ's body and blood to those who
killed him and spilled Christ's blood, who heaped contumely and injury upon him
when he was among the living to the extent they could, and who now – as he is
seated in the glory of eternal divinity – do not cease wounding him with verbal
blasphemies to the extent they dare. The sacred vessels held captive among them
as I have indicated, as in olden times [other sacred vessels were held captive]

among the Chaldeans, suffer shame, even though they are inanimate. Indeed, Christ feels the Jewish abuse of these insensate vessels sacred to him.[12]

Here Jewish past and present are fused. In both periods, Jews express vigorously and viciously their hatred of Christ, initially by their hostility toward him and direct infliction of violence upon him and presently by their blasphemies and their abuse of sacred vessels dear to Christ.

Peter suggests that the appropriate anti-Jewish action required by the onset of the crusades should be related to the economic activities that set the stage for Jewish mishandling of Christian *sancta*. Given this allegedly harmful economic activity, Jews should be forced to contribute their ill-gotten gains to the sacred military endeavor. Such action on the part of the king would be doubly beneficial. It would first of all be the appropriate response to Jewish enmity. Muslims suffer military violence during the crusades; Jews cannot be subjected to such military violence; they can at least suffer economic harm. Happily, this economic harm would at the same time add resources to the Christian campaign against Islam, thus providing a second benefit as well. It does not seem likely that King Louis of France responded to Peter's urging. The Second Crusade did have implications for Jewish moneylending business, but these implications seem to have been oriented toward protection of crusaders, rather than punishment of the Jews.[13]

Peter's claims of past and present Jewish crimes and the need for appropriate punishment offer an interesting foil to the 1096 crusaders and to Bernard of Clairvaux. He locates himself between the radically negative view of the 1096 crusaders and its rationalization of anti-Jewish violence and the protective stance of Bernard of Clairvaux. In addition, there is a striking contrast between Peter the Venerable and his ranking of the Jews as the worst of Christianity's enemies and the earlier admiration for Jews as superior to pagans, noted in Paul and the two Church Fathers we have discussed. For Peter the Venerable, Muslims are superior to Jews, because they accept at least some key Christian beliefs and they are passive in their opposition to Christian doctrine (crusading rationales notwithstanding). In the new and different context of twelfth-century medieval western Christendom, Jews constitute – for Peter the Venerable – the more detestable of the two alternative monotheistic communities, as a result of the alleged extent and activism of contemporary Jewish opposition.

The negativism expressed by Peter the Venerable to his Jewish contemporaries in the context of the Second Crusade is striking; it serves as a useful introduction to his more extensive treatment of Judaism and Jews in his lengthy polemical treatise against them.

At about the same time as he was composing his letter to King Louis VII, Peter was also involved in authoring a lengthy polemical treatise against the Jews. The title is in and of itself revealing: *Adversus Iudeorum inveteram duritiem (Against the Inveterate Obtuseness of the Jews)*. The title suggests immediately an assault on the Jews, rather than an effort to persuade them of Christian truth or to reinforce Christians in their beliefs. As we have seen in his letter to King Louis VII, Peter was convinced of the unceasing enmity of the Jews toward Christianity, which extended from antiquity down into the twelfth century. His polemical treatise is steeped in this same sense of long-term obtuseness and enmity and the desire to exhibit this obtuseness and enmity to his Christian audience.

Dominique Iogna-Prat has utilized Peter the Venerable as the vehicle through which to illuminate the accelerating twelfth-century commitment of the Church to combating both internal dissidents and external opponents. For Iogna-Prat, Peter's lifelong efforts at battling the Church's enemies both internal and external exhibit in microcosmic form the macrocosmic tendencies of the twelfth-century Church. Iogna-Prat entitled his important work *Ordonner et Exclure: Cluny et la societe chretienne face a l'heresie, au judaisme et a l'islam 1000–1500*, which has subsequently been made available in English as *Order and Exclusion: Cluny and Christendom Face Heresy, Judaism, and Islam (1000–1500)*.[14] This book joins a number of other recent efforts at identifying and analyzing the evolving internal intolerance and external aggressiveness of medieval western Christendom that began to surface in appreciable measure during the twelfth century.[15]

What is especially effective in Iogna-Prat's study is his treatment of the accelerating intolerance and aggressiveness through the prism of one representative figure, the abbot of Cluny. As indicated in his subtitle, the Cluniac movement in many ways spoke for Christendom, and Iogna-Prat further suggests that Abbot Peter in many ways spoke for Cluny.[16] For Iogna-Prat, the new thrust in the medieval Church involved an effort at internal purging and external combat. Early in the book, Iogna-Prat treats the issue of ordering Christian society and the world and shows the two to be related. For Christian thinkers of the twelfth century, order was ubiquitous – in the universe, in the human sphere, and in Christendom. God was responsible for the order of the universe; humans bore responsibility for order in the human sphere and especially in Christendom. These latter two forms of order are by no means easy to achieve, but they constitute the highest duty of Christians. They require relentless intellectual clarity and willful aggressiveness for their achievement.

Iogna-Prat organizes his analysis of Peter's efforts at ensuring proper order in two large segments. The first is Part II of the book and is entitled "Christian Society: Peter the Venerable's *Contra Petrobrusianos* and Its Background." It focuses on internal order in Christendom and specifically on Peter's 1139/1140 treatise against the dissident group founded by Peter of Bruis. Peter the Venerable identifies five major elements in the heretical views of Peter of Bruis, clarifies these five elements, and then refutes them by proving the truth of the normative Church views. The tone of presentation is harsh. The Petrobrusians constitute a serious threat to the Church, and the sense of danger elicits sharp condemnation, alongside serious intellectual engagement.

The second and outward thrust of Peter's activities constitutes Part III of the Iogna-Prat book and is entitled "Christian Universality: Peter the Venerable's *Adversus Iudeos* and *Contra sectam Sarracenorum.*" This third part shows Peter's commitment to Christian ordering of all of human society. Early in this section, Iogna-Prat argues that the new Christian commitment to proper order went beyond the internal structures of Christian society and extended out into the human world in its entirety. For Peter, Christianity was well on its way to subsuming all of human society, and thus part of his responsibility lay in clarifying Christian truth for all of known humanity, which significantly is now conceived of as the world of Islam and the Jews. Paganism, which loomed so large in the thinking of the Church Fathers, is no longer projected as a significant factor on the world scene; monotheism has been victorious, in the form of the Christian vision of the one God and two alternative and deficient visions of that God.

For Peter, Iogna-Prat projects internal intolerance and external aggressiveness as intimately linked; they both reflect the fundamental concern with proper order on the human scene. In *Order and Exclusion*, the Jews and Peter's treatise against them fall into the section on Christian universality, which is perfectly reasonable. At the same time, had Iogna-Prat decided to make them part of his discussion of Christian society, that would have been above reproach as well, since Jews were a constituent element in medieval western Christendom. It is striking that in Iogna-Prat's subtitle, *Cluny and Christendom Face Heresy, Judaism, and Islam (1000–1500)*, Jews occupy the middle position between internal heretics and external Muslims, suggesting that they in fact might find their place among the internal and/or external enemies of Christendom.[17] This median position may well have exacerbated Peter's antipathy toward the Jews.

Yvonne Friedman has provided a critical edition and careful analysis of Peter the Venerable's treatise against the Jews.[18] She has shown that it was composed in two stages. In the first stage of his composition, Peter identified four major Christological teachings that Jews reject: that Christ was predicted to be the son of God; that Christ was predicted to be God; that Christ was predicted to be different from human kings; that Christ as predicted Messiah has already appeared. Jews have denied and continue to deny these four tenets of Christianity; they have taken the opposite stance on each of these four critical issues, to their detriment. According to Peter, the four Christian truths were clearly predicted in the Old Testament, but Jews misread the crucial texts that foretell these truths. Thus, Peter sets out to make the correct reading of the biblical prophecies clear to his Jewish contemporaries or at least to his Christian readers. If Jewish contemporaries fail to grasp these correct readings, then at least Christian readers can see how firmly their faith is anchored in Scriptural prediction and how profoundly misguided their Jewish contemporaries are.

There is of course nothing unique or new in the broad thesis that Jews fail to grasp the meaning of biblical prediction. This notion was well developed in the Gospels themselves and was emphasized by the Church Fathers, as we have seen. Nor is there anything revolutionary in the four specific issues that Peter addresses. The notions that the Redeemer has already come, that he was not intended to be a human king, that he was intended to be the son of God, and that he was in fact intended to be divine were normative to Church thinking and had been well explored previously. Finally, the biblical proof-texts that Peter suggests for these four Christian doctrines denied by Jews are by no means innovative. The only aspect of the Peter's presentation that is noteworthy is its vituperative and demeaning quality.

Christian-Jewish argumentation over the ages bore the potential for frustration, annoyance, and anger. We have seen Augustine occasionally slip into moments of dismay at Jewish inability to grasp what was so blatantly obvious to him. However, despite these occasional outbursts, the overall tone of Augustine remained warm and sympathetic, grounded in a Pauline determination to bring truth to the Jews, who will ultimately accept this truth. Augustine made it clear throughout his composition that his ultimate goal was to convince Jews of biblically grounded truth. Not so with Peter the Venerable. In his case, there does not seem to be the Pauline certainty of eventual reconciliation between the Jews and God, and thus annoyance and anger predominate. They form the leitmotif for the entire initial segment of Peter's treatise and were in fact markedly augmented in the second segment of his composition.

Peter's sense of inveterate obtuseness on the part of Jews, suggested in the title, was amply demonstrated and denigrated throughout the first four chapters of his composition. On the four Christological issues addressed by Peter, the Jews had been and continued to be inveterately obtuse, despite the overwhelming proofs from the Hebrew Bible amassed by earlier Christian thinkers and reinforced by Peter. In this sense, the focus of Peter's treatise is the Jewish present, which is marked for him by an ongoing failure to grasp the obvious truths revealed in the Hebrew Bible, which the Jews revere and study diligently, but cannot correctly comprehend.

To be sure, the present-day Jewish incapacity is merely a continuation of a historic disability. Jews over the ages have not changed. The Jews of Jesus' day were unable to see in him the fulfillment of the predictions of their own prophets and related to him with enmity. Their descendants maintain the same failure and the same enmity. Thus, while Augustine may have occasionally expressed frustration and anger, Peter's sense of ongoing Jewish intransigence that extended for more than a few centuries, indeed for well over a millennium, filled him with rage and evoked the harshness of his polemic. Although the treatise was supposedly intended to convince, it in fact was oriented far more toward denunciation.

This intense denunciation suggests a measure of uncertainty as regards the Jewish future. Despite Paul's profound convictions as to the future reconciliation of God and the Jews, Peter's unyielding insistence on Jewish obtuseness raises reasonable questions as to eventual Jewish acknowledgment of the truth. To some extent, this retreat from the Pauline position might be ascribed to the lengthy lapse of time – more than a millennium – between the advent of Jesus and the twelfth century; however, this retreat also stems from the new atmosphere of internal intolerance and external aggressiveness that was increasingly palpable in western Christendom.

According to Yvonne Friedman, the original four-part treatise was subsequently enlarged by a second part to the fourth chapter, devoted to the issue of miracles. In this addition, Christian miracles were compared to the prior miracles performed for and by their Israelite predecessors, with the Christian miracles projected as far more impressive. Thus, the Jews of the past were indeed favored by God, but this divine favor was inferior to the subsequent divine concern for the people of the new covenant. Emphasis on the shortcoming of the Israelite/Jewish past contrasts markedly with the lavish praise of that past expressed by the Church Fathers whom we have examined.

The truly innovative addition to Peter's original four-chapter opus is the fifth chapter, in which Peter cites and attacks the Talmud. Christians and Jews both revered the Hebrew Bible as divinely revealed truth. At the same time, each community elevated a second corpus of writings to authoritative status. For Christians, this second corpus was the New Testament, the set of writings that trace the activities of Jesus and his followers. For Jews, the supplementary corpus was the Oral Torah, the legal writings that were first codified in Palestinian Jewry in the early third century as the Mishnah and then expanded over the ensuing centuries in both Palestine and Mesopotamia as the Talmuds. These Oral Torah documents spell out the detailed demands of the covenant that was revealed in the Hebrew Bible and include broader nonlegal materials as well, materials projected as necessary for living a fully Jewish existence.

Both Christians and Jews were convinced that the original Hebrew Bible and their additional sacred corpus complemented one another seamlessly and originated in the same divine source. For a long time, Jewish intellectual leadership remained more or less unaware of the New Testament, although the growing numerical strength of Christianity meant that its Scripture forced its way at least to an extent into Jewish consciousness.[19] Since Jews initially constituted a very small minority community in medieval Christian Europe, it was easier for the intellectual leadership of the Christian majority to remain unaware of the Jewish second corpus.

With the growth of the Jewish population of medieval western Christendom from the early eleventh century on, awareness of the other community's complementary corpus of sacred literature expanded rapidly among both Jews and Christians. For the Jews of western Christendom, immersed in the thoroughly Christian environment of medieval Europe, the symbols of Christianity were ubiquitous, pervading the public space of the towns in which they lived. As a result, Jews began to absorb more fully and more readily the knowledge of Christianity and its New Testament. One of the earliest of the Jewish polemicists in medieval western Christendom – Jacob ben Reuben – included in his work a chapter (not unlike the fifth and closing chapter of Peter's treatise) devoted to the citation of verses from the New Testament and to attack on these verses.[20] As Jewish polemicists took the offensive against the dominant religion, attack on the New

Testament became an accepted element in the literature they provided for their coreligionists.[21]

Christian familiarity with the Jewish complementary sacred texts was far more limited, since the Jews continued to constitute a relatively small minority community in an overwhelmingly majority Christian environment. However, as western Christendom's commitment to expansion deepened and moved well beyond the merely military during the twelfth century, familiarity with the writings of the Jewish and Muslim external foes became increasingly important. Peter the Venerable was a major figure in the drive to enrich Christian knowledge of Islam, commissioning a translation of the Quran into Latin, so that European Christians might become familiar with its contents. Precisely how Peter came to his knowledge of the talmudic passages he cites and denigrates is not yet known.[22] It is clear, however, that he had some access to this Jewish sacred literature and that he was determined to make it part of the case he was bringing against his Jewish contemporaries. In this closing chapter, it becomes obvious that the ultimate purpose of Peter's treatise was not to convince Jews, but rather to convict them yet again of inveterate obtuseness.

As we shall see more fully in the next chapter, knowledge of the Talmud could be exploited for a number of purposes. Peter's purpose was simple and primitive. The Jewish obtuseness he had been establishing by adducing compelling arguments for biblically grounded Christian truth was now reinforced considerably by bringing evidence from the Jews' own postbiblical tradition that exposed further – in Peter's mind – the intellectual disabilities his Jewish contemporaries suffered. Again, this disability involved more than present-day Jews. The Talmud was a destructive legacy of the Jewish past and suggests once again continuity in disabilities that began in the past, continued into the twelfth-century present, and were likely to be maintained into the Jewish future as well.

Peter the Venerable opens the fifth chapter of his treatise with stunning denunciation of the Jews and the Talmud they venerate. He begins with the Jews.

O Jew! It seems to me that I have provided satisfaction on those issues that have been placed in question – through both [sacred] authorities and through reason – for any man. If indeed for any man, then likewise for you – if in fact you are a man! Indeed, I dare not designate you a man, lest I lie. For I see that in you is extinguished, indeed buried, that which separates man from animals and beasts and raises man above them – reason.[23]

Peter announces grandly that he has laid out a full case for the truth of Christianity in the preceding four chapters and that the failure of his Jewish contemporaries to grasp these obvious Christian truths reveals these Jews to be less than human. This reflects the growing twelfth-century sense of Christianity as totally reasonable, thus stigmatizing those who deny Christian truth as less than human.[24]

Peter buttresses his denunciation of the Jews by his appeal to Scripture. He cites Psalm 49, which speaks of the man who does not understand as being compared to a beast and in fact being transformed into one.[25] He then follows up by citing the dispiriting message from Isaiah 6, which has God telling the prophet that he will speak and his Jewish audience will not grasp his message. The Acts of the Apostles made citation of this same verse the final note of Paul's castigation of the Jews of Rome in its closing episode.[26] Thus once more Peter projects continuity between Jewish failure in the days of Isaiah, again during the first century, and now during the twelfth century. Peter is convinced that, by his time, Jewish obtuseness had lasted nearly two full millennia and thus seems incorrigible.

Peter pillories not only his Jewish contemporaries; he turns the same vituperation upon the sacred literature of these Jews, the Talmud. He indicates that, in addition to his first four books, which he believes proved conclusively the truths of Christianity and the errors of the Jews, he will now in a fifth book indicate yet further the lack of reason on the part of the Jews.

I shall lead forth that monstrous beast from its lair and shall exhibit it in the view of all the world and in the sight of all peoples to be ridiculed. I shall present before all – O Jewish beast – that book of yours, your book, that Talmud of yours, that reprehensible doctrine of yours, which you prefer to the prophetic books and to all authentic teachings.[27]

The Jews and their Talmud are alike in their utter lack of reason, which means ultimately their inhumanity.

Iogna-Prat, in his close analysis of the fifth chapter of Peter's treatise, notes that it focuses on three major shortcomings of the Talmud: its demeaning, even blasphemous depiction of God; its ridiculous portrayal of the afterlife; and its low moral standards.[28] For our purposes, it is sufficient to note Peter's citations and observations with regard to the first of these three issues. Within the Talmud, there are numerous stories about the deity that are obviously designed to reinforce key religious values in the Jewish community.[29] Peter cites a sequence of these tales that show: God reading the Talmud and discussing it with the rabbis (T.B.,

Berakhot, 8a, and *Avodah Zarah*, 3b); God disputing with the rabbis and admitting defeat at their hands (T.B., *Baba Mezia*, 86a); God's anger (T.B., *Berakhot*, 7a); and finally God's anguish over the dire circumstances of the Jews (T.B., *Berakhot*, 59a, 3a, and 71).[30] All these tales – intended to advance spiritual teachings and values – elicit ridicule and rage from Peter the Venerable. They and the remainder of the talmudic material he cites serve to complete his case for the inveterate obtuseness of the Jews.

Jewish failure to interpret properly the teachings imparted by their divinely appointed prophets had long been a central theme in Christian argumentation with and about Jews. Peter the Venerable argued this case vigorously in the first four chapters of his treatise. In his fifth chapter, he opened a new front in the battle, claiming that historical Jewish obtuseness is reflected as well in the Talmud, which Jews mistakenly venerate as an element in divine revelation. In whatever direction we look – Peter's sense of Jewish present, Jewish past, or Jewish future – the same bleak picture emerges. Jews are simply incapable of grasping clear and obvious truths. Indeed, this obtuseness puts their very humanity in question.

The twelfth century is widely projected as a turning point in the evolution of medieval western Christendom. The vitalization on the material level that commenced toward the end of the tenth and the beginning of the eleventh century accelerated markedly. This vitalization now generated a profound commitment to achieving internal homogeneity and to engaging more fully – both militarily and spiritually – the external world, now characterized as an enemy world. This commitment had significant implications for the perceptions of twelfth-century Jews, their past, and their future and eventually for both popular perceptions of and ecclesiastical and governmental policies toward Europe's Jews.[31]

Viewing the external world as the enemy implied a sharp sense of clear-cut right and clear-cut wrong, the powerful conviction that Christianity was truth and that the competing monotheisms Judaism and Islam – to say nothing of paganism – were steeped in error. While this conviction of error applied to both Muslims and Jews, the early sense of Muslims being far-off and Jews being nearby, first expressed inchoately by the popular crusaders, made the Jews a more immediate target of the intensified conviction of Christian truth and the error of all others. Moreover, the vibrancy of twelfth-century European civilization produced new lines of Christian thinking and spirituality, perceived by many in the leadership of the Church as heretical and dangerous. Thus, yet another battle front was opened for the Church, and this new battle front served to deepen yet further the sharp cleavage in perceptions of (Christian) truth and (Jewish, Muslim, and dissident Christian) error.

With regard to the Jewish present, Bernard of Clairvaux softened somewhat crusading negativity, projecting a sense that Jews have at least committed themselves to accepting their subjugation and living peacefully in Christian society. For Peter the Venerable, however, no such change has taken place. For Peter, the obtuseness that characterized the Jews of Jesus' day has been maintained by the Jews of twelfth-century Europe. These twelfth-century Jews continue to resist the obviously accurate Christian readings of the biblical predictions in which they thoroughly but erroneously immerse themselves. Moreover, examination of their own sacred writings in the Talmud indicates just how muddled and misguided they are in their thinking.

According to Peter, Jewish error is by no means theoretical and passive. In his view, the Jews of Europe exhibit aggressively against twelfth-century Christians and Christianity the same animosity and enmity they expressed so stunningly in first-century Jerusalem. Nothing has been learned by the Jews, and nothing has changed. As twelfth-century Christendom committed itself to protracted battle against its external foes, Peter insisted that unyielding Jewish hostility to Christianity must be recognized and acknowledged and that the battle against the Jews must be vigorously waged.

With respect to the views on the Jewish past expressed by popular crusaders, Bernard of Clairvaux, and yet more fully Peter the Venerable, the encomia to the early period of Israelite/Judean history noted in Paul and the Church Fathers almost completely disappeared. Only Bernard, in his letter making the case for Jewish safety, mentions some of the positives of the Jewish past. The popular crusaders and Peter the Venerable dwell exclusively on the shortcomings of the Jews of antiquity, with emphasis on Jewish enmity to Christ and his followers. This enmity was of course a major element in the New Testament, but even that was mitigated to a significant extent. The Church Fathers softened the sense of historic Jewish enmity even further. There is little or no such mitigation on the part of the popular crusaders and Peter the Venerable.

The Pauline sense of eventual Jewish recognition of the truth and return to the covenant, properly comprehended, could not be overturned. Nonetheless, the popular crusaders offered the stark alternatives of conversion or death. As noted by Bernard, those Jews illegitimately killed would lose all possibility of enjoying eventual salvation. Readers of Peter's treatise have to at least wonder a bit about his sense of the Jewish future. Could the people who have remained so intransigently opposed to obvious Christian reading of the biblical legacy eventually achieve real truth? Paul was convinced that they could and would, and Peter the Venerable was not about to contradict him. However, the prospects were hardly encouraging.

A new context, with new constellations of popular thinking and power, had begun to create new perceptions of the Jewish present, past, and future. As this new context became more firmly established, the negativity of these new perceptions was intensified. Precisely what was to be done with the hostile and blaspheming Jews was by no means certain. The Augustinian position that Jews must be preserved in Christian society was too strongly grounded to be overtly rejected. On the other hand, the negative portrait of Jewish present and past and the doubts as to the Jewish future had to take a toll on medieval Christians and medieval Christian thinking. Exactly how the increasingly negative perspectives on Judaism and Jews might be expressed and augmented subsequent to the twelfth century will be addressed, at least to an extent, in the coming chapters, along with the practical conclusions to which these ever more negative majority perspectives could lead.

Notes

1 For further detail on the emergence of northern European Jewry during the second half of the Middle Ages, see Robert Chazan, *The Jews of Medieval Western Christendom* (Cambridge: Cambridge University Press, 2006; *Cambridge Medieval Textbooks*) and my forthcoming study of the history of Jewish migrations.

2 On the millenarian expectations associated in some quarters with the First Crusade, see Jay Rubenstein, *Armies of Heaven: The First Crusade and the Quest for Apocalypse* (New York: Basic Books, 2011), and Robert Chazan, "'Let Not a Remnant or a Residue Escape:' Millenarian Enthusiasm in the First Crusade," *Speculum* 84 (2009): 289–313.

3 Robert Chazan, *European Jewry and the First Crusade* (Berkeley: University of California Press, 1987), 287–293.

4 Ibid., 225.

5 See n. 2.

6 For full details on the 1096 violence, see Chazan, *European Jewry and the First Crusade*, 50–84.

7 Robert Chazan, *Church, State, and Jews* (New York: Behrman House, 1980), 103. All citations from this letter will come from ibid., 103–104.

8 Robert Chazan, *Medieval Stereotypes and Modern Antisemitism* (Berkeley: University of California Press, 1997), 49.

9 Ibid.

10 Ibid.

11 Robert Chazan, *Reassessing Jewish Life in Medieval Europe* (Cambridge: Cambridge University Press, 2010), chapter 6.

12 Chazan, *Medieval Stereotypes and Modern Antisemitism*, 51.

13 Chazan, *European Jewry and the First Crusade*, 179–191.

14 Dominique Iogna-Prat, *Order and Exclusion: Cluny and Christendom Face Heresy, Judaism, and Islam (1000–1500)*, trans. Graham Robert Edwards (Ithaca: Cornell University Press, 2002).

15 See the Prologue.

16 Iogna-Prat entitled his introductory chapter "A Journey through Christendom via Cluny."

17 Note that the treatise against Jews falls chronologically between the other two as well.

18 Peter the Venerable, *Adversus Iudeorum inveteram duritiem*, ed. Yvonne Friedman (Turnhout: Brepols, 1985; *Corpus Christianorum: Continuatio Mediaevalis*).

19 See Peter Schafer on the minimal reflections of Jesus in the Talmud – *Jesus in the Talmud* (Princeton: Princeton University Press, 2007).

20 See Robert Chazan, *Fashioning Jewish Identity in Medieval Western Christendom* (Cambridge: Cambridge University Press, 2004), chapter 13.

21 In fact, the Jewish lines of attack on the New Testament are strikingly parallel to the Christian lines of attack on the Talmud.

22 Iogna-Prat, *Order and Exclusion*, 302, notes that Peter – normally scrupulous in his citation of sources – does not do so with respect to his Talmud materials.

23 Peter the Venerable, *Adversus Iudeorum inveteram duritiem*, 125.

24 This aspect of twelfth-century thinking is emphasized by Anna Sapir Abulafia, *Christians and Jews in the Twelfth Century Renaissance* (London: Routledge, 1995).

25 Peter's citation is of course from the Vulgate, which diverges somewhat from the Hebrew original.

26 Acts 28:25–28.

27 Peter the Venerable, *Adversus Iudeorum inveteram duritiem*, 125–126.

28 Iogna-Prat, *Order and Exclusion*, 301–316.

29 A great deal of scholarly attention has been directed of late to the narrative style of the Talmud. See especially Jeffrey Rubenstein, *Talmudic Stories: Narrative Art, Composition, and Culture* (Baltimore: Johns Hopkins University Press, 1999), and idem, *Stories of the Babylonian Talmud* (Baltimore: Johns Hopkins University Press, 2010). Yaakov Elman has embarked on an effort to understand the Babylonian Talmud against its broad Mesopotamian cultural backdrop, which will likely produce further advances in understanding its narrative styles and these talmudic tales.

30 Interestingly, Jacob ben Reuben – cited in n. 20 – attacks verses from the New Testament along precisely the same lines. He claims that attribution of human feelings to Jesus constitutes an inappropriate portrayal of a being that Christians claim to be divine.

31 The studies on accelerating anti-Jewish sentiment in medieval Europe cited in the Prologue all focus heavily on developments during the twelfth century.

6

The Discovery of Jewish Sources

The Pugio Fidei

Peter the Venerable amassed unusual information on the Talmud for a twelfth-century Christian thinker. Although we do not know the ways in which this information reached him, the usual conjecture is that it came via converts from Judaism to Christianity, since knowledge of Hebrew was rare among Christians in twelfth-century western Christendom. Peter's use of the talmudic material at his disposal was limited; in effect, he used it in order to further denigrate his Jewish contemporaries. Over the subsequent century, the number of converts with serious Jewish learning multiplied; Christian knowledge of rabbinic tradition expanded considerably; and utilization of this knowledge moved in new directions. Not surprisingly, this budding familiarity with the teachings of the rabbis impacted Christian perceptions of the trajectory of Jewish history significantly.

By the middle of the thirteenth century, important new campaigns grounded in knowledge of the Talmud had emerged across western Christendom. The initial figures in these campaigns were converts to Christianity, who brought their command of Hebrew and Jewish sources with them into the Christian fold and used it against their former coreligionists. The first such activist convert was Nicholas Donin, a shadowy figure of whom we know little. Donin seems to have originated in the Jewish communities of southern Europe, although he seems to have eventually settled in Paris and from there extended his activities to the broader European scene.[1]

Nicholas Donin's view of the Talmud was far harsher than that of Peter the Venerable. Whereas Peter exploited talmudic passages to demean Jewish thinking, Nicholas Donin argued to the leadership of the Church that the Talmud was much worse than simply silly; according to

Donin, the Talmud was intolerable, that is to say that it literally should not be tolerated by Christian society. Our first sources for the anti-Talmud campaign Donin set in motion consist of letters sent by Pope Gregory IX to major monarchs and key ecclesiastical leaders all across western Christendom and a related set of thirty-five accusations against the Talmud, in all likelihood composed by Donin himself.[2]

The thirty-five allegations leveled against the Talmud, seemingly by Donin himself, fall into six broad categories: (1) the power allocated to the rabbis by the Talmud; (2) anti-Christian behaviors sanctioned by the Talmud; (3) antisocial behaviors permitted by the Talmud; (4) talmudic materials that demean God; (5) talmudic teachings that demean Jesus and the Church; (6) talmudic statements that are simply ludicrous (along the lines portrayed by Peter the Venerable).[3]

These six categories are reflected in more cursory fashion in the papal letters, which highlight the following elements:

- The Jews "are not content with the Old Law, which God gave to Moses in writing"; they "affirm that God gave another law that is called Talmud."
- This Talmud "contains matter that is so abusive and so unspeakable that it arouses shame in those who mention it and horror in those who hear it."
- This Talmud "is said to be the chief cause that holds the Jews obstinate in their ~~perfidy.~~"[4] *deceitfulness*

These papal letters do not make clear which of these statements constitute charges against the Talmud. Probably only the first two accusations were to be investigated, utilizing the categories and materials presented by Nicholas Donin.

The papal request of the monarchs of western Christendom was to support collection of exemplars of the Talmud and turn them over to churchmen, specifically the Dominicans and Franciscans of Paris. To the leadership of the Church in Paris, especially the Dominicans and Franciscans, the pope spelled out the ultimate objective of the collection of the books. "Those books in which you find errors of this sort you shall cause to the burned at the stake."[5] Copies of the Talmud were to be gathered and carefully examined. When the charges made against the Talmud – whatever they might have precisely been – were substantiated, the books were to be destroyed.

In the event, the papal orders were carried out only in northern France, with collection of the Jewish books supported by the pious King Louis

IX and with examination of the Talmud carried out by the distinguished theologians of Paris's great university. Copies of the Talmud were gathered in large quantities; in some kind of inquisitorial proceeding, the Talmud was put on trial and found guilty; the papal order of burning was eventually carried out multiple times in Paris in the 1240s, to the consternation of the Jews of northern France and indeed of all of northern Europe.

At this point, the story grows more complicated. In 1244, the new pope, Innocent IV, commended King Louis IX for his support of the anti-Talmud campaign and urged him to continue his valuable assistance.[6] Then, somewhat surprisingly, Pope Innocent IV in 1247 reversed course. Approached by the rabbis of France, the pope accepted their argument that without the Talmud Judaism could not be practiced, meaning that the papal stance on the Talmud undercut the Augustinian doctrine of tolerating Jewish life in Christendom. Convinced by the Jewish argumentation, Pope Innocent IV addressed the ecclesiastical leaders in Paris and urged them to reexamine the Talmud, to return to the Jews harmless talmudic material, and to excise talmudic material deemed offensive.[7] The reexamination was carried out by the Parisian theologians, but they rejected the papal plan, insisting that the Talmud in its entirety could not be tolerated. The new Paris commission ordered continuation of the confiscation and destruction of exemplars of the book.[8] Burning and prohibition of the Talmud remained thereafter the norm in France. However, in most of the rest of Europe the common practice became censorship of the Talmud, along the lines suggested by Pope Innocent IV. For our purposes, what is crucial is growing awareness of the Talmud, with a focus on its negative characteristics, when viewed from the Christian perspective.[9]

Nicholas Donin in effect introduced to Christian Europe a new perspective on the Jewish present in the 1230s. From early on – indeed from the Gospels on – Church thinkers had accused the Jewish authorities of leading the Jewish masses astray. Now, Nicholas Donin introduced evidence from the Talmud itself to show that the rabbis had arrogated to themselves unwarranted religious authority that demeaned the sacred books of the Bible and – more important yet – brought their Jewish followers to grievous error. The long-standing Christian condemnation of Jewish religious leadership took on a new reality. Indeed, the Jewish present and the Jewish past were intimately linked in this malpractice, since the roots of the Talmud lay well in the past but continued to influence Jewish life decisively in the present.

[handwritten margin note: Rabbis got too much power / led Jews in wrong direction]

In addition, Donin's charges lent new substance to Peter the
Venerable's allegation of ongoing Jewish blasphemy. Peter had used
his limited knowledge of the Talmud essentially to demean it (Nicholas
Donin in fact provided far fuller evidence of the kind of talmudic thinking that Peter had excoriated). At the same time, Peter had accused the
Jews of maintaining the hatred they bore to Jesus by regularly blaspheming the sacred objects of the Christian faith; he did not, however,
link this alleged blasphemy to the Talmud. Now, Donin provided to
Christian Europe talmudic statements that allegedly reflected precisely
such blasphemy.

[handwritten margin note: hating Jesus Christ]

Thus, the picture of present-day Jews and their forebearers advanced
by Nicholas Donin – on the basis of careful citation of talmudic sources –
substantiated the most negative allegations we have encountered as to
Jewish present and past. Donin represents a major milestone in the projection of negative imagery of Jewish present and past in medieval Europe.

Peter the Venerable and Nicholas Donin make the contrasting approach
of Friar Paul Christian to the Talmud all the more remarkable. Friar Paul
used his familiarity with the Talmud in opposite fashion; rather than
denigrating or condemning the Talmud, he was determined to exploit it
for proselytizing purposes. For him, present-day Jews – mired in religious
error – might be made to see the truth by reexamining the teachings of
their rabbis. These rabbis, to be sure, had led their followers astray, as
argued regularly by Christian thinkers over the ages and as documented
by Nicholas Donin. However, the teachings of the Talmud might nonetheless be turned to useful purposes. Although Friar Paul would have
surely agreed to Donin's negative views of the Jews and their Talmud, in
another sense he was far more positive in both respects. Like Paul and
Augustine (and the early Luther, whom we shall later encounter), Friar
Paul harbored genuine hopes for convincing Jews of Christian truth,
which betrays a more positive view of his Jewish contemporaries. He
was convinced that these thirteenth-century Jews bore the potential for
encountering and absorbing the truths of Christianity, if confronted with
evidence from their own religious tradition.

Friar Paul's strategy was simple. Since – as we have seen – the
Christian-Jewish argument revolved so heavily around the understanding of key biblical verses, rabbinic exegesis of these key biblical verses
might – somewhat surprisingly – strengthen the Christian case. In general
of course, Christian thinkers had condemned the rabbis for misleading
their followers, and Friar Paul would have concurred. However, he was

convinced that on occasion the rabbis provide useful evidence that buttresses the Christian case.

Isaiah 52:13–53:12, the so-called Suffering Servant passage, provides a striking example of Friar Paul's approach. For Christians over the ages, this powerful passage constituted an obvious prediction of Jesus – persecuted for no sin on his part and eventually risen to great heights. Medieval Jews, on the contrary, rejected the notion that the Suffering Servant was intended to refer to the Messiah; for Jews, the referent of the Suffering Servant passage was clearly the Jewish people, abused for no reason and ultimately – in the future – to be raised to great heights. Friar Paul argued to thirteenth-century Jews that their own rabbis of yore understood this passage as a reference to the Messiah, thereby buttressing the traditional Christian exegesis and undercutting the standard medieval Jewish view.

Free-standing rabbinic dicta were also adduced by Friar Paul in his proselytizing efforts. The rabbis, for example had recurrently linked the appearance of the Messiah to the destruction of the Temple. These linkages would seem to suggest that the Messiah has already come, indeed at approximately the same time as the advent of Jesus. Jews confronted with rabbinic materials that seemed to support the Christian case would – it was assumed by Friar Paul – raise serious doubt and uncertainty, which is of course the beginning of the process of loss of identity and conversion.[10]

Friar Paul seems to have begun his preaching career in the synagogues of southern France. The high point – although by no means the end point – of his career was a disputation arranged between himself and a distinguished Catalan rabbi, Moses ben Nahman of Gerona.[11] The ground rules of the engagement were simple: Friar Paul was to present rabbinic sources that he believed make the Christian case, and the rabbi was permitted to respond to the friar's claims.[12] The issues to be investigated were time-honored points of dispute between Christians and Jews. Friar Paul set out to prove (1) that the Messiah had already come; (2) that the Messiah was intended to be both divine and human; (3) that the Messiah was intended to suffer and die; and (4) that, with the advent of the Messiah, Jewish law had lost its validity. What was innovative in this disputation was Friar Paul's intention to prove these age-old Christian contentions from rabbinic writings.

In the course of the give-and-take at Barcelona, Friar Paul regularly introduced consideration of the Jewish past and the Jewish future. These projections of the Jewish past and future were intended to prove to the Jews the hopelessness of their circumstances. Thus, for example, the very first exchange revolved about Genesis 49:10, widely advanced as a verse critical to the Christian case for Jesus as Messiah. Friar Paul was – in one sense – very traditional in his use of this verse. He hoped to show Jews that Jesus clearly fulfilled this prediction of the patriarch Jacob, that Jesus was therefore the promised Messiah, and thus that the Jewish future was bleak so long as Jews hoped for a future messianic advent. What was innovative in the case made by Friar Paul was his utilization of talmudic materials in fleshing out his case that the Jews had lost their political authority and thus that the Messiah has already arrived.[13] In a more general way, the first and most important agenda item at Barcelona – that the Messiah has already arrived – is a critically important assertion with respect to the Jewish future and its hopelessness.

A sketchy Latin source presents the engagement as an unmitigated Christian success, with Friar Paul besting Rabbi Moses at every turn, until the rabbi fled Barcelona in ignominy. Rabbi Moses himself – a writer of great skill – penned a beguiling Hebrew narrative in which he depicts himself as turning back every source advanced by Friar Paul in a manner that showed his personal superiority to the friar and the truth of the Jewish position he represented.[14] Looking beyond these inflated claims from the two sides, it is clear from the aftermath of the disputation that both could claim a measure of achievement, but that neither achieved total success.[15] *neither won*

On the Christian side, the new approach of utilizing rabbinic materials was by no means discredited by Rabbi Moses. Friar Paul continued his preaching efforts subsequent to 1263. He was in fact invited in the late 1260s by King Louis IX to bring his innovative proselytizing campaign to Paris. At the same time, the encounter with Rabbi Moses ben Nahman clearly exposed weaknesses in the specifics of Friar Paul's argumentation, which led to a massive effort at refining the new approach. The result of this massive effort was a remarkable missionizing manual composed by Friar Raymond Martin under the title of the *Pugio fidei*.

By the middle of the thirteenth century, the commitment to learning Hebrew and plumbing Jewish sources for a variety of purposes – but especially for missionizing – had extended beyond the original cadre of converts from Judaism. Schools of Hebrew and Arabic as well were established, and serious Christian scholarship in Jewish sources emerged. One of the finest of the thirteenth-century Christian Hebraists was Friar Raymond, again of the Dominican Order. Exhibiting serious knowledge of the Hebrew language and of Jewish sources and at the same time well trained in Scholastic thinking and procedures, Friar Raymond took the innovative thrust developed by Friar Paul to a far higher level of sophistication and achievement.

Friar Raymond's *magnum opus* – the *Pugio fidei* – is remarkable in three ways. In the first place, the *Pugio fidei* is distinguished for the sheer quantity of rabbinic sources cited. Some of these sources are no longer extant, leading occasional modern scholars to suggest that some of these sources were in fact fabricated. With the passage of time, this view has become increasingly dubious, with the no-longer-extant sources now assumed to reflect the simple loss of materials over time. The second distinguishing characteristic of the *Pugio fidei* is its meticulous treatment of the rabbinic sources adduced. Friar Raymond translated his talmudic passages with exquisite care. When a key word might seem to be problematic, he justifies his translation by citing a major medieval Jewish exegete on the given word or phrase, in an effort to obviate any challenge from Jews as to the accuracy of his presentation of the rabbinic sources. Finally, the *Pugio fidei* addresses the broadest possible range of Christian doctrines. We have noted the four key issues addressed by Friar Paul; Friar Raymond went far beyond these four items and created in effect an entire Christian theology grounded in Jewish sources. The *Pugio fidei* is a remarkable achievement and attests to the seriousness of the thirteenth-century Christian proselytizing effort.[16]

Friar Raymond depicts his book as the *Pugio Christianorum ad impiorum perfidiam jugulandum, et maxime Judeorum* – *The Dagger of Christians for Slaying the Perfidy of the Impious and Especially the Jews.* Those impious whose perfidy he is determined to destroy obviously consist of enemies internal to Christendom, since he does not really address the Muslim world at all. Book I of the *Pugio fidei* is broadly addressed and philosophic. Modern scholars have speculated about the addressees of the philosophic arguments of Book I and have seen in them evidence of Friar Raymond's familiarity with the philosophic skepticism of the mid-thirteenth century and aspects of the Scholastic response.

Quickly, however, Friar Raymond moves from the philosophic plane to address "especially the Jews." Philosophic speculation is replaced with immersion in the texts honored by the Jews, that is to say adoption of the tactic innovated by Friar Paul Christian. Friar Raymond begins Book II of his opus by defining the term Jew, which means in effect explaining who Jews are in terms of their past. The key claim to be made to Jews, in Friar Raymond's view, is that the Messiah has already appeared, and thus the entirety of the argumentation in Book II of the *Pugio fidei* is devoted to this issue. As noted, this contention had long stood at the center of the Christian-Jewish debate; it was – as we have seen – the opening issue addressed by Friar Paul in the Barcelona disputation. Friar Raymond argues this point from a wide range of biblical verses, traditional Jewish interpretations of these verses, and free-standing rabbinic dicta. Friar Raymond also presents and rebuts numerous Jewish objections to the claim that the Messiah has already come. Book III in turn addresses a broad range of Christian doctrine, all elements of which are proved through citation of Jewish sources. The very last two chapters are devoted to the sinfulness of the Jews and their dolorous circumstances from the advent of Jesus until the end of the world.

Friar Raymond shared with Friar Paul the standard Christian criticism of contemporary Jewish failure to accept Christianity. Like Friar Paul, he at the same time believed that his Jewish contemporaries had the capacity to engage and accept Christian truth, if the argumentation advanced to them was appropriate and convincing. He further shared Friar Paul's conviction that the key to this appropriate and convincing argumentation was utilization of Jewish sources. Friar Raymond was clearly convinced that Friar Paul was very much on the right track, but that his innovative approach required much fuller documentation and needed to move well beyond the bare-bones Barcelona agenda. Friar Raymond's convictions moved him to compose the *Pugio fidei*, with its unique characteristics.

We have already seen that polemical/missionizing texts regularly involved historical arguments about the appearance of Jesus, arguments that involve constructions of the Jewish past and important implications for the Jewish future. This tendency is manifest in Friar Paul's missionizing argumentation, and it dominates Book II of the *Pugio fidei*. There are two necessary components in advancing Christian proofs of Jesus' fulfillment of messianic predictions. The first is accurate reading of the biblical predictions; the second is reconstructing the historical circumstances of his advent, especially the Jewish history involved.

Let us begin with Friar Raymond's use of key biblical predictions and related Jewish history. Book II of the *Pugio* in its entirety attempts to prove from biblical prophecy that the Messiah promised by God has in fact already appeared. Part of Friar Raymond's effort was necessarily directed toward exegetical issues. What precisely did key biblical prophecies mean? How are difficult terms or verses to be understood? To be sure, clarification of the biblical prophecies themselves constituted only half the task. Equally important was reconstruction of historical realities, in order to show that biblically predicted time periods had elapsed or that biblically predicted events had already taken place.

The very first substantive chapter in this effort – chapter 3 of Book II – is the lengthiest in the entire book; it focuses on the prediction of seventy weeks found in Daniel 9:24–27. For both Christians and Jews, this prophecy is the most direct statement available in Scripture for the time of the advent of the Messiah. It is brief and has no imagery associated with it. The only problem – and it is a huge problem – involves plumbing the ambiguities of four dense Hebrew verses and identifying the events referred to elliptically in these four difficult verses. The challenge is overwhelming. Despite the difficulty in parsing Daniel 9:24–27, numerous Christian and Jewish exegetes and polemicists devoted themselves to the task, and Friar Raymond took his place in this company as well.[17] His treatment is exceedingly full, cites numerous rabbinic sources, and builds what is for the friar an inescapable conclusion. Although Friar Raymond had to devote considerable energy in chapter 3 of Book II to clarifying the meaning of the seventy weeks indicated in Daniel 9, he also had to identify the historical realities that purportedly corresponded to the biblical prediction of seventy weeks. Friar Raymond had to reconstruct in considerable detail the progression of Jewish history from the starting point of the seventy weeks down through their conclusion, and he in fact did so.[18]

Chapter 4 of Book II centers around yet another famous verse in the Christian-Jewish debate – Genesis 49:10, Jacob's prophecy concerning Judah: "The scepter shall not depart from Judah, nor the ruler's staff from between his feet, until *Shiloh* comes and the homage of people be his."[19] As we have already seen, this verse has regularly been projected by Christian expositors as an obvious reference to Jesus, with whose coming the descendants of Judah – that is the Jews – lost all political and religious authority.[20] For Jewish readers, this simplification of the history of Jewish political and religious authority was wholly incorrect. Genuine Jewish political authority, in the form of kingship, had been lost long before the advent of Jesus. At the same time, other forms of Jewish religious authority, such as the Jewish courts and the rabbis, lasted well beyond the lifetime of Jesus. Thus, whatever form the scepter and the ruler's staff might take, Genesis 49:10 could not – according to Jewish polemicists – sustain the Christian case.[21]

Here we can highlight clearly Friar Raymond's sophisticated use of rabbinic sources, in a manner more adroit than that of Friar Paul, his predecessor. Friar Raymond sets out to define carefully the nature of Jewish authority and to amass multiple Jewish sources that prove the disappearance of genuine Jewish authority at precisely the time of the advent of Jesus. The combination of disappearance of Jewish authority and advent of Jesus must surely – according to Friar Raymond – mean that Jesus was the Messiah predicted in Genesis 49:10. This is a point in the age-old Christian-Jewish debate that would seem particularly amenable to Friar Raymond's utilization of rabbinic sources, and Friar Raymond's movement far beyond traditional Christian argumentation and even the original argumentation of Friar Paul is patent.

In the vivid report of the Barcelona disputation penned by Rabbi Moses ben Nahman, Genesis 49:10 is – as noted – the very first text advanced by Friar Paul. Friar Paul, well aware of prior Jewish perceptions of this verse and standard Jewish responses to the Christian case drawn from it, formulates his claim rather carefully.

The verse says: "The scepter shall not depart from Judah nor the ruler's staff from between his feet, until Shiloh comes," who is the Messiah. Thus, the prophet says that Judah will enjoy power up until the Messiah, who will descend from him. Thus, today, when you lack a scepter and a ruler's staff, the Messiah – who is a descendant of his [Judah's] – has already come, and he enjoys power.[22]

This is a subtle formulation that reflects Friar Paul's awareness of prior Jewish rebuttal of Christian claims.[23] In the first place, Friar Paul avoids focusing on kingship and thus eliciting the standard objections raised by Jews that kingship had disappeared long before Jesus; he speaks only of power in a more abstract sense. Second, he does not attempt to create an immediate juxtaposition between Jesus and loss of Jewish power. Rather, he simply points to a contemporary reality, which is Jewish powerlessness, and argues that Jewish powerlessness means that the Messiah has already come, without specification of the exact moment of his appearance. Finally, Friar Paul's formulation includes a sharp thrust at Jewish sensitivities, as he emphasizes that the Messiah has already come – obviously meaning in the person of Jesus without making the explicit connection, that this Messiah and his followers enjoy power, and that the Jews of the thirteenth century are utterly powerless. Thus, Friar Paul highlights the sharp contrast between contemporary Jewish powerlessness and Christian power, which is a major theme in thirteenth-century Christian missionizing argumentation.[24]

Interestingly, Nahmanides does not contest the meaning of Shiloh as Messiah. He seems comfortable in understanding Shiloh as a reference to the Messiah or at least chooses not to dispute the point.[25] Rather, he focuses on the meaning of the Hebrew verb *la-sur*, which is usually translated as "to depart." Rabbi Moses argues that the prophecy of Jacob assures ultimate royal authority to descendants of the tribe of Judah. However, he claims that this should not be taken to mean uninterrupted kingship; rather, it means that Judah's right to royal authority over the Jews shall never be abrogated.

[margin handwriting: Jacob meant an uninterrupted royal lineage; therefore not Jesus]

It was not the intention of the prophet [Jacob] to say that the kingship of Judah would not be suspended at any time. Rather, he said that it would not depart and cease totally from him [i.e. Judah]. The meaning is that, at all times that Israel enjoys kingship, it would properly belong to Judah. If it were to be suspended because of sin, it would return to Judah. Proof of my words [lies in the fact] that there were many years prior to Jesus when kingship was suspended from Judah but not from Israel and there were many years when kingship was suspended from both Israel and Judah. For during the seventy years that they [the Jews] were exiled to Babylonia, neither Judah nor Israel exercised kingship. During [the period of] the Second Temple, only Zerubbavel and his sons ruled for a number of years. After them elapsed three hundred eighty years until the destruction [of the Second Temple], during which the priests of the Hasmonean family and their servants ruled.[26] All the more so [is this true] when the nation has been in exile, for if there is no nation there can be no king.[27]

Royal authority during most of the Second Temple period did exist for the Jewish people, but it was not exercised by the tribe of Judah; during the period of Babylonian exile and the lengthy exile in which the Jews now found themselves, there was no exercise of royal authority at all. Such suspensions – argues Rabbi Moses – did not and do not mean abrogation of the promise of rule by the tribe of Judah.

Despite Friar Paul's careful statement that eschewed the language of kingship, Nahmanides reintroduced the terminology of royal authority. In his response to the rabbi, Friar Paul builds on his opening formulation that did not refer to royal authority, insists on redefining the terms "scepter" and "ruler's staff," and introduces a talmudic source that provides a redefinition.

In all those times [i.e., the Second Temple period and the subsequent period of exile], even though you lacked kings, you did exercise authority. For thus did they explain in the Talmud: "'The scepter shall not depart from Judah' – these are the exilarchs in Babylonia, who subjugate the people with the rod. 'Nor the ruler's staff from between his legs' – these are the descendants of Hillel who teach Torah publicly." Today, when you do not have the ordination known in the Talmud, that authority as well has been abrogated.[28]

Here, innovation is clear in a double sense. In the first place, a new authoritative Jewish source has been introduced. The talmudic explication of Genesis 49:10 has been inserted into the fray. Moreover, the force of Friar Paul's initial formulation is now fully clear. He is arguing that the scepter and the ruler's staff of Genesis 49:10, as defined by the rabbis of the Talmud, constitute a reference to authority in general and not simply royal power. Thus, the argument advanced by Rabbi Moses ben Nahman for periodic suspensions of royal power loses its impact. According to the talmudic statement, as understood by Friar Paul, Jewish governance – in the form of rabbinic authority – had existed unbroken all the way from the patriarch Jacob through the rabbis of the Talmud. Given the abrogation of this rabbinic authority – and Friar Paul insists that Nahmanides's title of rabbi is not genuine – the scepter and the staff have truly and fully departed from the Jewish people, which must mean that the Messiah had come at some prior point in time. This conclusion constitutes an innovative Christian argument, grounded in citation of the Talmud.

However, the case advanced from the combination of Genesis 49:10, and the talmudic statement about it suffered a serious weakness, which was not exploited by Rabbi Moses in this first set of interchanges, but was addressed by him subsequently. In Friar Paul's introduction of Genesis 49:10 and the rabbinic explication of it, there is an obvious chronological problem, which Nahmanides did not immediately attack. Granting this argument for the moment, the result would have been the following: Jews enjoyed rabbinic authority until well into the first half of the Middle Ages, that is to say until the abrogation of the authority of the Babylonian exilarchs; the lack of this authority in the thirteenth century means that the Messiah has already come. However, this messianic figure would hardly square with Jesus, for in his day and well beyond there remained – according to Friar Paul's claims from Genesis 49:10 and the rabbinic statement about it – rabbinic authority within the Jewish community.

Friar Raymond's case from Genesis 49:10 was built on a much larger set of rabbinic sources and avoided the weakness in Friar Paul's argument just now described. It is a fine example of the way in which Friar Raymond built upon, but moved well beyond his predecessor. Not surprisingly, given what we have learned of the exchanges at Barcelona, Friar Raymond opens with a discussion of the meaning of scepter and ruler's staff in the biblical verse. Like Friar Paul, he too was anxious to make the definition more inclusive than simply royal authority and thus to avoid the standard Jewish rebuttal. Again like Friar Paul, the direction pursued is to redefine the scepter and ruler's staff of Genesis 49:10 as internal leadership of the Jewish people, whatever form that internal leadership might take. What is sharply different in the *Pugio fidei* is the nature of the redefinition and the Jewish sources adduced for it. Whereas Friar Paul cited one rabbinic statement, which Nahmanides argued was not really a rabbinic definition of scepter and ruler's staff, but simply a passing reference in discussion of a complex legal issue, Friar Raymond cites multiple rabbinic passages, which obviously involve rabbinic efforts at defining the scepter and ruler's staff of Jacob's prediction. The key sources cited are the Targum to Genesis 49:10 and Bereshit Rabbah on Genesis 49:10.[29]

Moreover, Friar Raymond buttresses his case by citing additional biblical verses that relate to the issue of authority within the Jewish community and a range of rabbinic commentaries upon them.[30] What results is a far stronger case for understanding the scepter and the ruler's staff to mean more than kingship, with an emphasis on internal Jewish judicial and rabbinic authority. In Barcelona, Friar Paul's rabbinic citation had quickly evoked the objection of Rabbi Moses ben Nahman that the talmudic passage cited did not constitute a rabbinic effort to define Jacob's scepter and the rod. In the face of the multiple passages adduced by Friar Raymond, this objection was obviated.

Friar Raymond then proceeds to remove the discrepancy between Friar Paul's rabbinic statement and Jesus of Nazareth. He does so in two ways. In the first place, defining the scepter and ruler's staff as judicial authority, Friar Raymond proceeds to a lengthy discussion of the Jewish court system, with a focus on the most authoritative of the Jewish courts, those empowered to judge capital cases. For Friar Raymond, these courts represented the apex of Jewish judicial power, as he shows in a number of talmudic citations. The first of these citations is the depiction at the beginning of Tractate Sanhedrin of the various strata of the Jewish court system, commencing with the common court of three and ascending eventually through the court of twenty-three and on to the court of seventy-one.[31] Friar Raymond portrays effectively a system with a range of lower and higher courts. He argues that the higher courts in this system – the ones empowered to adjudicate capital cases – constitute an important manifestation of the scepter and ruler's staff of Genesis 49:10.

After establishing the reality of this court system and its highest levels, Friar Raymond proceeds to cite two talmudic passages – one from the Palestinian Talmud and the second from the Babylonian Talmud – that portray the dissolution of the apex of the Jewish court system forty years prior to the destruction of the Second Temple.[32] Let us note the brief formulation in the first of these sources. "Forty years prior to the destruction of the [Second Temple], capital cases were taken away from Israel."[33] Thus – claims Friar Raymond – precisely at the point of the advent of Jesus, a monumental change took place in Jewish judicial authority. The combination of the loss of the most significant judicial prerogative of the Jewish court system, which defined the scepter and ruler's staff of Genesis 49:10 for Friar Raymond, and the advent of Jesus as Messiah constitutes clear fulfillment of Jacob's prediction. Friar Raymond has created a precise nexus between loss of Jewish authority as he has defined it and the advent of Jesus as Messiah.

The second such precise nexus created by Friar Raymond shifted from the Jewish court system to the rabbinic leadership that was in fact reflected *inter alia* in this court system. Friar Raymond discusses, again at length and with citation of numerous talmudic passages, rabbinic ordination as practiced during the Second Temple period, the central role played by the rabbis in Second Temple Jewish life, and the distinguished qualities of these rabbinic leaders.[34] His admiring description would have been totally acceptable to the Jewish thinking of the thirteenth century (and most other centuries as well). Having established the rabbis of the Second Temple period as an alternative manifestation of the scepter and staff of Jacob's prophecy, he advances sources that portray the dissolution of the rabbinate at the time of Jesus.

Friar Raymond adduces a number of rabbinic passages that highlight persecution of the rabbinic authorities of the first and second centuries by the Romans. The key passage cited by Friar Raymond involves the Roman proscription of ordination, according to which the rabbi who confers ordination is to be killed, the student ordained is to be killed, the town in which the ordination takes place is to be destroyed, as is the district within which the ordination takes place.[35] Once again, for Friar Raymond this constitutes clear juxtaposition of the advent of Jesus and Jewish loss of the scepter and staff, in this line of reasoning meaning the true rabbinic leadership of the Jewish people.

Friar Raymond then concludes this set of arguments by presenting in orderly fashion the historical truths he claims to have elicited from the rabbinic sources. The scepter and staff of Jacob's prediction are by no means restricted to royal authority. The scepter and staff are defined in broader terms in the rabbinic corpus and include prominently the most important of the Jewish courts and the rabbinic leadership of the Jewish people. Toward the end of the Second Temple period, that is to say at the time of the advent of Jesus, the crown jewel in the Jewish court system disappeared. Likewise, at the same time, genuine rabbinic leadership was uprooted by the Roman authorities. The combination of the loss of these forms of scepter and staff and the advent of Jesus prove that Jesus was in fact the messianic figure predicted in Genesis 49:10.[36]

In the process of constructing this sequence of conclusions, Friar Raymond overcame the major weakness of the case laid out by Friar Paul on the basis of Genesis 49:10. The Barcelona rebuttals formulated by Rabbi Moses ben Nahman, on the one hand, assisted his Jewish contemporaries in meeting the challenge of the new Christian missionizing argumentation. At the same time, the rabbi's rebuttals also served the Dominicans as well, in their effort to repair the shortcomings in Friar Paul's argumentation and to create a more convincing case for Jewish conversion.

Friar Paul had already been aware of traditional Jewish objections to Christological readings of Genesis 49:10 and used a talmudic source to obviate these objections. Friar Raymond learned from the weaknesses of his predecessor's argument and fashioned a far tighter Christological case from a much wider selection of rabbinic materials. In the process, he also constructed a full picture of the loss of Jewish power and authority in late antiquity. Jews had lost their royalty rather early on, but had retained significant internal authority nonetheless. During the first century, they had lost all forms of genuine internal authority, suggesting major decline in Jewish circumstances concurrent with the appearance of Jesus as the divinely predicted Messiah.

Friar Raymond addressed a number of additional biblical prophecies in the same way, defining the terms of the prophecy and then adducing rabbinic sources to show the fulfillment of these prophecies at the time of Jesus. Let us turn our attention, however, to his broader construction of Jewish past and future at the beginning and end of the *Pugio fidei*.

Beyond the use of Jewish history for proving messianic advent, Friar Raymond was committed to presenting an overarching portrait of the Jewish past and future. Indeed, he made this historical portrait the opening and closing themes of his missionizing manual. Once again, the novelty in Friar Raymond's composite history of the Jews stems from his use of rabbinic materials, alongside the biblical sources more traditionally cited by Christian thinkers and leaders. As we shall see, on occasion this new source material results in innovative and distinctive presentations of aspects of the Jewish past and future, which tended to be pejorative. The rabbinic sources were introduced largely to cast aspersions on the Jewish past and future.

Friar Raymond makes the briefest of transitions from Book I to Book II of the *Pugio fidei* by indicating that the first book of his opus was devoted to those who lack a revealed law. Book II – he then tells us – was to be devoted to those who do have a revealed law, specifically to the Jews, who claim primacy of place among those possessing a revealed law. This leads Friar Raymond, in a reasonable way, to define the term "Jew." The term "Jew" (*Judeus*) identifies those who derive from the tribe of Judah. The term distinguishes the descendants of the tribe of Judah from the descendants of the ten northern tribes, who split off from the Davidic monarchy and maintained for themselves the designation "Israel."

It is certainly reasonable of Friar Raymond to begin with a definition of the term "Jew." However, his very brief remarks at the beginning of chapter 1 of Book II would surely have sufficed. Clearly, however, Friar Raymond's concern was far broader than a simple definition of terms. He in fact devotes the bulk of chapter 1 of Book II to observations on the Israelite kingdom of the north and all of chapter 2 to the Judean kingdom of the south, from which the term "Jew" derived. He obviously had wider purposes in mind. It is hardly accidental that he chose to open his missionizing assault on the Jews with important – and damning – observations on the Jewish past.[37]

Friar Raymond begins his discussion of the southern kingdom in traditional fashion by pointing to the split in the wake of the death of Solomon, as described in I Kings 12. He cites in particular I Kings 12:28, the decision of the founding king of Israel, Jereboam, to create two golden calves, announcing to his people: "You have been going up to Jerusalem long enough. This, O Israel, is your god, who brought you up from the land of Egypt." For Friar Raymond, as for the author of Kings, this act was nothing other than blatant idolatry.[38] Friar Raymond then moves on to the story of the destruction of the northern kingdom and the exile of its people, as recounted in II Kings 17. Friar Raymond does not quote the entire lengthy passage of condemnation – II Kings 17:7–23 – that serves as the biblical author's explanation for the destruction and exile; however, he quotes enough – II Kings 17:21 – to provide a full sense of the sins that brought about divine wrath. It is striking, as we shall see, that Friar Raymond's citation begins and ends with Jereboam and the two purportedly idolatrous calves that he created.

Having cited the biblical story, Friar Raymond proceeds to offer rabbinic clarification for the sins of the northern kingdom. He first quotes the commentary of Rabbi Solomon ben Isaac (Rashi) on Hosea 3:5, which elaborates on the sins of the northern kingdom. These sins involved three specific acts of rejection on the part of the Israelites. They rejected the Davidic king, the Jerusalem Temple, and – most significantly by far – God himself, by substituting false deities for the one true divinity.[39] This

specification takes on important meaning in chapter 2 of Book II of the
Pugio fidei.

Friar Raymond next cites a passage from Deuteronomy Rabbah,
which explicates yet further the sins of the northern kingdom. What is
especially striking about this next source is its identification of a number
of divine blessings that the Israelites of the north forfeited. The last in
this sequence involves God's pleasure with the building of the Temple
and his resultant intention to maintain Israel in its promised land forever.
However, the Israelite decision to separate from the Davidic kingdom
elicited – according to Deuteronomy Rabbah – the divine decision to
exile the Israelites of the north.[40]

Although Friar Raymond makes no direct observations on this passage, he introduces it in his table of contents to chapter 1 as showing that
the divine promises to Israel were conditional.[41] For serious shortcoming, God could withdraw assurances previously given. This is of course a
major bone of contention between Christians and Jews, with Christians
insisting on the conditional nature of divine promises and Jews arguing that certain divine promises were unconditional. In his overview of
the destruction of the northern kingdom, Friar Paul claims that rabbinic
sources indicate explicitly the conditional nature of divine assurances.
Israelite sins were sufficiently weighty to undo God's promised blessing
of unending settlement in the Promised Land.

From this argument for the conditional nature of divine promises,
Friar Paul proceeds to further clarification of the punishment meted out
to the northern kingdom, which he finds illuminated in a citation from the
Babylonian Talmud, tractate Sanhedrin. This rich passage suggests that
the punishment of the northern kingdom would be everlasting. The rabbinic statement is forthright. "The ten tribes [of the north] have no portion in the world-to-come and will never return [to the Land of Israel]."[42]

This conclusion is derived from a midrashic reading of Deuteronomy
29:27. Prior to this important verse, Moses had laid out the terrible punishments that abandoning the covenant would entail. These punishments
would be so terrible as to occasion questioning by latter-day observers,
who would ask: "Why did the Lord do thus to this land? Wherefore this
awful wrath?"[43] The answer points to the heinousness of abandoning
God and his covenant. The passage ends with Deuteronomy 29:27: "The
Lord uprooted them from their soil in anger, fury, and great wrath and
cast them into another land, as is still the case." Each segment of this
verse is subjected in the Talmud to midrashic interpretation. In a fairly
standard way, the two verbs – "uprooted" and "cast" – are taken to refer

to two different spheres. "'The Lord uprooted them from their soil in anger, fury, and great wrath' – in this world; '[the Lord] cast them into another land' – in the world to come." The closing "as is still the case" is, in the simplest terms, a reference to the circumstance that the question as to the intensity of divine wrath would be posed many generations after the fact and that the divine punishment was to remain in effect until that later date. Midrashically, however, the expression elicited alternative ruminations. "'As is still the case [literally to this very day]' – just as this day departs and does not return, so too they [the sinning Israelites] go and do not return" – the view of Rabbi Akiba; Rabbi Eliezer says, "just as the day darkens and then lights up, so too with respect to them [the sinning Israelites] – just as things darken for them, so will they lighten for them."[44] Thus, the difference in midrashic interpretation involves alternative views of the ultimate fate of the Israelites of the north.

The essential message that Friar Raymond wishes to draw from this rabbinic material is the devastating nature of Israelite sin and the all-embracing and everlasting quality of the punishment. Particularly important is the eternality of the divine rejection, insisted upon by the distinguished Rabbi Akiba. Friar Raymond's overall emphasis is upon everlasting damnation. This is the closing note to chapter 1 altogether, where he quotes Hosea 1:6: "For I shall never again show mercy to the house of Israel; I shall obliterate them."[45]

While the overall message is the sinfulness of Israel and its eternal damnation, the statement of Rabbi Eliezer adds an extremely important nuance for Friar Raymond. Friar Raymond does not see Rabbi Eliezer as rejecting the general thrust of Rabbi Akiba's conclusion. Rather, the friar sees Rabbi Eliezer as establishing an exception to the everlasting damnation projected by Rabbi Akiba. "Note that this last statement, that of Rabbi Eliezer, was verified at the time of Christ and his disciples, when many gentiles, who were of the ten tribes, were illuminated by the light of the Christian faith."[46]

This exception is important to Friar Raymond, and he adduces a number of further rabbinic passages to solidify the point. He attempts to prove from these new passages that the Israelites had in fact abandoned their faith and community and had become, in every way, gentiles. The simplest proof in this direction is the statement that "the Israelites did not go into exile until they had become gentiles."[47] These former Israelites were then, according to Friar Raymond, part of the gentile following of Jesus. This means that, despite the eternal damnation decreed by God for the Israelite kingdom of the north as concluded by Rabbi Akiba, salvation could still be achieved through accepting the message of Christianity as further clarified by Rabbi Eliezer.[48]

Thus, chapter 1 of Book II the *Pugio fidei* makes a number of important assertions with respect to the Israelite kingdom of the north, its history, and its subsequent fate. Its history was a saga of failure; the sins committed involved rejection of the divinely ordained dynasty of David; even more reprehensible was the substitution of other gods for the true one God, with the calves of Dan and Bethel emblematic; God's wrath was intense and his punishment extreme; this punishment was intended to be eternal; there could be only one exception to this eternal punishment; that exception involved acceptance of Jesus as Christ. This account of the Israelite kingdom of the north is rooted, to a significant extent, in the biblical narrative and prophetic passages. To a yet greater extent, this narration draws upon the corpus of rabbinic explication of the Bible. Again, herein lies the innovation of Friar Raymond's *Pugio fidei*.

Let us proceed with Friar Raymond into chapter 2 of Book II and his treatment of the southern kingdom of Judea. This treatment of Judean history is deeply rooted in the common medieval assumption of historical parallels and prefigurations. For Friar Raymond, the key to understanding the fate of the Judeans/Jews lay in the recognition of these historical parallels and prefigurations. Just as the Solomonic kingdom was divided into an errant northern branch and a truth-embracing southern branch, so too during the seventieth week predicted by the prophet Daniel was the Judean community divided into two parts – errant Jews and truth-embracing Christians. Just as the northern kingdom had erred grievously in rejecting the Davidic dynasty, so too did the Jews reject the divinely appointed scion of the Davidic line, acknowledging instead the Roman emperor. Again more importantly, just as the Israelites of the north had sinned by establishing two idolatrous calves for themselves in place of the one true God, so too the Jews had sinned by establishing for themselves two false Messiahs (a disconcerting detail to be discussed shortly).

As the sins of the northern kingdom and the Jews ran parallel, so too did their punishments. Just as God had damned the Israelites of the north eternally for their sins through the agency of the Assyrian king Sennacherab, so too did God reject eternally the Jews, this time through the agency of the Roman rulers Vespasian and Titus. Finally, and by now predictably, just as a segment of the northern community had won salvation through recognition of Jesus as Christ, so too did a small portion of the Jewish community achieve salvation in the same way.[49] For Friar

Raymond, the parallels and prefigurations could hardly have been more obvious or more convincing. Again, the theory is not at all new; what is so striking about this construction of the history of the Jews is its mining of rabbinic materials in order to establish the desired picture.

By opening with a depiction of the Israelite kingdom of the north, Friar Raymond begins with a fairly easy target. The Israelite kingdom had been excoriated by a number of the prophets and had been depicted in decidedly negative terms by the authors of Kings. To be sure, Friar Raymond provides a fuller portrait of the errant kingdom of the north, focusing especially on the eternal quality of its condemnation, while allowing at the same time for salvation for those who accepted the truth of Christianity. The more ambitious – and somewhat more difficult – step was to argue that precise parallels could be found between the Israelites of the north and their Judean brethren. The key to this parallelism lay in turning the messianism associated with the Bar-Cosba uprising of the 130s into an act of idolatry and then positing a double messianic idolatry.[50] The rewriting of the two Jewish rebellions against Rome – that of 66–70 and 132–135 – into two messianic ventures, each one led by a false Messiah named Bar-Cosba, feels quite forced, but the move was necessary in order to create the precise parallelism that Friar Raymond's case demanded.

The most curious detail in Friar Raymond's case for Israelite-Jewish parallels – two messianically inspired uprisings against Rome – is fully explicated in chapter 4 of Book II of the *Pugio fidei*. This curious detail involves the claim that the Jews had reenacted the sin of the northern Israelites through two idolatrous acts, the creation of two false messianic figures, each with the name Bar-Cosba. Friar Raymond, who in the early parts of chapter 4 of Book II went to great lengths to detail the demise of the Jewish court system and the extermination of the rabbis, pressed forward from his report on the destruction of the rabbis to clarify what he saw as the two Bar-Cosba-led rebellions. We might reasonably suggest that this analysis of the purported Bar-Cosba rebellions is not really germane to the case he is immediately making from Genesis 49:10. The reader could readily proceed from chapter 4's paragraph 16, in which the friar completes his case for the destruction of the rabbis *en masse*, to paragraph 28, in which he dismisses the suggestion that the scepter of Genesis 49:10 is to be understood as a reference to the exilarchs of Babylonia. This shortened version of chapter 4 would have covered all the points relevant to an understanding of Genesis 49:10 and its Christological implications. Paragraphs 17 through 27 represent a separate agenda – completion of the construction of Friar Raymond's damning history of the Jewish past.[51]

On the face of it, Jewish readers would have been mystified by the claim of two Bar Cosba-led rebellions. To be sure, Jewish readers were well aware that their ancestors had twice attempted to free themselves from Roman domination, the first time through the rebellion of 66–70 and the second time through the rebellion of 132–135. The first rebellion, as traditionally understood by Jews, involved a wide-ranging coalition of Jewish militants; no central figure emerged as the leader of this uprising. By contrast, the second rebellion is thoroughly associated with a powerful central figure, identified by something like the Bar-Cosba designation utilized by Friar Raymond. Although relatively little is known of the specifics of the uprising and its suppression, it took its place in Jewish historical awareness as a second and significant – albeit unsuccessful and hence in retrospect misguided – effort to throw off the yoke of Roman domination.[52] For Jewish readers, two rebellions were a certainty; two messianic Bar-Cosba leaders would have been a puzzle.

The figure who occupies center stage in Friar Raymond's account of the two rebellions was identified by a number of names. Modern scholars have concluded, based on newly available evidence, that this militant leader's name was actually Simon Bar-Cosiba, with the designation "Bar-Cosiba" probably a patronymic.[53] The designation Bar-Cochba, Son of the Star, was seemingly given to him by the distinguished Rabbi Akiba, who was a major supporter. Subsequent to the failure of the rebellion led by this Jewish militant, the rabbis generally referred to him as Bar-Coziba, meaning the deceiver.[54] Although Friar Raymond regularly designates this figure as Bar-Cosba (which I am doing as well, since my focus is Friar Raymond's treatment of this figure and incident), he adopts fully the rabbinic sense of this figure as a deceiver.

The key to Friar Raymond's case for two separate Bar-Cosba figures lies in his discussion of the spiritual giant who is regularly depicted in rabbinic sources as the chief supporter of Bar-Cosba and his messianic pretensions. That giant figure is Rabbi Akiba, whose interpretation of Deuteronomy 29:27 has already been cited and who was one of the formative figures in the rabbinic community of first- and second-century Palestine. Friar Paul amasses considerable information on Rabbi Akiba. Crucial is the rabbinic tradition according to which Rabbi Akiba spent the first forty years of his life as a merchant, the second forty years of his life as a student, and the third forty years of his life as a rabbi, teaching – according to Friar Raymond – the Talmud in Betar.[55] Friar Raymond concludes, reasonably enough, that in sum Rabbi Akiba lived a lengthy life of 120 years. The long and varied life of Rabbi Akiba then leads Friar Raymond to suggest that, "in approximately the seventieth year of his life, while still in Jerusalem, he made himself the shield-bearer for the aforesaid false Messiah, twisting the words of the prophets spoken with respect to the true Messiah to him [Bar-Cosba]." According to the friar, the rest of the rabbis lent Rabbi Akiba their advice and assistance in the misguided uprising of 66–70.[56]

This then leads Friar Raymond into a full depiction of the first Jewish rebellion, which culminated in the destruction of Jerusalem. Friar Raymond cites at length Lamentations Rabbah for a description of the war with Rome; he supplements this description with a lengthy report from Eusebius's *Ecclesiastical History* (which we have already noted); he completes this set of accounts by citing *Yosippon*, which medieval Jews and Friar Raymond saw as the Hebrew version of Josephus. To be sure, none of these sources, as rich as they are, invokes the figure of Bar-Cosba. Thus, Friar Raymond introduces into the middle of his lengthy depiction a brief statement from Tractate Sanhedrin, with respect to the rabbis and Bar-Cosba. According to this brief statement, "Bar-Cosba ruled for three and one-half years. He said to the rabbis: 'I am the Messiah.' They said to him: 'With regard to the Messiah, it is said that he will judge by his sense of smell. Let us examine you and see if you can judge by your sense of smell.'[57] Since they saw that he could not judge by his sense of smell, they killed him." According to Friar Raymond, this bizarre incident took place during the first rebellion, led by the first Bar-Cosba.[58]

According to Friar Raymond, subsequent to the destruction of Jerusalem at the end of the first rebellion, the Jews created a new center for themselves at Betar.[59] "There, fifty-two years after the destruction of Jerusalem, they [the Jews] made for themselves another false Messiah."[60] According to Friar Raymond, they gave this second false Messiah the very same name they had given to the first. This second false Messiah led them into yet another disastrous rebellion against the Romans. The Romans, led by Hadrian, pitilessly destroyed the Jewish rebels. In support of all this, Friar Raymond provides an array of rabbinic sources that describe the second rebellion. This collection of rabbinic sources is, in its own way, quite remarkable; medieval Jewish historians were not nearly so assiduous in collecting materials on the poorly documented second Jewish rebellion against Rome.[61]

In these varied sources (unlike the sources utilized for telling the tale of the first rebellion), Simon Bar-Cosba and Rabbi Akiba figure prominently. Friar Raymond cites, for example, the Jerusalem Talmud, tractate *Ta`anit*: "Rabbi Akiba would explain: 'A star rises from Jacob' – Bar Cochba [The Son of the Star] arises. When Rabbi Akiba would see Bar-Coziba, he would say: 'This is the King Messiah!' "[62] The explanation for Rabbi Akiba's enthusiasm is given in the following terms: "And what did Bar-Coziba do [to merit the messianic designation]? He would catch the catapult stones with one of his knees, would throw them [back], and would kill many of them [the Romans]."[63] Friar Raymond cites a number of rabbinic sources that then depict the failure of the rebellion and the extraordinarily bloody destruction imposed by the Romans.[64]

Friar Raymond accords special attention to the post-rebellion Hadrianic decrees and to the martyrdoms recorded in rabbinic sources, martyrdoms in which Rabbi Akiba figured prominently. Friar Raymond quotes these rabbinic sources at length, but subjects them to his own interpretation. "It should be noted that this Rabbi Akiba, killed shortly before, and the other Jews [likewise martyred] were not killed because they studied the law of Moses, but rather because – in contravention of the law of Moses – they made two false Messiahs, one after the other, as has been shown in the aforecited, and because they rebelled against the Romans, and because they denied that the Lord Jesus was the Messiah. He [Rabbi Akiba] was thus a martyr to the devil, not to God. For the punishment does not make a martyr to God, rather the [proper] cause [makes a martyr to God]."[65] Involved here is a fairly limited, but highly interesting piece of counter-history. Friar Raymond tells the tale of seeming Jewish martyrdoms, based on internal Jewish sources. At the conclusion of this tale, he then imposes his own counter-interpretation of these martyrdoms, in effect turning what Jews have traditionally seen as the most laudatory of acts into repulsive service of the devil.

Thus, Friar Raymond has elaborately reconstructed the history of the Jews of the first and second century, fully grounded in rabbinic sources. According to the rabbinic sources he has amassed and his reading of these sources, what Jews traditionally perceived as a creative period in the development of rabbinic leadership and Jewish law was in fact a period of religious blindness. Rabbi Akiba, one of the great heroes of rabbinic Judaism, is turned by Friar Raymond into a deceived and deceiving supporter of false messianism, and his martyrdom – venerated through the ages by Jews – is transformed into idolatry.

Although the New Testament and the Church Fathers condemned first-century Jews and their leaders for the rejection of Jesus, Friar Raymond filled out a far fuller picture of religious error on the part of these first-century leaders. Surveying this history of error, Friar Raymond suggests striking parallels to the shortcomings of the leadership of the northern kingdom of Israel. History in effect repeated itself. Given the case he had built on the basis of rabbinic sources for the intense divine anger sparked by the idolatry of the northern kingdom and the decree of everlasting punishment enacted against it, Friar Raymond's reconstruction of the parallel Judean idolatry clearly means that the Judeans/Jews were subject to the same divine anger and eternal rejection, except of course for those who chose the path of conversion and truth.

Book III of the *Pugio fidei* is divided into three sections. The first makes the Christian case for the Trinity; the second begins the Christian case for Incarnation; the third completes the case for Incarnation and proceeds in a number of further directions. These two related doctrines – Trinity and Incarnation – encountered especially intense objection on the part of Jews. Christian and Jews both believed that God had promised to send a divinely ordained Messiah. Thus the Christian-Jewish debate about the Messiah – the heart of Book II of the *Pugio* – revolved about the specifics of Jesus' timing, life, and activity and whether or not he fulfilled the characteristics of the promised messianic redeemer. This debate was spirited and important, but at least began with shared assumptions. Such was not at all the case with the doctrines of Trinity and Incarnation; Jews rejected these related doctrines out of hand. The notion of a Trinity occasioned intellectual Jewish derision; this derision often has an air of condescension about it. The doctrine of Incarnation was yet more objectionable to Jews. It seemed to them blasphemous to suggest that the one God of the universe might take on human form and flesh. As a result, the doctrine of Incarnation required far fuller argumentation from the Christian side. In fact, in Jewish polemical literature there is often a sense of the doctrine of Incarnation as an obviously fatal flow in Christian thinking, to be attacked vigorously by the Jewish side.[66]

The second section of Book III of the *Pugio fidei* sets the stage for the doctrine of Incarnation. It focuses on the human condition and its shortcomings. The closing chapters of section 2 of Book III show humanity unable to achieve paradise and inevitably consigned to hell. The suggestion is that only a God-human could be successful in breaking this cycle. The third and final section of Book III begins with full exposition of the doctrine of Incarnation. Since the focus of this case for Incarnation lies with the human need for salvation, it is natural, to an extent, for Friar

Raymond to complete his case for salvation only through Christ, the God-human, by noting that the Jews were excluded from this salvation.

In one sense, this conclusion is an obvious one. If it is only through Christ that salvation can be achieved, then obviously the Jews – who reject Christ – must necessarily be excluded from that salvation. Yet, clearly this issue is treated by Friar Raymond as much more than a simple ramification of the Christian doctrine of Incarnation. He in fact devotes the closing two chapters of Book III – and hence of the *Pugio fidei* in its entirety – to the claimed rejection of the Jews. Thus, Books II and III of the *Pugio fidei* – the books devoted specifically to the missionizing argumentation against the Jews – open and close upon the same note, the appalling sinfulness of the Jewish people in the past and their subsequent damnation.

The closing chapters of Book III of the *Pugio fidei* are exceedingly rich in the excoriation of the Jews, richer than the opening chapters of Book II. Although Friar Raymond by no means abandons his earlier claim of Jewish idolatry in accepting two false messiahs, he does demote that issue considerably. The core of his discussion of Jewish sinfulness and resultant divine punishment revolves around the rejection of Jesus by the Jews. Early in chapter 21 of Book III, Friar Raymond asks the question as to the sin of the Jews that occasioned their expulsion from Jerusalem, the Holy City, and the Holy Land in its entirety and the end of divine concern for the Jewish people. For Friar Raymond, the answer, taken from a number of rabbinic sources, was quite straightforward. This horrendous punishment was the result of gratuitous hatred (*sin'at hinam* in Hebrew; *odium gratis* in Latin), which for the friar meant the hatred that led the Jews to reject Jesus and indeed to persecute him.

Again, there is nothing innovative in the claim that rejection of Jesus was the occasion of Jewish misfortune. We have seen this repeatedly in Paul and the Church Fathers. What is highly innovative is Friar Raymond's terminology of *sin'at hinam*, gratuitous hatred, and his amassing of rabbinic materials intended to buttress this claim. Friar Raymond adduces a series of rabbinic texts in order to lay out his case, which in effect constitutes another element – in many ways the key element – in his rabbinically grounded history of the Jewish people.

The first and most important of these texts is from the Babylonian Talmud, tractate Yoma. In this lengthy text, a number of contrasts are drawn between the Jews of the First Temple and those of the Second Temple.[67] The first contrast seems to work to the advantage of the former; it notes that, despite the rather similar length of time that the two temples stood, the first was served by a mere eighteen high priests, while the second was served by more than three hundred high priests. Indeed, a close look at the priesthood of the Second Temple suggests that most of the high priests did not even serve out a full year in their position, surely a negative reflection on the religious leadership of the Second Temple.

The second contrast works seemingly in opposite fashion, much to the advantage of the Jews of the Second Temple. The question is raised as to the grounds for the destruction of the two temples. The destruction of the First Temple is said to have been occasioned by three major sins – idolatry, gross sexual misbehavior, and bloodletting. By contrast, it is known that, during the period of the Second Temple, Jews "occupied themselves with Torah, with [fulfillment of] the commandments, and with acts of charity." Why then was the Second Temple destroyed? The answer given in this talmudic passage is that the cause for destruction was baseless hatred (*sin'at hinam*; *odium gratis*). The point of this, in traditional Jewish thinking, is to teach that baseless hatred – ostensibly a minor infraction – is grave indeed.

There are two further contrasts advanced in the Yoma text. The first builds on the obvious nature of Jewish shortcoming during the period of the First Temple and the lack of clarity on Jewish shortcoming during the period of the Second Temple. "Rabbi Yohanan and Rabbi Elazar both said: 'For the early ones [the Jews of the First Temple], for whom their sin was revealed, their end [that is the time of their return] was revealed. For the latter ones [the Jews of the Second Temple], for whom their sin was not revealed, their end [i.e., the time of their return] was not revealed.'" In terms of evaluation, this contrast seems relatively neutral. It is simply a matter of clarity; clarity of sin entails clarity of the period of punishment; lack of clarity in sinfulness entails lack of clarity about the period of punishment.

The final contrast addresses directly the issue of relative merit of the two periods of the Jewish past and involves a disagreement. "Rabbi Yohanan said: 'The fingernail of the early ones was greater than the belly of the latter ones.'" The view of Rabbi Yohanan is disputed by Resh Lakish, who says: "The latter ones [the Jews of the Second Temple period], even though they suffered imperial subjection [a reference to the reality of Persian, Greek and Roman domination for most of the Second Temple period], they occupied themselves with Torah." Rabbi Yohanan then buttressed his case for the superiority of First Temple Jewry by pointing to the reality of return and rebuilding in the wake of the destruction of the First Temple, while no such return and rebuilding were evident in the wake of the destruction of the Second Temple. Resh Lakish is given no rejoinder to this argument by Rabbi Yohanan.

Evident in this lengthy passage is a difference of opinion on the part of later rabbis as to the relative merits and shortcomings of the two Jewries, that of the First Temple and that of the Second Temple. This overt disagreement is reflected in the final segment of the citation, with Rabbi Yohanan preferring the earlier Jewry and Resh Lakish valorizing the later Jewry. Overall, the passage takes a number of positions, with some segments reflecting the superiority of the First Temple Jews and some portraying the superiority of the Second Temple Jews. The First Temple priesthood was more stable, and the redemption of its members was predicted and realized. On the contrary, the contrast between the sins of idolatry, sexual immorality, and bloodshed on the one hand and baseless hatred on the other seems to tip the scales very much in favor of the later group. For Friar Raymond, however, this passage does not reflect indeterminacy on the part of the rabbis with respect to the two periods of the Jewish past; for the friar, the contrasts are quite consistent, as we shall soon see.

Friar Raymond introduces yet another talmudic text that wrestles with the sinfulness of earlier Jewries. This second text, taken from the Jerusalem Talmud, again tractate Yoma, is briefer and more focused. Here three groups of Jews are compared, the Jews of the First Temple northern kingdom, the Jews of the First Temple southern kingdom, and the Jews of the Second Temple period. In the case of the first two, there is again ample biblical testimony to heinous sins. With respect to the third group of Jews, the question is posed sharply. "With regard to the [Jews of the] Second [Temple], we acknowledge that they were deeply occupied with Torah and were careful about the commandments and the tithes and that all good qualities were in evidence among them. However, they loved money and hated one another gratuitously." This leads to a moral observation: "Gratuitous hatred is weighty, for it is equal to idolatry, gross sexual misbehavior, and bloodletting."[68]

This second passage, from the Jerusalem Talmud, closes with a definitive statement, rather than a disagreement. Rabbi Elazar was asked as to the relative merits of the Jewries of the two temples, suggesting again that this was an uncertain issue in the minds of later Jews. His answer focused on the reality of return and rebuilding in the wake of the destruction of the First Temple and the lack of such return and rebuilding in the wake of the destruction of the Second Temple. For Rabbi Elazar, this was decisive evidence in favor of the earlier Jews, those of the First Temple.

Friar Raymond complements these two crucial texts with a series of further rabbinic passages that expatiate on the sins of the Jews of the First Temple period. He focuses in particular on evidence that shows these Jews regularly and cruelly assaulting the messengers sent by God himself to the Jewish people. This shocking sinfulness on the part of the Jews of the First Temple period was critical to the overall construction of Second Temple Jewish history that was the friar's ultimate goal.

Friar Raymond's case involves the following. First, it is obvious that the Jews of the First Temple period were utterly perverse. They were acknowledged by their own descendants to have sinned through idolatry, gross sexual misbehavior, and bloodletting. They broke God's law and were bereft of virtues. By contrast, the Jews of the Second Temple period were acknowledged by their descendants to have been free of these gross behaviors and to have been committed to the study of Torah and observance of the commandments. Nonetheless, the evidence of history suggests that there was something worse about the later Jews, as indicated by their lack of return and redemption. Indeed, the rabbis themselves indicate that, despite the obvious shortcomings of the Jews of the First Temple, they were more meritorious – perhaps less reprehensible would be better – than the Jews of the Second Temple. What could possibly have tipped the scales? What could account for the weightier punishment leveled against the Jews of the Second Temple and the obvious denigration of these Jews by most rabbis? Friar Raymond formulates the question in the following stark terms: "What then was the evil in the behaviors of the later Jews, for which Jerusalem was overthrown and the temple completely destroyed, for which the beginnings of their captivity took place so cruelly, first by Titus and Vespasian and then by Hadrian, for which the duration of their captivity has been so lengthy and its completion so unknown?"[69] While this is a rather traditional Christian question, in Friar Raymond's formulation we can hear obvious echoes of the rabbinic texts he brought before his readers.

For Friar Raymond, the answer was perfectly obvious. "Gratuitous hatred [again *sin'at hinam*; *odium gratis*], which was to be found among them and which outweighed all the aforecited crimes of the earlier Jews, was the cause of their exile and destruction."[70] Friar Raymond goes on to introduce the evidence he adduced from rabbinic texts as to the horrible crimes of the Jews of the First Temple period, including the persecution and killing of God's messengers, an extreme instance of gratuitous hatred. There could be only one worse instance of gratuitous hatred and that involved – in the friar's view – the killing of God himself. Since this

chapter is still part of the third section of Book III of the *Pugio*, in which
Friar Raymond makes his extensive case for Jesus as both divine and
human, he could comfortably point back to that recently completed case
in claiming that the Jews had done something worse than killing God's
messengers. Picking up a rabbinic theme, he concludes that, because the
Second Temple Jews did not acknowledge their sin, they were denied
return and rebuilding. This is the carefully constructed case built by Friar
Raymond from rabbinic sources. These sources – he believed – do not
exhibit uncertainty and disagreement; they were consistent in condemning Second Temple Jewry, although without articulating – as he was
doing – the precise nature of the shortcoming.

Friar Raymond does not abandon his notion of a double idolatry on
the part of the Jews in supporting two false messiahs, both named Bar-
Cosba. Rather, he demotes this idolatry to an extent. For the friar, the
ultimate sin of the Jews was rejection, persecution, and killing of Jesus.
By contrast, everything else paled somewhat. Nonetheless, Jews were further guilty of idolatrous behavior in following the purported two Bar-
Cosbas. They were, according to Friar Raymond, guilty of anticipating
false messianic redeemers, failing to understand that the Messiah had
already arrived.[71]

While this is the heart of Friar Raymond's rabbinically based history
of the Second Temple period and, by extension, of the history of Jewish
sinfulness, he does add a multiplicity of rabbinic sources to show the
extent of the catastrophe suffered by the Jews and the ongoing Jewish
refusal to grasp the truth. Lest it be suggested that the tragedy of the Jews
flowed from the misdeeds of one particular group of Jews, the Jews of the
Second Temple period, Friar Raymond concludes chapter 21 of Book III
by adducing a number of rabbinic sources that suggest the steady process
of attrition of the generations.[72] These sources advance a rather standard
set of tropes in the thinking of late antiquity and the Middle Ages, suggesting the superiority of past generations over those of the present. For
the friar, these sources obviate any suggestion of one-time Jewish error.
His Jewish contemporaries are, according to his view of the sources he
cites, even worse – if possible – than their sinning ancestors.

Given the history of the Jews he laboriously constructed from rabbinic sources, it will come as no surprise that Friar Raymond ends the
Pugio fidei with a sequence of sources intended to show that the eventual
hope of the Jewish people resides in conversion. The sad story of the
Jewish past, as delineated by Friar Raymond, can have only one satisfac-
tory outcome, and that is the acceptance of the religious faith they have

so steadfastly and mistakenly rejected. That rejection was the cause of Jewish misfortune; repudiating that rejection will offer the only path to redemption.

Introduction of the Talmud into medieval western Christendom might theoretically have led to an amelioration of the Christian perspectives on the Jewish present, past, and future. This, however, was not at all what actually happened. Talmudic materials were utilized to forge even more negative imagery of the Jewish present, past, and future. With Nicholas Donin, this process was relatively simple. Committed to bringing to Christian attention the intolerable aspects of talmudic literature, Donin highlighted all the negative elements in it, as he saw them – demeaning the Bible, God, Jesus, and the Church; promoting behaviors that are anti-Christian and antisocial; and proposing doctrines that are an affront to human intelligence.

Friar Raymond and the *Pugio fidei* are considerably more complex. The overall purpose of the *Pugio fidei* was to mount effective arguments anchored in rabbinic sources for the truth of Christianity. In part, this necessitated – for Friar Raymond – projecting the Jewish past and future in ways that would convince Jews of their historical errors, the everlasting punishment decreed for these errors, and the only available option for avoiding this everlasting punishment, that is to say by acknowledging (even though belatedly) Christian truth. As noted recurrently, Friar Raymond was hardly an innovator in forging new themes in Christian histories of the Jews. His innovative contribution lay in utilizing a wholly new set of sources, in fact Jewish sources in creating his history.

The overarching portrait of the Jewish past in the *Pugio fidei* follows very much along the lines set much earlier in Christian thinking vis-à-vis the Jews. Within that range of traditional thinking, Friar Raymond comes out very much toward the pejorative end of the spectrum. He suggests none of the dignity assigned by Eusebius and Augustine, for example to early Jewish experience and creativity. Friar Raymond's history is detailed, is totally based on rabbinic sources, and is unrelievedly negative.

Did such a history really serve the missionizing purposes of the *Pugio fidei*? Was it productive or counterproductive to reformulate the Jewish past as Friar Raymond did? Would not such denigration of the Jewish past alienate eventual Jewish auditors, rather than convince them?[73] I would suggest that, despite the danger of alienating eventual Jewish listeners, Friar Raymond's counter-history was not without its missionizing potential. The travails of Jewish history, especially the destruction of Jerusalem and the lengthy exile that followed Roman domination, had long played a role in Christian thinking and in Christian missionizing argumentation. As Jewish presence in medieval western Christendom increased markedly from the eleventh century on and as Christian proselytizing efforts accelerated during the closing decades of the twelfth century, the argument from dolorous Jewish circumstances took on heightened meaning. Jewish polemicists of the twelfth and thirteenth centuries accorded very special attention to this Christian thrust.[74] Friar Raymond's rabbinically grounded history of the Jews featured prominently the argument that the sinfulness of the Second Temple Jews is revealed, above all else, by the intensity of their punishment and the suffering of their descendants. Thus, his history very much accorded with the central thrusts of the thirteenth-century Christian missionizing endeavor.

At the same time, it must be noted that the *Pugio fidei* was written in Latin for use by Christian – probably essentially Dominican – missionizers. The impact of the argument mounted by Friar Raymond and the materials he amassed to support that argument surely deepened the animosity and antipathy of these missionizers toward their Jewish targets. Reinforcement of the Christian sense of the Jews as a hopelessly misguided, deeply malevolent anti-Christian grouping in society was surely one of the by-products of the intensive proselytizing efforts of Friar Raymond Martin.

Notes

1   See the important suggestions of Andre Tuilier, "La condemnation du Talmud par les maitres universitaires parisiens," in *Le brulement de Talmud a Paris 1242–1244*, ed. Gilbert Dahan (Paris: Les editions du Cerf, 1999), 59–78.
2   The sources – both Latin and Hebrew – for the assault on the Talmud that began in the 1230s have been collected in John Friedman, Jean Connell Hoff, and Robert Chazan, *The Trial of the Talmud: Paris 1240* (Toronto: Pontifical Institute of Mediaeval Studies, 2012). For this volume, I composed a lengthy historical essay, which can be found at 1–92.
3   Ibid., 102–121.
4   Ibid., Letters 2 and 3, 93–95.
5   Ibid., Letter 4, 95.
6   Ibid., Letter 5, 95–97.
7   Ibid., Letter 6, 97–98.
8   For this reply, see ibid. and Letter 8, 100–101.
9   For a fuller depiction of the aftermath of the trial, see ibid., 80–92.
10 Robert Chazan, *Daggers of Faith* (Berkeley: University of California Press, 1989), chapter 5.

11 Robert Chazan, *Barcelona and beyond the Disputation of 1263 and Its Aftermath* (Berkeley: University of California Press, 1992).

12 In his engaging narrative account of the proceedings, Rabbi Moses ben Nahman – the Jewish protagonist – portrays himself as regularly flaunting these ground rules and taking the offensive.

13 I shall analyze Friar Paul's use of this verse in more detail shortly.

14 Chazan, *Barcelona and Beyond*, chapter 2.

15 Ibid., chapter 3.

16 I have treated the *Pugio fidei* in an earlier and more limited way in *Daggers of Faith*, chapter 7.

17 For some of the complexity of this brief passage and efforts to penetrate this complexity, see Robert Chazan, "Daniel 9:24–27: Exegesis and Polemics," in *Contra Iudaeos: Ancient and Medieval Polemics between Christians and Jews*, ed. Guy G. Stroumsa and Ora Limor (Tubingen: Mohr-Siebeck, 1996), 145–161, and "Rashi's Commentary on the Book of Daniel: Messianic Speculation and Polemical Argumentation," in *Rashi et la culture juive en France du Nord au moyen age*, ed. Gilbert Dahan et al. (Paris, 1997), 111–121.

18 In quoting the *Pugio fidei*, I will cite from the 1687 Leipzig edition, reprinted Farnborough, 1967. Friar Raymond's lengthy discussion of the Daniel passage can be found at 269–294, with considerable digression in the course of the discussion.

19 This is an extremely difficult verse to translate, since translations already involve exegesis. Exegesis of this verse has an especially tortured history.

20 Eusebius focused on this verse. For the medieval period, see Robert Chazan, "Genesis 49:10 in Thirteenth-Century Christian Missionizing," in *New Perspectives on Jewish-Christian Relations*, ed. Elisheva Carlebach and Jacob J. Schacter (Leiden: Brill, 2012), 92–108.

21 See Adolf Posnanski, *Schiloh: Ein Beitrag zur Geschichte der Messiaslehre* (Leipzig: J. C. Hinrichs, 1904).

22 Nahmanides's account of the Barcelona disputation, generally identified as *Vikuah ha-Ramban*, was edited critically by Moritz Steinschneider (Stettin: Shrentsel, 1860); it was republished by Reuben Margulies (Lwow: Ksieg, n.d.) and again by Chaim Chavel in his collection of the writings of Rabbi Moses ben Nahman (2 vols.; Jerusalem: Mossad ha-Rav Kook, 1971), 302–320. For a list of many of the editions and translations of this very popular work, see Chazan, *Barcelona and Beyond*, 244. For the convenience of the reader, I shall cite the Chavel edition; this passage can be found on p. 304

23 See Chazan, "Genesis 49:10."

24 Robert Chazan, *Fashioning Jewish Identity in Medieval Western Christendom* (Cambridge: Cambridge University Press, 2004), chapter 8.

25 Some medieval exegetes do contest the identification of Shiloh with the Messiah – see Chazan, "Genesis 49:10."

26 During this lengthy period, Israel – that is, the Jewish people – had kings who were not of the tribe of Judah.

27 *Vikuah ha-Ramban*, 304.
28 Ibid.
29 *Pugio fidei*, 313.
30 Ibid., 312–314.
31 Ibid., 314. Friar Raymond cites the opening Mishnah of Tractate Sanhedrin in truncated form.
32 Ibid., 314–315.
33 Ibid. This passage can be found in T. P., Sanhedrin, 24b.
34 *Pugio fidei*, 315.
35 Ibid., 315–316, citing T. B., Sanhedrin, 14a.
36 Ibid., 316.
37 See Robert Chazan, "Defining and Defaming Israelites and Judeans: Jews in the *Pugio Fidei*," *Iberia Judaica* 2 (2010): 105–119.
38 According to most modern scholars, I Kings represents the Judean and anti-Israel perspective on the actions of Jereboam.
39 *Pugio fidei*, 261.
40 Ibid., 261–262.
41 Ibid., 260.
42 Ibid., 262, citing T. B., Sanhedrin, 110b. Friar Raymond conflates here the mishnah and the subsequent baraita.
43 Deut. 29:23.
44 *Pugio fidei*, 262, citing T. B., Sanhedrin, 110b.
45 This is a difficult verse, as reflected in the wide range of modern translations.
46 *Pugio fidei*, 262.
47 Ibid. The citation is from T. P., Sanhedrin, 53b.
48 *Pugio fidei*, 262.
49 Ibid., 264–265.
50 I shall explain my use of the designation "Bar-Cosba" shortly.
51 Again, see Chazan, "Defining and Defaming Israelites and Judeans."
52 For a recent overview of this rebellion, see Hanan Eshel, "The Bar Kochba Revolt, 132–135," in *The Cambridge History of Judaism*, ed. Louis Finkelstein et al. (4 vols.; New York: Cambridge University Press, 1984–2006), 4: 105–127.
53 For the most authoritative edition of this new evidence, see Yigael Yadin et al., eds. *The Documents from the Bar Kokhba Period in the Cave of Letters* (Jerusalem: Israel Exploration Society, 2002), 277–366.
54 See further for Friar Raymond's awareness of both designations.
55 *Pugio fidei*, 321.
56 Ibid.
57 Based on Isa. 11: 3.
58 *Pugio fidei*, 322. The passage cited is from T. B., Sanhedrin, 93b.
59 Friar Raymond uses the designation "Bitter"; I will use the more recognizable transliteration "Betar."
60 Ibid., 325.
61 Ibid., 325–329. Fuller examination of these sources would constitute an excellent topic for further investigation.

62 Ibid., 326, citing T. P., Taanit, 24a. Note the appearance in this passage of the adulatory "Bar-Cochba" and the deprecatory "Bar-Coziba."

63 *Pugio fidei*, 326, citing Lamentations Rabbah to Lamentations 2:2.

64 *Pugio fidei*, 328–329.

65 Ibid., 329.

66 For a sense of this opposition, see Daniel J. Lasker, *Jewish Philosophical Polemics against Christianity* (2nd ed.; Oxford: Littman Library, 2007), chapters 4 and 5, and Chazan, *Fashioning Jewish Identity*, chapter 12.

67 The entire lengthy passage can be found in the *Pugio fidei*, 895–897, citing T. B., Yoma, 9a–9b.

68 This passage can be found in the *Pugio fidei*, 897–898, citing T. P., Yoma, 1:1, 38c.

69 *Pugio fidei*, 902.

70 Ibid.

71 Ibid., 908.

72 Ibid., 918.

73 I am not suggesting that the *Pugio fidei* was written directly for a Jewish audience. Clearly, it was intended as a missionizing manual for Christian preachers. This means that its message would eventually reach a Jewish audience.

74 Chazan, *Fashioning Jewish Identity*, chapters 9–11.

7

Introduction of Medieval Slanders

The Fortalitium Fidei

During the almost two centuries that elapsed between Friar Raymond Martin's late-thirteenth-century *Pugio fidei* and Friar Alphonso de Espina's mid-fifteenth-century *Fortalitium fidei*, much changed on the European scene in general and for European Jews in particular. On the general European scene, the homogeneity that marked the mid-thirteenth-century environment of Friar Raymond had begun to disintegrate. Although reformist voices were regularly heard by the middle of the thirteenth century, they became increasingly strident during the fourteenth and fifteenth centuries. These reformist voices were raised within the Church itself, calling for less material ostentation, less legalism, and more spiritual and moral sensitivity. A mere half century after Friar Alphonso, these internal reformist voices would break through the medieval Catholic Church's monopoly on ecclesiastical authority and create a new and religiously fragmented Europe.[1] Also, by the fifteenth century, humanistic learning on the Italian peninsula had begun to create a different kind of challenge, attacking the Church in the name of alternative patterns of thinking altogether. This external challenge intensified during the fifteenth and succeeding centuries, culminating in the eventual Enlightenment assault on traditional Church belief and practice.

The growing strength of these critical perspectives moved the Church into a more defensive frame of mind and into increasingly reactionary postures. These changes within the Church are illustrated by the title of the work that dominated the previous chapter and the work that dominates this chapter. Friar Raymond – still in a relatively self-confident and aggressive mode – called his opus the *Pugio fidei*, the *Dagger of Faith*, and intended it for slaying the enemies of Christianity by convincing them – especially the Jews – of Christian truth. Friar Alphonso shaped his composition more defensively, entitling it the *Fortalitium fidei*, the *Fortress of Faith*, devoted to a description of the dangers threatening the beleaguered fortress of Christianity and to plans for protecting it.

Jewish circumstances in fifteenth-century Europe showed signs of important change as well. In the first place, the demographic patterns of European Jewry had been radically altered by the fifteenth century. Jews had been expelled from England in 1290 and from royal France in 1306. Although Jews were permitted to return to royal France in 1315, vibrant pre-1306 French Jewry was not reconstituted, and in 1394, a final and definitive expulsion took place. Thus, by the fifteenth century, Spain housed the only set of significant Jewish settlements left in the westerly and more advanced sector of Europe. The Jewish population of Europe was maintained and in fact continued to grow, but the center of gravity in European Jewish life shifted into the more backward areas of central and eastern Europe, where economic need continued to make Jews useful. As these backward areas strove to catch up to their more westerly neighbors in economic achievement and political sophistication, the Jews as potential agents of economic and political advancement became – if anything – more valuable. For a Spanish clerical thinker like Friar Alphonso, the fact that only Spain of all the western European kingdoms still housed a Jewish community was distressing. The ongoing existence of Jews within the Spanish kingdoms under these new demographic circumstances raised issues that would not have been on the Spanish Church's agenda in earlier centuries.

Within Spain, there was a more specific development that complicated Jewish life and Christian perceptions of Jews dramatically. In a sense, the dream of Friar Raymond had begun to materialize on the late-fourteenth-century Iberian peninsula, where Jews converted in very large numbers. There were, however, complications associated with the realization of this long-cherished dream. The first complication was the role of violence in this massive conversion. The large-scale abandonment of the Jewish community and Judaism in 1391 was the result of widespread assaults against Jews that broke out all across the peninsula. As Jewish communities were attacked and Jews were offered the traditional choice between death and conversion, significant numbers of Jews opted for the latter.[2] In many cases, Jews choosing baptism did so with full awareness of the long-standing Church prohibition of forcible conversion and with the conviction that – when order would be restored – their conversions would be nullified. Unfortunately for these former Jews, their conversions were not in fact annulled by the late-fourteenth- and fifteenth-century Church, and they were forced to remain in the Christian fold. Some made peace with their new circumstances; others did not and continued to resist – in one way or another – the new identity that had been forced upon them.

Thus, a second complication was created – the problem of insincere and even relapsing converts. Insincerity and relapse among these former Jews were stimulated in part by those Jews who had converted under false pretenses, that is to say had assumed that their forced baptism would not be binding. There were two additional factors affecting the recent converts. The first was simply the normal difficulty of adjusting to a new religious identity. When the number of converts was small, as was generally the case with Jews opting for Christianity during the Middle Ages, the process of assimilation of a limited number of converts went smoothly.[3] In post-1391 Spain, the large number of converts complicated the process of integration considerably. There were enough of these converts to enable the creation of a self-sustaining social milieu, and many of the post-1391 converts became part of such separatist milieux. Such converts could comfortably live and socialize among themselves. Although the objective of this self-segregation was to make adjustment to new realities and new identity smoother and less traumatic, it impeded the process of integration markedly.

This social reality created a second issue, which was the perception within the Old Christian majority that the converts from Judaism – labeled variously as New Christians or *conversos* or Marranoes – in fact constituted a separate and problematic subcommunity within Spanish society. Indeed, the emergence of a widely used set of terms to identify and distinguish these new members of the Church suggests in and of itself problems with their assimilation. In theory, there should have been only one group of Christians in Spanish society, since baptism was supposed to efface prior identity. The very fact that there were now Old Christians and New Christians indicates that the religious amalgamation assumed by ecclesiastical theory encountered serious social obstacles.

Resistance to this group of new additions to the Christian fold intensified throughout the fifteenth century, to the point that anti-New-Christian violence broke out in key Spanish cities by the middle of the fifteenth century, and laws excluding New Christians from numerous sectors of economic and civic life began to proliferate. As this resistance intensified, some of the New Christians who had initially embraced their Christian identity came to question it. If Old Christian society would not accept them, many New Christians came to resent their circumstances and their problematic Christian identity. Thus, by the time that Friar Alphonso began to write his book in the 1460s, the Spanish Church was confronted by a serious and multidimensional problem of relapsing New Christians, who were perceived as a new kind of internal Jewish/Judaizing threat to Spain's Christianity and Christian society.

It is against this pan-European and more specifically Spanish backdrop that Friar Alphonso composed his *Fortress of Faith*. Like a number of the figures with whom we have dealt – Nicholas Donin, Friar Paul Christian, and even Friar Raymond Martin, Friar Alphonso is not all that well documented. He is known in fact simply as a member of the Franciscan Order, as a dedicated preacher, and – most significantly – as the author of the *Fortress of Faith*. The importance and contours of the *Fortress of Faith* have suggested over time to some observers that he was a royal advisor (a suggestion for which there is no solid evidence) and that he himself came out of New Christian background. The latter assumption was widely shared among Spanish scholars, non-Spanish students of Spanish history, and students of medieval Jewish history. The religious background of Friar Alphonso is of considerable importance for our investigation of the *Fortress of Faith*. Whether the author was a Spanish Old Christian or a Spanish New Christian will influence substantially our evaluation of the book's construction of the Jewish past, present, and future.

Fortunately, the issue of Friar Alphonso's background was investigated fully and convincingly by Benzion Netanyahu in the mid-1970s.[4] Netanyahu's conclusion is that Friar Alphonso was definitely not a New Christian, and the case he lays out is exhaustive and convincing. Netanyahu begins by simply ranging the two camps – those asserting that the friar was a New Christian and those asserting that he was not – one against the other. He then proceeds to examine the two camps chronologically. He notes tellingly that there are no sources from the fifteenth, sixteenth, or early seventeenth century that identify Alphonso de Espina as a New Christian. This identification first surfaced in the 1640s and was then increasingly repeated thereafter. Netanyahu argues that this late evidence hardly constitutes a solid basis for the identification of the friar as a New Christian.

Netanyahu then turns to internal evidence. The *Fortalitium fidei* is extremely rich in the citation of Jewish sources.[5] Netanyahu asks whether this knowledge of Jewish sources indicates a background of genuine Jewish learning or might have been gleaned from translations of rabbinic sources readily available in mid-fifteenth-century Spain. In the most

impressive section of his article, Netanyahu traces the available translations for every one of the many citations of rabbinic sources, leading to
the following conclusion: *"Not a single rabbinical statement cited in the
Fortalitium was taken by Espina from the original sources"* (italics in
the original).[6] Netanyahu discusses at length Friar Alphonso's rework-
ing of his sources as well. The result of this massive investigation is the
definitive statement just now cited. Recent students have fully accepted
Netanyahu's findings, have simply noted the paucity of information
about Friar Alphonso, and have focused on what is known, that is to say,
the *Fortress of Faith*.[7] Although Friar Alphonso was not a New Christian,
we shall see that New Christians were very much on his mind.

The *Fortress of Faith* is a lengthy and richly documented preacher's
manual.[8] Although it bears resemblance to the thirteenth-century *Pugio
fidei*, especially in its focus on Jewish sources, both talmudic and medieval, in many important ways the two works are radically different. Friar
Raymond's composition was clearly intended for Christian preachers
who would aggressively carry its message to Jewish audiences, in hopes
of convincing Jewish listeners to convert to Christianity. Friar Alphonso
also intended his book for Christian preachers, but in the hope that they
would carry his message to Christian audiences, would convince them
of the truth of their faith, would alert them to the dangers threatening
them, and would propose necessary steps for meeting these dangers.
The eventual audiences for the preaching of the mendicant friars using
their compositions constitute a major difference between the efforts of
Friar Raymond and Friar Alphonso, as do the alternative messages to be
delivered to these differing audiences. In the case of Friar Raymond, his
message to eventual Jewish audiences was the necessity to acknowledge
Christian truth and convert; in the case of Friar Alphonso, the message to
eventual Christian audiences was the failure of conversion and the need
to remove the Jews entirely from Spain.

Friar Alphonso divided his composition into five books, the first
devoted to the fortress of Christianity and the remaining four to the
enemies that endanger it, the threats posed by these enemies, and the
measures that Christians must take to protect their endangered fortress.
The four enemies are heretics, Jews, Muslims, and demons. A modern
observer would probably rank the importance of these enemies in something like the following order: Muslims, heretics, Jews, and demons
or – alternatively – heretics, Muslims, Jews, and demons. In either case,
Jews might well seem to constitute a minor threat to the allegedly embat-
tled fortress of Christianity. Friar Alphonso, however, saw things quite

differently; he devoted more space to the Jewish enemy than to the other three combined.[9] This is certainly a striking move on the friar's part and indicates clearly that his deepest concern lay with the Jewish enemy.

In fact, although the basic five-book structure of the *Fortalitium fidei* might suggest that Jews and Judaism would be treated in Book III only, this is in fact not the case. Book III is, to be sure, entirely devoted to the Jews. However, Judaism and Jews play a major role in Book I and Book II as well. In Book I, where Friar Alphonso sets out to present the bases of Christian faith, he regularly depicts Christian truth as grounded in, but superior to, Judaism. In defining the Christian fortress, he projects it as founded upon, but thoroughly superseding Judaism. At the simplest level, Friar Alphonso adduces Hebrew Bible sources as proofs for Christian truth, while at the same time insisting that Christianity had in all ways exceeded its Jewish matrix. Such argumentation is recognizable to us from previous authors, going all the way back to the New Testament. However, there is more. In presenting the truth of Christianity, Friar Alphonso regularly combines his arguments on behalf of Christianity with dismissal and denigration of Judaism, which is curious. Moreover, Friar Alphonso – as noted – also cites at great length talmudic and medieval Jewish sources in making his case for the truth of Christianity, which is likewise strange. These unusual features of the *Fortalitium fidei* will occupy us extensively.

Book II of the *Fortalitium fidei* is devoted to the dangers from heresy. Although Friar Alphonso had at his disposal considerable knowledge of the history of heresy (recall the concern of Eusebius and Augustine over the heresies of their own days and their provision of considerable information on these heresies), it is clear that the heresy upon which he is most fully focused involves the former Jews of the Iberian peninsula, who have joined the Christian fold, but are far from integrated into their new faith and community.

Thus, in order to grasp fully Friar Alphonso's views of the Jewish past, present, and future, we must examine Book I, Book II, and Book III of the *Fortalitium fidei*. From this combination we will derive a fuller sense of Friar Raymond's disquiet over, indeed fear of his Jewish contemporaries; his heavily negative perspectives on the trajectory of Jewish history, that is his Jewish contemporaries, their predecessors, and their successors; and his harsh suggestions for countering the dangers presented by the former Jews and overt Jews of fifteenth-century Spain.

Book I of the *Fortress of Faith*, which carries no title, projects the imagery of a beleaguered fortress – which is Christianity and Christian Spain – and the elements required to defend it. This opening book is clearly intended as a positive preamble to the description of the threats posed by the enemies of the fortress and the responses required to these threats. In the first chapter of Book I, Friar Alphonso describes the spiritual armor that every Christian must wear in order to repulse the attacks on the fortress of Christianity.[10] The depiction of the requisite spiritual armor is fairly standard, involving the cultivation of intellectual, spiritual, and moral strengths.

In the second chapter of Book I, Friar Alphonso addresses the special role of preachers, which creates the sense of this composition as a preacher's manual. Friar Alphonso speaks of the failures of Christendom's leaders and preachers and the resultant havoc caused to the Christian populace. Strikingly, the very first enemy group insufficiently addressed by these leaders and preachers consists of the Jews. "For the most part, there is none concerned about the faithless Jews, who blaspheme your name and secretly practice unheard of cruelties, because their bribes have blinded the eyes of prelates and judges among the clergy and the people."[11] Notable here is the focus on the Jewish present and the reference to Jewish blasphemy, which is reminiscent of Peter the Venerable, and "unheard of cruelties," which the friar will clarify fully and innovatively in Book III. Also striking is the claim that Jewish bribes have blinded the clerical and political leadership of Spanish society to the frightful dangers the Jews pose. Just as Book III of the *Fortress of Faith* exceeds by far all the other three books devoted to the enemies of Christianity and Christendom, so too does this early statement in Book I highlight immediately the special threat posed by the Jews.

In the third chapter of Book I, Friar Alphonso turns to the key principles that undergird the Christian fortress. Here, his deep concern with Judaism and Jews of both the present and the past is yet more fully manifest. Although this chapter (*consideratio*) is intended to discuss "the nobility and excellence of the Catholic faith," every one of the six subchapters (*articuli*) introduces Judaism and the Jews in one way or another.[12] In fact, Judaism becomes an increasingly dominant theme as Friar Alphonso proceeds through the six subchapters of the third chapter of Book I of the *Fortress of Faith*. Proving "the nobility and excellence of the Catholic faith" seems to require highlighting the sources of Christianity in the Hebrew Bible and then distinguishing between the true Christian fulfillment of the Hebrew Bible and its debased Jewish offshoot.

Although appeal to the Hebrew Bible for establishing "the nobility and excellence of the Catholic faith" makes perfect sense and was a

well-established foundation of Christian thinking, Friar Alphonso's tendency to highlight the biblical grounding of Christianity and then demean
Judaism and the Jews is noteworthy. Given the fact that the remaining
four books of the *Fortress of Faith* are devoted to identifying the enemies
of Christianity and that Judaism and Jews are treated at great length in
this subsequent portion of the composition, it is striking that Judaism
and Jews should be so regularly mentioned and attacked in Book I. The
friar's strange compulsion to begin his assault on Judaism already in
Book I suggests something of an obsession on his part with Jews of both
the present and the past. Book I reinforces the sense that Friar Alphonso
perceived the Jews to be the most dangerous of the enemies attacking the
Christian tower of faith.

   Sub-chapter 1 of the third chapter of Book I sets out to show "that
Jesus is the son of the living God." The first two arguments in this sub-
chapter, however, immediately invoke the Jews. The first of these arguments involves the Jews when they killed Jesus, and the second involves
the same Jews when they rose up against the disciples of Christ after his
death. Thus, even in this first subchapter, seemingly focused on Jesus, the
Jews play a key role.[13] The next four subchapters of Book I, chapter 3,
all proclaim the superiority of Christian truth over Judaism. "The second sub-chapter [shows] that the faith of Christ is older than the law of
Moses. The third sub-chapter [shows] that the faith of Christ is more stable than the law of Moses. The fourth sub-chapter [shows] that the faith
of Christ is nobler than the law of Moses. The fifth sub-chapter [shows]
that the faith of Christ is more useful than the law of Moses."[14] Thus,
throughout these middle four subchapters of Book I, chapter 3, Christian
truth is repeatedly portrayed through contrast with Jewish error and inferiority. Once more, Friar Alphonso's overwhelming concern with Judaism
and Jews is obvious.

   At this point, we might well pause and ask as to the reason or reasons for this curious focus on the Jews in Book I of the *Fortalitium fidei*,
devoted to a positive exposition of Christian truth. The answer would
seem to lie in the special circumstances of Spanish Christian society.
Within Spanish Christian society, there was – as noted – by the time of
Friar Alphonso a significant segment of New Christians, who had themselves or whose parents had been reared in the Jewish community and
faith. Friar Alphonso's outreach to an eventual Christian audience was
very much colored by this reality. Presentation of Christian truth for
an audience that included many New Christians involved a double tactic – the traditional grounding of Christian belief in its Hebrew Bible

moorings and simultaneous denigration of the Jewish alternative that was so much a part of the heritage of these New Christians. In this sense, the New Christians represented an internal threat to the fortress of Spanish Christianity, and this internal threat had to be addressed – even in the first book of the *Fortalitium fidei* devoted to Christian truth. The New Christian threat had to be presented somewhat obliquely, but it had to be presented nonetheless. Hence the ubiquity of dismissal of Judaism throughout Book I.

The closing subchapter of Book I, chapter 3, is extremely lengthy and detailed. Its overarching purpose is defined by Friar Alphonso as proving that "the law of Moses is now no longer law, but that it has ceased to be a law."[15] This formulation is again quite strange. The actual content of this very long and important subchapter of Book I, chapter 3, is fulfillment of biblical promise by Jesus and the Church. It is difficult to comprehend why this critical subchapter – which in fact presents the fundamentals of Christian truth – should be defined by Friar Alphonso in terms of dismissing Jewish law. The first two sections of this subchapter do in fact discuss the deficiencies of Jewish law. But in the third section Friar Alphonso turns his attention to the genuine focus of this subchapter, which is fulfillment of biblical prediction by Jesus and the Church. Friar Alphonso's treatment of this fulfillment is rich and detailed, which makes his opening with the attack on Jewish law all the more striking and reinforces the sense that affirmation of Christian truth and negation of Judaism go hand-in-hand for the *Fortalitium fidei* and the suggestion that concern with the New Christian population of mid-fifteenth-century Spain is the reason for this unusual combination.

The fourth and final section of the closing subchapter of Book I, chapter 3, is devoted to proofs that all the biblical predictions about the Messiah were fully realized in the advent of Jesus. This final section is once again richly detailed; it is divided into twelve subsections, many of which are then subdivided into numerous points. Once more, however, the Jews are highlighted in the very first subsection. Again, a broad Christian issue – in this case the argument that the biblical predictions concerning the Messiah were all fulfilled by Jesus – opens with the attention to and attack on the Jews. In this instance, the very first subsection is devoted to proof that the Messiah was destined to come at the point of the destruction of the Second Temple, the removal of the scepter of authority from the Jews, and fulfillment of the seventy weeks prophecy of Daniel 9. Presentation of the Christian case begins with attention to the unfavorable fortunes of the Jews, assumed to reflect divine rejection.

Close scrutiny of this subsection shows further interesting aspects of Friar Alphonso's treatment of Judaism and Jews. Let us examine carefully the arguments in Book I, chapter 6, subchapter 4, section 1, devoted to proving that "the true Messiah ought to arrive in the course of the destruction of the Second Temple or thereabouts, the removal of the scepter of Israel, and the completion of the seventy weeks of Daniel."[16] Friar Alphonso opens this subsection with Malachi 3:1: "Behold, I am sending my messenger to clear the way before me, and the Lord whom you seek shall come to his temple suddenly." Friar Alphonso extracts from this verse clear proof that, at the time when the predicted messenger would arrive, "the temple would be built and in good condition."[17] To this, Friar Alphonso adds Isaiah 56:1 and its gloss by the medieval Rabbi Moses *ha-darshan*, which relates the verse to the Messiah, and Zachariah 9:9, which the friar sees as having obviously been fulfilled by Jesus. For the friar, "it causes much admiration how all these prophets were in harmony, so that with one voice all proclaimed that the arrival of the Messiah was so near at hand."[18]

Friar Alphonso has in fact extracted more than one lesson from the concatenation of these three verses; he has concluded that the Messiah would come close to the time of the three prophets (meaning close in terms of the unfolding of universal history), that the Temple would be standing at the time of his arrival, and that Jesus fulfilled quite literally one major element in the prophecies. It is especially noteworthy that the friar quotes a medieval Jewish exegete on Isaiah 56:1. As noted, the *Fortalitium fidei* – unlike the *Pugio fidei* – was intended ultimately for a Christian audience, yet Friar Alphonso saw fit to cite a Jewish exegete in his argumentation. Friar Alphonso's tendency to cite Jewish exegesis becomes increasingly pronounced as he proceeds through this lengthy subsection.

Citation of the exegetical comment of the medieval rabbi indicates that the innovation introduced by Friar Paul Christian during the middle decades of the thirteenth century and reinforced by the *Pugio fidei* had become, by the middle of the fifteenth century, standard procedure. As indicated, Netanyahu has proven conclusively that Friar Alphonso did not have immediate access to the Talmud itself and that he used materials readily available, again suggesting how fully the new technique had taken hold. However, we have noted a major difference between Friar Raymond and Friar Alphonso, with the former intending his preacher's manual to be used with Jewish audiences and the latter intending his to be utilized with Christian audiences. Why would a Christian audience be at all interested in the views of a medieval Jewish exegete? Once again, I believe we must be aware of the presence of New Christians in the eventual audience for the *Fortalitium fidei*. Such former Jews would find a Jewish exegete supporting Christian views of considerable interest and importance.

Friar Alphonso in fact proceeds further and advances a Jewish objection to the case laid out to this point. This objection notes that there is no necessary correlation between the short time predicted by the three prophets and the last days of the Second Temple, and Friar Alphonso sets out immediately to answer the objection. He cites Isaiah 9:6–7, with its lavish titles for the child that will be born, and argues that "it is impossible that that some mortal man, in whom there is no divine nature, could be so entitled with these most excellent names."[19] The friar then immediately introduces once again rabbinic exegesis on the verse, claiming that in fact two talmudic sources and a medieval Jewish exegete bear witness to the fact that the Isaiah verses were predictions of the Messiah. The citation of rabbinic sources here is by means incidental; rather, it is crucial to the friar's argument. Indeed, Friar Alphonso's arguments from this point in the lengthy subsection to its end are dominated by citations from rabbinic literature, reflecting once again the importance of formerly Jewish New Christians in the eventual audience for Friar Alphonso's argumentation on behalf of the truth claims of Christianity.

In terms of our investigation of Christian constructions of Jewish present, past, and future, this aspect of Book I of the *Fortress of Faith* is telling. Jews were of vital significance in the past. They were the people of the covenant and the prophets, although Friar Alphonso does not dwell to any extent on praising this role. In terms of the past, the friar's interest lies with Jewish error and Christian truth, although the projection of Jewish error is mitigated to an extent by rabbinic acknowledgment of Christian truth in glosses on the Hebrew Bible and in free-standing rabbinic dicta. The Jewish past is – at this point in time and for Friar Alphonso – the most important history outside of Christianity itself. Indeed, the two histories – that of Christianity and that of Judaism – are so intimately linked with one another that the friar's case for the truth and glory of the former cannot be advanced without regular and extensive denigration of the latter.

Book I of the *Fortress of Faith* has less to say with respect to the Jewish present, but its observations are significant. The Jews of fifteenth-century Spain are – not surprisingly – very much a continuation of the Jewish past and its errors. They maintain faithfully but foolishly the misunderstandings of their ancestors. More important, they are the key voices of spiritual opposition to Christianity on the fifteenth-century scene. Presentation of the truth of Christianity must be made with full reference to this dissenting voice and its errors. There is, to be sure, more than simply continuity with prior Jewish dissidence and error. Like Peter the Venerable (and unlike Bernard of Clairvaux), Friar Alphonso is convinced of active Jewish enmity in his fifteenth-century milieu, expressed through regular blasphemy by the Jews. More frightening yet, they express their enmity by perpetrating unheard-of cruelties, which will be fully depicted in Book III of the *Fortress of Faith*.

Jews are extremely important in Book I of the *Fortalitium fidei*, despite the fact that this book is ostensibly focused on Christianity itself. Friar Alphonso can seemingly not portray the truth of Christianity without indicating its roots in early Jewish history and writings (which is standard), without highlighting Jewish error in understanding this literary legacy (which is still standard, but nonetheless a bit intense), without contrasting the shortcomings of Judaism with the virtues of Christianity (which is not all that standard), and without citing rabbinic and medieval Jewish thinkers in a work intended for a Christian audience (which is most unusual).

With Book II, Friar Alphonso begins the important task of identifying the enemies of the Christian fortress, depicting the dangers they present, and sketching the requisite steps to minimize or eliminate these dangers. In Books II and III of the *Fortalitium fidei*, the friar's focus with regard to Jews shifts from the Jewish past, which was his central concern in Book I, to the Jewish present, where the Jews and the related ex-Jewish New Christians pose – in his view – profound dangers to contemporary Christian society.

In Book II, Friar Alphonso identifies the first and ostensibly most serious enemy as heretics, which is perfectly reasonable. In the Hebrew Bible, internal dissidents constitute the most dangerous foes, since fulfillment of the covenantal relationship with God was the driving force in history, and internal dissidents disrupted this covenantal relationship. External enemies were perceived as far less significant, since such external enemies functioned merely as agents of divine wrath and nothing more. When we examined Eusebius's views on the history of the Church, he adduced as the first of the negative forces in that history those that "through a passion for innovation have wandered as far as possible from the truth, proclaiming themselves the founts of knowledge, falsely so called, while mercilessly like savage wolves making havoc of Christ's flock."[20] According to Eusebius, these innovators – working against the established traditions and truths of the Church – were extremely destructive. We have noted as well Augustine's experimentation with a variety of heretical points of view and his subsequent obsession with heresy. Thus, Friar Alphonso's decision to begin with heretics makes good sense.

Book II of the *Fortalitium fidei* represents more than simply a shift from the positive depiction of the Christian fortress of faith to a description of the enemy forces threatening it. It also involves a move from essentially theological considerations to the realm of societal life. The enemies that Friar Alphonso portrays of course disagreed with Christian religious doctrine, as indicated clearly in Book I. With Book II and the subsequent three "enemy books," however, the issues at stake go far beyond theoretical disagreement. Each of the four enemy groups threatens Christianity on more than simply the intellectual plane; each enemy grouping represents a serious threat to the stability of Christian society and in many cases to the everyday lives of Christians. The first group depicted – the heretics – threatens the very fabric of Christian society; their dissidence disrupts the normal order of Christian life and encourages other members of society to emulate them, thus creating chaos within the Christian fold. For the health of Christendom, heretics must be carefully identified and rooted out.

Friar Alphonso begins Book II, devoted to heretics and the dangers they pose, with general considerations relative to the phenomenon of heresy. In the opening chapters (*considerationes*), he defines heresy and distinguishes it from simple error, discusses the origins of heresy, and proposes methods for identifying a heretic as such.[21] These introductory observations are useful, but essentially fairly general and bland. It is with the sixth chapter of Book II that Friar Alphonso begins to hone in on the immediacy of contemporary heresy, its specific characteristics, and the serious dangers it portends.

Chapter 6 of Book II identifies fourteen major contemporary forms of heresy, and the list is rich and instructive.[22] The fourteen contemporary heresies identified by Friar Alphonso begin rather surprisingly with those Christians who resort to circumcision. This is surely an unusual form of heresy, especially when listed as the very first category of heretical behavior adduced. By focusing on this particular form of heresy, the friar serves notice immediately of his concern (once again) with Spain's New Christians, for these are the deviants in Christian society who in fact might be likely to resort to circumcision. We have already noted the role that Spain's New Christians/ex-Jews play in the friar's thinking in

Book I. He indicates immediately that they are foremost in his mind in Book II as well. To be sure, the focus in Book I was convincing these New Christians of Christian truth; the focus in the Book II treatment of New Christians is specification of heretical behavior and thinking, indication of the damages they inflict, and identification of the means of purging Christian society of this destructive internal element. Choosing the resort to circumcision as the very first form of heresy constitutes a clear signal of Friar Alphonso's special and intense concern with backsliding on the part of the Spanish New Christian/ex-Jewish population.

A number of the subsequent forms of heresy further reinforce the sense of the friar's concern with backsliding among the New Christians. The immediately following second category of heretics involves those who negate the New Testament. Once again, this points to New Christians, brought up in a Jewish environment rich in attacks on the New Testament.[23] Standard Christian heretics would not have dismissed the New Testament; to the contrary, most medieval Christian heresies involve the sense that the New Testament was absolutely true and furnished the genuine guide to Christian thinking and living. Most medieval movements defined as heretical by the Church involved an insistence on returning to the pure and noble ideas and ideals of Jesus, as expressed in the Gospels. To highlight denial of the New Testament once again reflects Friar Alphonso's focus on a certain class of dissidents – those brought up within the Jewish community and unable to break with their prior Jewish behaviors and thinking.

The next four categories of heretics identified by Friar Alphonso all revolve around the issue of confession. The friar indicates four different types of attack on the institution of confession.[24] To be sure, there was discomfort in certain medieval Christian circles with confession as demanded by the Church; however, confession was a special target of medieval Jewish polemics. Medieval Jewish polemicists lampooned the Christian practice of confessing to a human being, indicating all kinds of negative ramifications of such confessing.[25] While not so clear-cut as the obvious New Christian targets of the friar's initial two forms of heresy, the heresies involving confession once again suggest a focus on the New Christian population.

The seventh form of heresy specified by Friar Alphonso involves those "who say that only God alone should be obeyed."[26] Once again, this is hardly likely to have been a contemporary heresy within the Old Christian population. New Christians, brought up in a Jewish environment intensely negative to the Christian emphasis on Jesus as part of the godhead, would be those who would have insisted on obedience to God alone and to have negated defiantly the role of Jesus and the Holy Spirit. Thus, the first seven forms of heresy specified in Book II of the *Fortalitium fidei* imply overwhelmingly in some instances or plausibly in others that the essential target of Friar Alphonso's ire and anxiety over heresy within Christian society consisted of those elements in the New Christian population that failed to break with their Jewish past and thus rejected and demeaned key Christian beliefs and practices.

The second half of the list of contemporary heresies introduces issues that were not at all specific to New Christians. Some of these issues involved anti-ecclesiastical propensities, which are in fact well documented among medieval heretics of many stripes; issues related to the afterlife, which were generally contentious throughout the Middle Ages; and issues of causation in human affairs, which were a constant irritant in Christian thinking, especially as the power and influence of science and philosophy were felt more keenly throughout Christian society. Thus, Friar Alphonso was fully aware of a wide range of heretical inclinations throughout fifteenth-century Spain. However, he was obviously especially attuned to the dissident thinking rampant within Spain's New Christian society and highlighted its particular heretical dispositions throughout the first half of his fourteen forms of contemporary heresy. His sensitivity to the New Christians is thus manifest in both Book I and Book II of the *Fortalitiiujm fidei.*

In the closing chapters of Book II, Friar Alphonso turns his attention to the means for dealing with the contemporary heretics. The key to his mind involves inquiry into heresy, identification of heretics, and appropriate punishment. By this time, the Church had a well-established court system for dealing with heresy, and Friar Alphonso saw the inquisitorial courts as essential to identifying contemporary heretics. These courts had also developed a system of punishments for those convicted of heresy, and Friar Alphonso projected this system of punishments as appropriate and effective, critical to reducing or eliminating the damage that heretics might inflict on Spanish society. Not long after the writing of the *Fortalitium fidei*, a special set of inquisitorial courts was established for Spain, and these courts in fact undertook the task assigned by Friar Alphonso.[27] Again, for the friar, the presence of heresy within Spanish society involved more than intellectual dissidence. For him, heresy was a frightening danger to the well-being of Spanish Christendom.

For Friar Alphonso, heretics dissented from normative Christianity, which was in and of itself lamentable; more importantly, they constituted a threat to the unity and stability of Christian society. The Jews as well – the subjects of Book III of the *Fortalitium fidei* – were dissenters from the truths of Christianity, and as in the case of the heretics, their impact went well beyond simple intellectual and spiritual dissent. To be sure, the threat posed by heretics and the threat posed by Jews differed markedly. Whereas heretics threatened the religious unity of Christian society and fostered spiritual fragmentation and societal chaos, the Jews – according to Friar Alphonso – constituted a physical danger to Christians.

Although earlier medieval figures we have discussed, especially Peter the Venerable, discerned the Jews as a threat to the *sancta* of Christianity through their blasphemous rejection of Christianity and its symbols, by Friar Alphonso's time a popular sense had developed in western Christendom of actual physical danger emanating from Jews. Friar Alphonso absorbed this sense and made it the cornerstone of his treatment of the Jewish enemy in his Book III. This absorption of popular perceptions of Jewish physical violence, which expressed itself in assault on Christians in a variety of forms, constitutes the major innovation of the *Fortalitium fidei* with respect to Christian perceptions of contemporary aspects of Jewish history. With Friar Alphonso, the growing popular fear of Jews and their alleged violence made its way into the projection of the Jewish present and past offered by an intellectual figure in medieval Christian society, leading ultimately to the advocating of a radical solution to the perceived problem.

As noted, Book III is the lengthiest of the "enemy books" of the *Fortalitium fidei*, in fact exceeding the length of the other three "enemy books" combined. It is richly detailed and draws much of its information from Jewish sources. In Book III, the citations from Jewish sources make much greater sense than in Book I, for in effect Friar Alphonso presents considerable data on the Jews from their own testimony. Jewish writings – according to the friar – provide much of the evidence he utilizes in order to construct his highly negative portrait of the Jewish present and past.

Book III begins with the rather standard trope of Jewish blindness, an allegation that Friar Alphonso had already advanced in Book I. From this, he proceeds in chapter 2 to depicting the demonic aspects of Jewish origins, citing talmudic material that discusses the early history of humanity.[28] This is hardly an impressive treatment of the background of the Jews, when compared with some of the more sophisticated views of the Jewish past we have encountered. Chapter 3 of Book III moves to what the friar projects as the internal shift that has taken place in Jewish life with the emergence of the Talmud and rabbinic Judaism. For this shift, he cites at length the important earlier convert Abner of Burgos/Alfonso de Valladolid, who was much concerned with the vicissitudes of the Jewish past in his numerous and penetrating polemical works. Beyond this, Friar Alphonso uses Jewish sources to show internal dissension within rabbinic Judaism.[29] Once again, there is striking parallelism between this Christian anti-Jewish argument and Jewish anti-Christian polemics. Jews regularly pointed to the internal fissures within Christendom as evidence of its lack of truth.[30]

The next three chapters of Book III shift to the Jewish arguments against Christianity. The friar's catalogue of Jewish arguments is rich and detailed; it provides a lengthy list of Jewish objections to Christianity drawn from the explication of the Hebrew Bible, another lengthy list of objections drawn from Jewish examination of the New Testament, and a third list drawn from philosophic consideration. All in all, Friar Alphonso provides three sets of Jewish arguments against Christianity, each consisting of twenty-four arguments and thus adding up to a total of seventy-two Jewish anti-Christian arguments.[31] Alphonso clearly intends his catalogue to be exhaustive in identifying Jewish intellectual attacks on Christianity, and he remains wedded to symmetrical lists that are grounded in the number twelve, which is the number of chapters in each "enemy book."

Friar Alphonso's catalogue of Jewish intellectual assaults on Christianity is distinguished by its completeness and its heavy utilization of rabbinic sources. Qualitatively, however, this rich catalogue does not break new ground; it asserts Jewish enmity in the realm of religious disagreement, which is perfectly obvious even without the friar's exhaustive data. Dramatically new ground is broken with chapter 7 of Book III of the *Fortalitium fidei*, in which Friar Alphonso details the "unheard of cruelties," to which he had alluded early in Book I. Reflecting the accelerating popular sense of the Jews of western Christendom as so deeply steeped in the hatred of Christianity that they regularly committed violence against their Christian neighbors, Friar Alphonso brought extensive evidence of this alleged violence and made it the strikingly innovative element in his depiction of Jewish enmity. Not only did the Jews disagree with and attack key beliefs of Christianity, as he had already argued in Book I and earlier in Book III, but they in fact committed violence against their Christian neighbors, especially against the weakest and most vulnerable of them. Understanding the background of the popular perceptions that Friar Alphonso absorbed so thoroughly requires some further familiarity with the development of European Jewry from the turn of the millennium until the middle of the fifteenth century.

We have noted earlier the remarkable growth and development of the Jewish communities of medieval Europe. As indicated, western Christendom in the year 1000 was not the site of large and well-rooted Jewish settlements. In the year 1000, the overwhelming majority of Jews lived within the boundaries of the Islamic world, with numerous Jews finding their homes in the Byzantine Empire as well; the Jewish population of Christian territories – limited to areas of southern Europe – was quite small. By the fifteenth century, this earlier Jewish demographic distribution had changed markedly, partly as the result of expansion of western Christendom at the expense of its Islamic and Byzantine neighbors and partly as the result of decisions made by large numbers of Jews who opted to improve their lot by migrating from traditional areas of Jewish settlement in southern Europe to rapidly developing centers of European life in the north and enjoying the opportunities they offered. During the four and a half centuries between the year 1000 and the composition of the *Fortalitium fidei*, the Jewish population of western Christendom had expanded rapidly, so that Jews had become a significant component in the population of medieval Christian Europe.[32]

Jewish decisions to remain in areas newly conquered by Christian forces or to migrate into areas previously lacking in Jewish settlements were stimulated by more than simply Jewish desire for economic betterment; these decisions were strongly encouraged by the rulers of medieval Europe. Those rulers who were annexing Islamic and Byzantine holdings on European soil were anxious to keep the Jewish inhabitants of their newly conquered territories in place, in order to maintain the level of civilization they had inherited. The rulers of northern Europe, into which Jews began to migrate for the first time, were interested in attracting Jewish immigrants, out of the conviction that these newcomers would bring advanced economic skills with them and would stimulate the economies of their new home areas.

A concerned cleric like Friar Alphonso might well have reacted negatively to these initiatives of the ruling class, seeing them as diluting the quality of Christian life in favor of material advantage, and in a sense he might well have been correct. Nonetheless, ever-accelerating Jewish population growth in medieval Christian Europe was a reality. Fairly early on, Church leaders became concerned with the Jewish population of western Christendom, since Jews were in most areas the largest non-Christian grouping in society. Although Jewish numbers were in fact quite limited and constituted only a small fraction of the total European population, the reality of being the only legitimate dissenting group in an otherwise homogeneous society was in and of itself problematic – as already noted, augmenting the traditionally negative imagery of Jews within the Christian majority.

Out of the confluence of Jewish immigration, deep-seated hostility in the majority population to the Jewish immigrants, and the intricacies of Church law emerged a significant complication in Jewish economic activity. As a result of the animosity they encountered as both Jews and newcomers, Jews in northern Europe were unable to fashion a normally diversified economic posture. Instead, they were shunted into limited areas of the economy, generally economic activities not yet fully developed. A special, important, and problematic sector of the European economy was eventually opened up to the Jews as a result of the twelfth-century Church drive against Christian usury. The Church understood the Deuteronomic prohibition of usury as involving lending by Christian to Christian against payment of interest. This meant *inter alia* that, in the Church view, Jews might give interest to Christian lenders or take interest from Christian borrowers. In this way, a new economic specialization was created for European Jews during the twelfth century. Jews became increasingly involved in and identified with the money trade. We recall Bernard of Clairvaux's criticism of Christian lenders as "Jewing worse than the Jews do."[33]

In a general way, banking has never been a popular profession. Those involved in financial transactions have regularly been seen as parasitic, benefitting from the constructive activities of others in society. More particularly, moneylenders were well thought of at the time of dispensation of the loan, but deeply resented when it came time to repay. When association of normal animosity toward the money trade was joined to Jewish newness and to the traditional New Testament imagery of Jewish enmity, this combination of ingredients produced a potential hatred and fear of Jews on the European scene.

During the twelfth century, this hatred and fear – with an emphasis on the fear – resulted in the development of a series of images of Jewish animosity and harmfulness. Although the perceived harmfulness of Jewish lending was implicit in the activity itself, the new images extended the notion of Jewish danger to Christian society into the realm of the physical. The most fundamental perception was that Jews took advantage of the opportunities to kill Christians, whom they hated simply because they were Christians. Since Jews could not overtly challenge the Christian majority among which they lived, the murders were projected as being carried out surreptitiously, and the victims were often reputed to be youngsters, projected as both innocent and defenseless. In the popular view, the innocence indicated that these killings were the result of the hatred of Christians, with no other motives involved; the defenselessness allowed the murders to take place and were taken as reflections of Jewish cowardice.[34]

The core notion of Jewish hatred translating into murder of Christians was quickly embellished in a number of ways. The two earliest embellishments introduced ritual elements into the murders. It was claimed in a number of cases that, in carrying out their murders of Christian youngsters, Jews were actually reenacting their historic role in the Crucifixion of Jesus. Once again, the victim was totally innocent, and once again Jews were motivated by groundless hatred. In these allegations, the first of which surfaced in the mid-twelfth-century English town of Norwich, the child victim was purported to have actually been crucified by his Jewish tormentors. The allegation of ritualized murder spread quickly, and numerous such claims appeared across northern Europe during the second half of the twelfth century.

During the middle decades of the thirteenth century, the basic sense of groundless Jewish murder of Christian youngsters took a new turn. Rather than associating the purported murders with Easter and the Crucifixion, the new charge shifted the focus to Passover – which normally fell quite close to Easter – and its rituals. The new charge was that, in order to fulfill their Passover ritual obligations, Jews killed Christian youngsters and utilized their blood for the holiday religious rites. Here, there were powerful biblical resonances – the death of the Egyptian firstborn; the sacrifice of animals by the Israelites poised to leave Egypt; and the spread of blood on the Israelite doorposts in order to spare the lives of Israelite children. This newer allegation of ritualized need for Christian blood struck deeper emotional roots than the Crucifixion imagery and became widely believed in medieval (and modern) Christian Europe, despite protracted efforts on the part of the established authorities of church and state to debunk the claim.[35]

Jewish hatred and violence became commonplace assumptions of European societies. When the overwhelming tragedy of the bubonic plague struck Europe in the middle of the fourteenth century, many European Christians, searching for ways to understand and thus perhaps control the catastrophe, concluded that human agents were playing a major role. The Jews were perceived by many as the human agents that had set the plague in motion. The widespread conviction of Jewish animosity and malevolence moved these Christians to initiate or at least accept this conclusion. Throughout plague-stricken Europe, Jewish communities were attacked, out of the sense that the Jews were responsible for the horror of death and destruction. Once again, the authorities of church and state attempted to intervene and restore reason, but the chaotic circumstances allowed for only limited success.

By and large, the leadership of medieval western Christendom rejected these popular allegations. Both ecclesiastical and secular authorities dismissed the claims of Jewish murder, ritualized Jewish murder, Jewish murder for access to Christian blood, and Jewish well poisoning. In many instances, these authorities intervened energetically to protect their Jewish subjects endangered by the popular canards. Such interventions were generally successful, except in periods of maximal societal stress. However, the efforts of the authorities to lay to rest the underlying conviction of Jewish murderousness was conspicuously unsuccessful. Despite pronouncements of all kinds, emanating from the highest level of secular government and the Church, the perceptions were steadily maintained throughout the closing centuries of the Middle Ages and indeed on into the early modern and modern centuries as well.

In this respect, Friar Alphonso represents an important innovation. He embraced wholeheartedly the anti-Jewish allegations that ecclesiastical and secular authorities had long been at pains to reject. Indeed, Friar Alphonso claims that the anti-Christian Jewish violence over the preceding centuries was a recognized reality, was well known to the Christian authorities, and moved these authorities to inflict upon the Jews the requisite punishment. The purported combination of acknowledgment of Jewish crimes and imposition of punishment constituted – for Friar Alphonso – an important lesson. For the friar, Jewish murderousness must be recognized by all, and the authorities of Spain – who had, according to Friar Alphonso, been regularly swayed by Jewish bribes – must be moved to shoulder their responsibility and take the necessary steps to eliminate the Jewish threat to Christian lives.

Chapter 7 of Book III of the *Fortalitium fidei* constitutes the first step in Friar Alphonso's innovative case, with its catalogue of Jewish anti-Christian violence. In a fascinating way, he lays the grounds for his listing of medieval Jewish murders by presenting at the outset of chapter 7 a dramatized retelling of the Crucifixion. In this dramatized retelling, the intense Jewish hatred of Jesus on the part of the Jews of Jerusalem is highlighted, along with their cruel insistence on his death.[36] In this way, Friar Alphonso sets the stage for the sequence of subsequent Jewish crimes he records, arguing in effect that Jewish hatred and murderous cruelty constituted a continuous pattern from antiquity down through the Middle Ages. According to the friar, the hatred and cruelty so well known from the Gospel accounts have been maintained by the Jews over the ages; they should be surprising to no one.

Medieval Jewish hatred and cruelty are copiously documented by the friar in seventeen examples, most but not all of which involve Jewish murder of Christian youngsters. The cases of alleged Jewish murder are chilling, as are the ancillary allegations of Jewish hatred expressed in alternative anti-Christian actions. Let us begin with the latter, which constitute six of the seventeen items in Friar Alphonso's catalogue of Jewish crimes. The very first of these ancillary allegations involves the traditional claim that the Jews of Spain in the early seventh century brought the Muslim conquerors to the peninsula and assisted in its conquest.[37] Repudiated by modern historians, this view of the Muslim conquest was widely credited during the Middle Ages. This allegation was advanced by Friar Alphonso in order to show continuity in Jewish hatred and anti-Christian action from antiquity through the early Middle Ages and then down into the High Middle Ages; it had the further virtue of arousing the ire of the friar's Spanish readers.

After citing eleven instances of Jewish murder, the friar concludes with five more general allegations of Jewish criminality.[38] The first of the five involves Jewish physicians, who allegedly harm Christian patients and who should be scrupulously avoided by Christians. Related to this is Jewish poisoning of Christians. The third general allegation focuses on Jewish prayers for the destruction of Christianity and its leaders. Next are anti-Christian teachings. The last of these general allegations, which concludes the list of seventeen Jewish crimes, involves Jewish usury, which was well known to all and which meant for the friar despoliation of Christians and Christendom. The list of Jewish crimes is artfully contrived by Friar Alphonso. It opens with Jewish treason against early Christian Spain, designed to enrage Spanish Christian readers; it proceeds to the heinous Jewish crime of killing Christians – especially but not exclusively youngsters, which is heavily documented; it concludes with the usury that was exceedingly well known and regularly resented.

The centerpiece of this lengthy catalogue is the list of eleven cases of direct Jewish killing of Christians. This list moves geographically, beginning with France, proceeding to Germany, then on to Italy, and concluding at home on the Iberian peninsula.[39] The sense conveyed by this geographic distribution of incidents is that Jewish murder is pan-European and ubiquitous, observable in every sector of medieval Christian Europe. The targets of and modalities of the Jewish crimes vary widely; they include killing Christians in a general way (#4), poisoning wells (#6), burning down Christian houses (#10), crucifying a Christian adult (#3). The bulk of the cases, however, involve Jewish killing – in one way or another – Christian children (#'s 2, 5, 7, 8, 9, 11, and 12). The killing of children, obviously foregrounded by the friar, is clearly intended to arouse the strongest revulsion among those exposed to the message of the *Fortalitium fidei*.

Besides the horror Friar Alphonso intends to inspire with his catalogue of Jewish crimes, there is a second important message as well, sounded in the first two medieval Jewish murders he depicts. Both incidents as described by Friar Alphonso are rooted in historical reality. In 1182, King Philip Augustus of France expelled the Jews from the royal domain. This was a very significant precedent, although it involved a fairly limited number of Jews, due to the small size of the royal domain at this early point in Philip's reign. Modern studies of this expulsion suggest that it was stimulated by the needs of the struggling royal treasury, which profited handsomely from confiscation of Jewish loans and Jewish real estate. The royal biographer Rigord, however, attributed the king's move to his concern for Christianity and Christians and introduced the claim that the king had heard of Jewish murder of Christian youngsters as a kind of reenactment of the biblical sacrificial system and had expelled his Jews out of outrage over this Jewish behavior.

Friar Alphonso knew of this view of the expulsion of 1182 through Vincent of Beauvais's *Speculum historialis* and featured it in his listing of Jewish crimes. For the friar, this report meant that the allegation of Jewish murder of Christian youngsters was unquestionably true. Moreover, it further pointed to the appropriate behavior for Christian kings in response to the reality of Jewish murder of Christian youngsters, which was to expel the offending Jews. The notion of King Philip Augustus expelling his Jews out of a concern for Christian safety would seem to be obviated by his decision in 1198 to readmit Jews to his domain. Had he been convinced of the murderousness of the Jews, it seems unlikely that the readmission would have taken place. Nonetheless, for Friar Alphonso Jewish murder of Christian children was a reality, and the appropriate governmental response to Jewish murderousness was clearly adumbrated by King Philip Augustus in 1182.[40]

The very next incident cited by Friar Alphonso was also taken from Vincent of Beauvais, involved a genuine late-twelfth-century occurrence, concerned once again King Philip Augustus, and showed the king accepting a report of Jewish murder and acting upon it. In 1192, while Jews were still banned from royal France, the king invaded the domain of a neighboring baron and put to death a large number of Jews belonging to the ruler of the principality. According once again to Rigord, Philip was moved to this action by the report of Jews murdering a Christian of this baron, with the murder involving overtones of the Crucifixion. Acting once more as a protector of Christianity and Christians, the king exacted vengeance for this anti-Christian act, according to Vincent and Friar Alphonso.[41] Yet again, however, the situation was considerably more complex. In the first place, there is a Hebrew account that offers a rather different perspective. According to this Jewish narrator, the Jews had a legal grievance against a Christian neighbor and brought the grievance to their overlord, who executed the Christian in question. Modern observers have seen Philip Augustus's action as a clever political ploy to intrude on an independent neighboring domain.[42] For Friar Alphonso, however, this was yet a second piece of evidence from twelfth-century France that substantiated Jewish criminality and that afforded an example of appropriate behavior on the part of Christian authorities.

Chapter 7 of Book III of the *Fortaltium fidei* makes a powerful case for Jewish crimes, ancient and medieval; it argues the ubiquity of these crimes and acknowledgment of them by medieval chroniclers and – more important – by medieval authorities; and it points to prominent Christian political leaders who took the appropriate actions in the face of Jewish crimes. Chapter 8 of Book III makes a curious detour away from the case for Jewish crime and its punishment. In chapter 8, Friar Alphonso amasses evidence for absurd Jewish teachings, evidence that is very much along the lines of Book V of Peter the Venerable's anti-Jewish diatribe.[43] While interesting and powerfully derogatory, chapter 8 interrupts the smooth flow from chapter 7 to chapter 9 of Book III of the *Fortalitium fidei.*

With chapter 9 of Book III, Friar Alphonso picks up the thread of chapter 7, which featured Jewish crimes and introduced Christian rulers who – according to the friar – responded appropriately to Jewish crimes. Chapter 9 focuses on four major expulsions in Jewish history.[44] As he had done with his catalogue of Jewish crimes, Friar Alphonso begins back in antiquity, with the early days of Christianity and related Jewish history. The first of the expulsions he depicts was the exile from the Land of Israel in the wake of the Jewish crime against Jesus. Interesting for our purposes is the friar's citation of Eusebius's lengthy and poignant description of Jewish suffering during the unsuccessful uprisings against Rome, which we have earlier noted. Once again, the message is that Jewish criminality extends through the ages and that instances of appropriate punishment can likewise be found all across time.[45]

From antiquity, Friar Alphonso proceeds down into the Middle Ages and depicts two major expulsions, first from France in 1306 and then slightly earlier from England in 1290. In both cases, he claims that the two monarchs – Philip IV of France and Edward I of England – were motivated (like their predecessor Philip Augustus of France) by the awareness of Jewish crimes, especially the murder of Christian youngsters. Like King Philip Augustus, these two later monarchs provide a positive example to their successors of recognition of the dangers Jews represent and of the steps that a committed Christian ruler must take in order to protect his Christian constituency from these dangers.[46] King Philip Augustus, King Edward I, and King Philip IV showed through their actions that truly Christian rulers protect their followers from Jewish violence by expelling the Jews from their kingdoms.

With chapter 9, Friar Alphonso completes his innovative construction of the Jewish present, which absorbs popular medieval imagery, depicts the Jews of medieval Europe as violent and ruthless enemies of Christian society, and portrays truly Christian rulers as determined to rid their realms of Jewish danger. Once again, Friar Alphonso – as with chapter 8 – meanders, with two further chapters that detract from, rather than augment the disturbing imagery he has presented of Jews and their present-day anti-Christian behaviors and of the actions that a determined Christian ruler should take. Meandering aside, the case he presents is innovative and powerful.

In fact, a few decades after the writing of the *Fortalltium fidei*, the monarchs of Spain decreed precisely the kind of expulsion that Friar Alphonso saw as appropriate. As was true for the expulsions from England and France, so too the expulsion from Spain in 1492 was not in fact motivated by the fear of Jewish physical violence. In all three expulsions, the monarchs expressed overtly their rationales for expelling their Jews. For the expulsions of 1290 and 1306, the rationale lay in the crime of Jewish usury, which governmental efforts had purportedly been unsuccessful in eradicating; for the expulsion of 1492, the Spanish king and queen pointed to the deleterious impact of Spain's Jews on the recalcitrant New Christian population. Modern scholars have attempted to move beyond these formal rationales and identify the more complex thinking behind the banishments.[47] None, however, has suggested royal acceptance of the allegations advanced in the *Fortalitium fidei*. At most, it is possible that the English, French, and Spanish rulers may have been aware that their edicts would find favor with large numbers of their subjects who subscribed to the views on present-day Jews advanced by Friar Alphonso de Espina.

There is but one more chapter of interest to us in Book III of the *Fortalitium fidei*, and that is the closing chapter, which treats the Jewish future. In chapter 12 of Book III, Friar Alphonso addresses the Jewish future in a way that reflects the Pauline perspectives that have played such a major role in the constructions of the Jewish future we have thus far encountered. However, his construction of the Jewish future represents – not unsurprisingly – an especially negative version of the Pauline views. The closing chapter of Book III is defined by Friar Alphonso as treating "the conversion of the Jews at the end of days." It opens with the issue of converting Jews in the present and ends with the eventual conversion of Jews at the time of ultimate redemption. The friar's treatment of both is illuminating.

The first half of chapter 12 begins with the question of why Jews do not in fact accept Christian truth. Although the discussion is lengthy, the underlying answer revolves around Jewish acceptance of the Talmud and its teachings. Subsequently, standard issues are raised, such as the use of force in conversion, acceptance of converts from Judaism, and what should be done with converts from Judaism who relapse back into their prior faith.[48] All these issues were, as noted, very much part of the friar's fifteenth-century ambiance, with its large population of formerly Jewish New Christians. The overall stance of Friar Alphonso involves support for the traditional Christian perspective of encouraging genuine conversion, but this support is tinged with awareness of the potential complications of the conversion process. In Book II of the *Fortalitium fidei*, the friar had dealt at length with such complications, and he was obviously cognizant of and concerned with the difficulties of assimilating converts from Judaism successfully into the Christian fold.

Friar Alphonso concludes chapter 12 and Book III in its entirety with a discussion of the eventual conversion of the Jews.[49] This discussion is hardly an enthusiastic encomium to this eventual conversion; rather, it focuses heavily on the ongoing Jewish resistance to Christian truth, Jewish attraction to the anti-Christ who will precede the eventual conversion, and Jewish acceptance of this seductive and dangerous figure.

Although all this accords with accepted doctrine, it is skewed once more toward the negative, in this case a negative appraisal of the Jewish future. Jews will finally and reluctantly accept Christ, but only after prolonging their rejection of him to the very last possible moment.

In his lengthy Book III of the *Fortalitium fidei*, Friar Alphonso paints a highly charged negative portrait of Jews. His focus is very much on the Jewish present, which for him is dominated by blindness and a consuming hatred of Christianity and Christians. Most strikingly, this hatred moves the Jews to acts of violence against their Christian contemporaries, which transforms them from religious dissidents into dangerously anti-social elements in Christian society. In the face of this danger, exemplary rulers in medieval Christendom have pointed the way toward protecting Christian society by expelling their Jews.

According to the friar, the destructive inclinations of the Jews are by no means new. In their destructiveness, the Jews of medieval Europe were in effect continuing the trajectory established by the Jews of antiquity who rejected the Messiah sent by God to redeem the Jewish people and all of humanity. The leaders who led this rejection of Jesus evolved as the rabbis of the Jewish tradition, and their teachings subsequently reinforced their Jewish successors in their blindness to Christian truth and their hostility to the Christian faith and its adherents. The Jewish future will end with the acceptance of Christian truth and faith, but only at the very last possible moment, with Jews maintaining their blindness and hostility until that climactic moment.

The *Fortalitium fidei* represents the most negative assessment of the Jewish present, past, and future we have thus far encountered, although the later writings of Martin Luther will compete with Friar Alphonso in this regard. Unlike Luther, the friar embeds his anti-Jewish observations in a work that is general in orientation, intended to identify the multiple dangers facing the beleaguered fortress of Christianity. However, the extent to which Jews dominate this general work is noteworthy. As Friar Alphonso surveys the situation of mid-fifteenth-century Spain, he sees Jews – both overt Jews and clandestine Jews who had ostensibly converted to Christianity – as the dominant danger threatening Spanish society. The general character of the *Fortalitium fidei* makes its negative perspectives on the Jewish present, past, and future all the more striking.

It might be tempting to see the progression of thinkers treated in this section of the book as simple movement toward enhanced negativity with respect to the Jewish present, past, and future, a process fated to continue down into the modern centuries and culminate in the Holocaust. I would urge resistance to this sense of ineluctable progression, in favor of an emphasis on changing contexts. For Friar Alphonso, fifteenth-century Christian Spain was a world in danger, surrounded by external and internal foes. The conquest of Constantinople, which took place shortly before the composition of the *Fortalitium fidei*, revealed just how vigorous and threatening the forces of Islam were. Internally, change was palpable within Spanish society, and this change was frightening to many, including the friar. Although the Jews were arguably not the real danger confronting fifteenth-century Spain, the focus on them is on some levels understandable. The Jewish enemy was the best known of the internal forces ranged against Spain and Spanish Christendom. There was surely great temptation to counter the general sense of foreboding by focusing on a well-known and ultimately rather weak enemy.

Out of this anxiety-ridden context, Friar Alphonso composed his portrait of the Jewish present, past, and future, dominated by blindness, hatred, and destructiveness. For the friar, the obvious solution to the dangers posed by present-day Jews was to drive them out of Christendom, as a number of rulers had already done and as the rulers of Spain would do in a few decades. Eventual Jewish redemption lay far off in the future, as part of the broader redemption that God would eventually usher in for all of humanity.

Notes

1 See Chapter 8.

2 The most recent treatment of the events of 1391 can be found in Mark Meyerson, *A Jewish Renaissance in Fifteenth-Century Spain* (Princeton: Princeton University Press, 2004), chapter 1. Although Meyerson focuses on the Jewish community of Morvedre in the Kingdom of Valencia, his treatment provides a broad and excellent description of the events of 1391 in general.

3 Recall the discussion in Chapter 6 of the leadership role played by converts such as Nicholas Donin and Friar Paul Christian in their new ambiance.

4 Benzion Netanyahu, "Alonso de Espina – Was He a New Christian?" *Proceedings of the American Academy for Jewish Research* 43 (1976): 107–165.

5 See further for a discussion of this phenomenon.

6 Netanyahu, "Alonso de Espina," 121.

7 The most extensive recent treatments of Friar Alphonso and his *Fortalitium Fidei* are Steven J. McMichael, *Was Jesus of Nazareth the Messiah?: Alphonso de Espina's Argument against the Jews in the Fortalitium Fidei (c. 1464)* (Atlanta: Scholars Press, 1994), and Alisa Meyuhas Ginio, *La Fortresse de la foi: La vision du monde d'Alonso de Espina, moine espagnol (?–1466)* (Paris: Les Editions du Cerf, 1998). Both accept the conclusions of Netanyahu regarding the religious identity of Friar Alphonso.

8   McMichael, *Was Jesus of Nazareth the Messiah?*, 605, notes one manuscript
    and four incunabula editions, which suggests considerable late-fifteenth-
    century interest in the work. There has not been recent interest in reprinting the
    Fortalitium fidei. I believe that the following analysis of the intensely negative
    perspectives on Judaism and Jews will clarify an important element in this lack of
    modern interest. I have been able to examine a number of printed versions of the
    Fortalitium fidei at the library of the Jewish Theological Seminary of America.
    I have also been aided by the remarkable generosity of Steven McMichael, who
    has shared with me a transcript he made some years ago of Book III of the
    Fortalitium fidei. I am profoundly grateful to him. Since there are so few copies
    of the *Fortalitium fidei* available, I will direct readers to Steven McMichael's
    Was Jesus of Nazareth the Messiah?, which is readily available and has a com-
    plete outline of the text, quoted from the original, and lengthy citations from
    Book I. For Book III, I will also cite Alisa Meyuhas Ginio, who has provided
    a Spanish summary of the contents of Book III in *De Bello Iudaeorum: Fray
    Alonso de Espina y su Fortalitium fidei* (Salamanca: Universidad Pontificia de
    Salamanca, 1998; *Fontes Iudaeorum Regni Castellae*).

9   McMichael, *Was Jesus of Nazareth the Messiah*, 8, indicates the pages
    devoted to the four enemies as: heretics – 29 pages; Jews – 150 pages;
    Muslims – 84 pages; demons – 21 pages. Thus, while the other three enemies
    are accorded a total of 134 pages, the Jews by themselves occupy 150 pages.

10 Friar Alphonso organized his composition very carefully (compulsively?)
    into books, sections, subsections, sub-subsections, and so on. The sequenc-
    ing of these divisions, which can be quite confusing, is as follows: *liber*;
    consideratio; *articulus*; *punctus*; *principale* or *thesaurus*; *punctus*. Literal
    translation of these terms will be of no assistance to the English reader. Thus,
    I have created the following paraphrases for Friar Alphonso's organizational
    scheme: *liber* = Book; *consideratio* = Chapter; *articulus* = Sub-Chapter;
    punctus = Section; *principale* or *thesaurus* = Sub-Section; *punctus* = Point.
    I have tried to make these paraphrases, which are essentially unrelated to the
    Latin, a vehicle for clearer understanding of the friar's organizational think-
    ing. For a very useful outline of the entire composition, *punctus* by *punctus*,
    see McMichael, *Was Jesus of Nazareth the Messiah?*, 297–325.

11 Ibid., 9.

12 The outline of this chapter can be found in ibid., 298–303. Note again my
    translation of the terminology used by Friar Alphonso in organizing his com-
    position, as spelled out in n. 10.

13 Ibid., 298.

14 Ibid.

15 Ibid.

16 Ibid., 329. Again, recall my paraphrase of the technical terms used in the
    organization of the *Fortress of Faith*, as indicated in n. 10.

17 Ibid., 330.

18 Ibid., 331.

19 Ibid., 332.

20 See Chapter 3.

21 McMichael, *Was Jesus of Nazareth the Messiah?*, 303–304.

22 Ibid., 304–305.
23 See Robert Chazan, *Fashioning Jewish Identity in Medieval Western Christendom* (Cambridge: Cambridge University Press, 2004), chapter 13, for early Jewish attacks on the New Testament. These attacks intensified throughout the subsequent medieval centuries.
24 McMichael, *Was Jesus of Nazareth the Messiah?*, 308–310.
25 Chazan, *Fashioning Jewish Identity*, 308–310.
26 Ibid., 304.
27 Ginio, *La Fortresse de la foi*, 130–132b discusses the relationship of the *Fortalitium fidei* to the subsequent Spanish inquisition.
28 McMichael, *Was Jesus of Nazareth the Messiah?*, 304–317 provides an outline of Book III. The length of this outline in comparison with the outlines of the other books of the *Fortalitium fidei* is notable. For chapter 2 of Book III, see McMichael, *Was Jesus of Nazareth the Messiah?*, 305, and Ginio, *De Bello Iudaeorum*, 15–17.
29 McMichael, *Was Jesus of Nazareth the Messiah?*, 305, and Ginio, *De Bello Iudaeorum*, 18.
30 Chazan, *Fashioning Jewish Identity*, 226–228.
31 McMichael, *Was Jesus of Nazareth the Messiah?*, 305–311, and Ginio, *De Bello Iudaeorum*, 18–58.
32 Robert Chazan, *The Jews of Medieval Western Christendom* (Cambridge: Cambridge University Press, 2006; *Cambridge Medieval Textbooks*), 1–9; idem, *Reassessing Jewish Life in Medieval Europe* (Cambridge: Cambridge University Press, 2010), 1–7.
33 See Chapter 5.
34 Robert Chazan, *Medieval Stereotypes and Modern Antisemitism* (Berkeley: University of California Press, 1997), chapters 3–5.
35 Ibid.
36 McMichael, *Was Jesus of Nazareth the Messiah?*, 311, and Ginio, *De Bello Iudaeorum*, 59–61.
37 McMichael, *Was Jesus of Nazareth the Messiah?*, 311, and Ginio, *De Bello Iudaeorum*, 61–62.
38 McMichael, *Was Jesus of Nazareth the Messiah?*, 312, and Ginio, *De Bello Iudaeorum*, 70–75.
39 McMichael, *Was Jesus of Nazareth the Messiah?*, 311–312, and Ginio, *De Bello Iudaeorum*, 62–70.
40 McMichael, *Was Jesus of Nazareth the Messiah?*, 311, and Ginio, *De Bello Iudaeorum*, 62. For a recent treatment of the expulsion of 1182, see Robert Chazan, *Medieval Jewry in Northern France: A Political and Social History* (Baltimore: Johns Hopkins University Press, 1973), 64–68, and William Chester Jordan, *The French Monarchy and the Jews: From Philip Augustus to the Last Capetians* (Philadelphia: University of Pennsylvania Press, 1989), 30–34.
41 McMichael, *Was Jesus of Nazareth the Messiah?*, 311, and Ginio, *De Bello Iudaeorum*, 63.
42 For a recent treatment of this incident, see Chazan, *Medieval Jewry in Northern France*, 69–70, and Jordan, *The French Monarchy and the Jews*, 35–37.

43 McMichael, *Was Jesus of Nazareth the Messiah?*, 312–313, and Ginio, *De Bello Iudaeorum*, 75–77.

44 McMichael, *Was Jesus of Nazareth the Messiah?*, 313–314, and Ginio, *De Bello Iudaeorum*, 77–81.

45 Although Rome suppressed vigorously the rebellion of 66 and the Jews of Palestine suffered grievously from this suppression, there was in fact no Roman expulsion of Jews in the wake of the rebellion. Both traditional Jewish and Christian thinking projected such an expulsion, but it in fact did not take place. During the subsequent decades, Palestinian Jewry remained demographically strong, as indicated in the capacity to mount yet another major rebellion in the year 132.

46 McMichael, *Was Jesus of Nazareth the Messiah?*, 314, and Ginio, *De Bello Iudaeorum*, 78–81. For recent views of the expulsion from France, see Jordan, *The French Monarchy and the Jews*, 200–238; for recent views of the expulsion from England, see Robin Mundill, *England's Jewish Solution: Experiment and Expulsion, 1262–1290* (Cambridge: Cambridge University Press, 1998).

47 See again Mundill, *England's Jewish Solution*, and Jordan, *The French Monarchy and the Jews*. On the expulsion from Spain, see Haim Beinart, *The Expulsion of the Jews from Spain*, trans. Jeffrey M. Green (Oxford: Littman Library of Jewish Civilization, 2002).

48 McMichael, *Was Jesus of Nazareth the Messiah?*, 317, and Ginio, *De Bello Iudaeorum*, 93–97.

49 McMichael, *Was Jesus of Nazareth the Messiah?*, 317, and Ginio, *De Bello Iudaeorum*, 97–98.

8

Looking Backward and Looking Forward

Martin Luther

Friar Alphonso de Espina wrote in a setting that seemed homogeneous and secure. However, Europe stood on the threshold of major change, and some of the virulence of the friar's view of Judaism and Jews may well have resulted from an inchoate sense of foreboding. To be sure, the major centers of sixteenth-century disruption and change lay outside the Iberian peninsula, especially but not exclusively north of the Alps in Germany, where a combination of humanism, ecclesiastical reformist sentiment, and societal upheaval convulsed political and religious life. Analysis of this disruption and change has proven difficult, since the major sixteenth-century thinkers present a confounding combination of continuity with the medieval, on the one hand, and significant break with the medieval on the other. Among the changes that have proven difficult to assess are evolving sixteenth-century stances toward Judaism and Jews. On this issue as well, it is not easy to disentangle the medieval from the innovative, and it has been argued that, with regard to the Jews, there is much more continuity than change.[1]

Surely the dominant figure in sixteenth-century religious change was Martin Luther. Although there were many other major figures, Luther was in many ways the most visible on the ecclesiastical/political scene and the most widely read on the intellectual scene. He was deeply committed to Christianity as it had evolved in medieval western Christendom, but at the same time he shared the discontents of many medieval Christians about the state of the Church and the direction provided by its leaders. Luther was certainly influenced by the new thinking in European circles; he mastered Hebrew and Greek out of the innovative concern for direct access to biblical sources. Nonetheless, many of the challenges he dramatically posed to the Church were not truly innovative. His major strictures followed the lines adumbrated by a series of medieval reformers from the twelfth century on, many of whom were persecuted as heretics. What was truly innovative was that Luther publicly posed his challenges, flaunted ecclesiastical authority, and was able to find protectors who safeguarded him from the normally successful efforts of the Church hierarchy to squelch such voices of dissent.[2] Luther's successes emboldened others as well to challenge Church doctrine and practice, and he thus set in motion the fragmentation of the heretofore homogeneous religiosity of medieval European civilization. This fragmentation established a new context for European life in general; for European Jewish life in particular; and for European perspectives on the Jewish present, past, and future.

Luther was a prolific writer, whose compositions benefitted from the new technology of the printing press. Of all the thinkers covered in this book, only Augustine could challenge Luther for literary output. Within the vast Luther corpus, Judaism and the Jews do not occupy anything like a position of centrality. They are at best of secondary concern. Nonetheless, Luther did repeatedly turn his attention and his pen to the issue of the Jews. In 1523, Luther wrote a reply to allegations against him, which he turned into an essay that simultaneously criticized the Catholic Church for its policies vis-à-vis Jews and urged a new and more sympathetic approach to them.[3] He began this call for a new approach to Jews by pointing out that Jesus himself was a Jew and that Jews should be honored for their closeness to Christ. This essay laid out a program for reaching out to Jews by confronting them with biblical truth, in effect urging that his insistence on direct and unmediated biblical truth for Christians be reprised with Jews as well. This proposed program provided an occasion for Luther to criticize the Catholic Church for its mistreatment of Jews, arguing that Catholic mistreatment was the key to Jewish intransigence, that Jews could hardly be attracted to a religious faith that was so callous and so foolish. Better treatment of Jews and more careful efforts to win them over intellectually and sympathetically would – Luther argued – result in successful conversion of at least some Jews.

Fifteen years later, in 1538, Luther once again turned his attention to the Jewish issue. In his essay *Against the Sabbatarians*, Luther ceased using the Jews against the Catholic Church and instead identified the rabbis with the Catholic Church in their shared disregard and in fact contravention of the Bible; at the same time, he continued to argue for confronting Jews with biblical truth. The tone of this second essay was noticeably cooler than that of the 1523 statement.[4] Toward the end of his life, in 1543, Luther wrote a series of viciously negative diatribes against the Jews.[5] Luther attacked Jewish belief savagely and held up all facets of contemporary Jewish existence to withering criticism and ridicule. Most scholars have found it somewhat difficult to believe that the same thinker authored the earlier and the 1453 writings.[6]

Given Luther's importance, what limited attention he did give to Judaism and the Jews has been very carefully examined and analyzed.[7] Scholars have pored over his essays, seeking to understand all facets of the Luther statements on Judaism and Jews – the key issues, the factors that inspired both the more positive and the highly negative statements, the nature of the shift, the reasons for the shift, and the impact of his pronouncements. They have been especially attentive to the disparity between the early "positive" Luther and the later vituperative Luther and have tried to identify and explain the curious change in Luther's perspectives on Judaism and Jews.

To be sure, some analysts have argued that there was in fact no ideational shift in Luther's essential view of Judaism and Jews. Rather, these scholars claim that there was merely a tactical shift, with the fundamental Luther perspective on Jews unchanged. In the formulation of Heiko Oberman: "This shift [in Luther] has not escaped modern scholarship any more than it did the Jews of Luther's time. Change, however, does not imply fundamental rethinking, and must not be taken as a sign that Luther had shifted his opinion of those Jews who wished to preserve their identity and evade the embrace of the Christian church."[8]

It seems to me that the Oberman view is clearly correct. Luther maintained the medieval Christian (and Muslim and Jewish) view that the one true God fashioned only one genuine covenant with one human community. Although alternative religious communities might be tolerated in limited ways, they were ultimately in error in their religious commitments. As noted regularly throughout this study, this sense of the Other – even the monotheistic Other – as wrong was especially intense in Christian views of Judaism and Jews. In this regard, Luther was decisively medieval. What he had argued in his 1523 and 1538 compositions was that there had been internal Christian mistakes in approaching the Jews. The Roman Catholic Church – steeped in error of all kinds – had approached Jews over the ages in utterly inappropriate ways. Luther, who was deeply committed to the teachings of Augustine, insisted on the Augustinian call to approach the Jews lovingly, out of a commitment to helping them overcome their errant religious views.[9]

I would venture even a bit further than Oberman. Luther's major 1543 statement – *On the Jews and Their Lies* – is grounded in much the same theological position and the very same biblical citations as his earlier statements. Thus, even the details of theological argumentation remained stable throughout. What is different is partially tactical: By 1543, Luther had given up on his earlier hope to win over Jews and had concluded that they were utterly incapable of a reasonable approach to the Bible and gleaning the truth from it. In addition, the 1543 essay shows a new set of views on the Jewish present and past, which is of course precisely the focus of the present study. What has most impressed posterity, both scholarly and popular, is Luther's portrayal of sixteenth-century Jews and – equally significant – the set of programmatic implications that Luther drew from his reassessment of the Jewish past and especially the Jewish present. The reassessment of his Jewish contemporaries once again presents some noticeable departures from standard medieval views; his programmatic suggestions are by and large dangerously innovative, in line with but even more radical than the suggestions advanced by Friar Alphonso de Espina in the *Fortalitium fidei*.

Once again, however, our objective is not to get to the heart of Luther's views of Judaism and Jews or the reasons for these views. Rather, our focus remains Christian perspectives on the Jewish present, past, and future, in this case the perspectives advanced by Martin Luther. Even if we accept the notion that the shift in Luther's stance was tactical only, his earlier and softer view projected one kind of Jewish present, past, and future, while his later view advanced another and far harsher trajectory of Jewish history. Luther's change of heart on the history of the Jews shows us the potential for Christian thinkers of focusing on certain aspects of Jewish history in one circumstance and alternative aspects in differing circumstances. As a result of his shift in stance, Luther provides us with a variety of perspectives on the trajectory of Jewish history.

I would further urge that in fact Luther's alternative projections of Jewish present, past, and future affords insight into the ongoing impact of the medieval on sixteenth-century thinking and the opening of new possibilities for the early modern period. On the one hand, Luther's 1543 essays highlight the growing awareness and criticism of the Jewish present bequeathed by medieval Europe. We saw an early stage of this tendency in Peter the Venerable, but the criticism reached its apogee in the *Fortalitium fidei*, which presents alleged medieval Jewish crimes,

Christian awareness of and horror at these crimes, and the allegedly resultant expulsions of Jews from a variety of areas of western Europe. Friar Alphonso de Espina was interested in using these materials to convince the Spanish authorities to follow suit and expel their Jews, which they eventually did in 1492. Luther summarizes many of the most important negative motifs in medieval Christian constructions of the Jewish present. The tendency to highlight the negative in the Jewish present generally obscures – as we have seen with Friar Alphonso – the positive elements in the Jewish past and optimistic hopes for the Jewish future.

At the same time, Luther's earlier and more positive statements will help us look at the changing European circumstances. Two vital factors underlie his more positive essays. The first is the fluidity of identity in this new epoch. As alternative options for religious identification emerged in the wake of the disintegration of medieval religious homogeneity, movement and change in religious identity became more prominent. This fluidity stirred hopes that Jewish religious identity, which for a long period had seemed more or less impervious to change, might begin to loosen as well. Jews – viewed through much of the medieval period as totally resistant to conversion – might be more amenable to it under the new circumstances. In addition, the creation of a number of religious alternatives for Christians meant a competitive environment, in which the Jews might once again become useful in intra-Christian debate. Luther could and did exploit the Jewish issue as a cudgel with which to beat the Roman Catholic Church. In his earlier and more positive letters, Luther exploited mistreatment of the Jews as yet one more example of the benighted policies of the medieval Church.

In multiple ways, the new period introduced by Martin Luther's successful revolt against the medieval Roman Catholic Church eventually established conditions somewhat reminiscent of the Roman Empire in late antiquity. The reality of an environment in which alteration of religious identity became common – as had been the case in Roman late antiquity – created a renewed sense of the possibility of winning Jews into the Christian fold. Likewise, the establishment of a variety of Christian religious movements vying with one another meant that the Jews might once more serve useful purposes within the intra-Christian debate, as they had in late antiquity. In a newly heterogeneous environment, the Jews could again be utilized as a weapon in majority dissensions, and Luther points the way in this direction. Because of this combination of implications, I have labeled this chapter "Looking Backward and Looking Forward."

Martin Luther's essays on the Jews provide us with a valuable sense of both directions.[10]

Luther's earlier and more sympathetic view of Jews was not initially intended as a statement on the Jews. His 1523 essay, "That Jesus Christ Was Born a Jew," was stimulated by rumors disseminated about his allegedly heretical teachings. "I am supposed to have preached and written that Mary, the mother of God, was not a virgin before or after the birth of Christ, but that she conceived Christ through Joseph and had more children after that. Above and beyond all this, I am supposed to have preached a new heresy, namely that Christ was [through Joseph] the seed of Abraham."[11] Although Luther portrays these as two allegations, in fact they are essentially one and the same, namely denial of the divine impregnation of Mary and imputation of her pregnancy and birth to a normal human relationship with her husband. Luther suggests that it was at first his intention to disregard these allegations, but that he eventually became convinced that they had to be addressed.

Luther also indicates that, given the absurd nature of the allegations and the unfortunate need to address them, he decided to add some useful content to his letter by addressing the issue of the Jews. In fact, however, there were substantive reasons to add the issue of the Jews to his defense against the false allegations. The supposed heretical statements of Luther, which he vigorously denies in the essay, both involve the issue of Jesus' genealogy. Thus, clarifying the issues of genealogy led Luther in a reasonable way to address the issue of the Jews. In effect, he set out to prove in his essay that he did not believe that Jesus was biologically fathered by Joseph; rather he subscribed to the traditional Christian belief that Mary was divinely impregnated and that the child she bore was thus of divine parentage. At the same time, this did not change the fact that Jesus was of the seed of Abraham – to be sure through Mary and not through Joseph.

Thus, the issue of Jesus' genealogy and the resultant conclusion of Jesus' Jewishness moved Luther to transition smoothly into a discussion of the Jews. He opens this discussion by claiming: "I will cite from Scripture the reasons that move me to believe that Christ was a Jew born of a virgin, that I might perhaps also win some Jews to the Christian faith."[12] In Luther's eyes, acknowledgment of Jesus as a Jew might well make Christianity somewhat more attractive to some Jews. Of course, emphasis on Jesus' Jewishness might well, at the same time, make Jews somewhat more attractive to Christians. Luther's sense of Jesus' Jewishness is neither innovative nor heretical; a focus on this reality would simply highlight a long-acknowledged Jewish virtue that was always in danger of being neglected.

Luther mounted a series of arguments to prove that Mary was a virgin before and even after the birth of Jesus. These arguments break no new ground. The first is based on Genesis 3:15, God's decree of battle between the serpent and Eve. For Luther, this battle was to be carried on at two levels – the first the natural level of serpent–human interaction and the second the cosmic level of struggle between the devil and a unique human being. With respect to the latter struggle, "the seed [that will crush the head of the devil] must be the natural child of a woman; otherwise it would not be called the seed of woman. On the other hand, as has been pointed out, human nature and birth does not produce such seed. Therefore, the solution must ultimately be that this seed is a true natural son of the woman – derived from the woman, however not in the normal way but through a special act of God."[13] For Luther, this is a compelling argument for the virgin birth of Jesus, a doctrine he obviously accepts and teaches, and clear evidence against the rumors of his heretical deviation from this doctrine.

Luther's second proof text is Genesis 22:18, in which God promises Abraham that, because of his willingness to sacrifice his beloved son Isaac, "all the nations of the world shall be blessed by your seed."[14] Here again the mother of God is proven, according to Luther, to be a pure virgin. "For since God cannot lie, it was inevitable that Christ should be the seed of Abraham, that is his natural flesh and blood, like all of Abraham's descendants. On the other hand, because he was to be the blessed seed that should bless all others, he could not be begotten by man, since such children, as has been said, cannot be conceived without sin because of the corrupt and tainted flesh, which cannot perform its function without taint and sin."[15]

Luther proceeds to add further verses from the later books of the Bible, specifically II Samuel 7:12–14 and Isaiah 7:14. With respect to the second of these verses, Luther engages in a protracted argument with Jewish exegesis, which claimed over the ages that the Hebrew term used by the prophet – `almah – does not denote a virgin, that it is simply a designation for a young woman. Luther carries on this argument with Jewish exegesis in a reasonable and restrained manner, exhibiting none of the vituperation that characterizes his 1543 essays. Noteworthy throughout this discussion of the doctrinal issue of Virgin Birth is Luther's regular dependence on the books of the Hebrew Bible, which he approaches in

the Hebrew original and which reflects admiration for the early period
of Jewish history. Since we are focused on Christian views of the Jewish
present, past, and future, Luther exhibits here traditional Christian reverence for the early Jewish past. He disagrees with current Jewish readings
of some of the verses he cites, but he does so respectfully.

Since he had engaged Jewish exegesis on the term `almah`, Luther concludes this segment of his essay by turning to the Jews on the substantive
issue of Jesus' virgin birth. "So certainly no one can doubt that it is possible for God to cause a maiden to be with child apart from a man, since
he has also created all things from nothing. Therefore, the Jews have no
ground for denying this, for they acknowledge God's omnipotence, and
they have the clear testimony of the prophet Isaiah."[16] Again the tone
is firm but civil, as Luther addresses his Jewish contemporaries. These
Jewish contemporaries are in error on the doctrinal issue of Virgin Birth,
as well as on the lexical issue of the key term in the Isaiah verse, but none
of these errors arouses hatred and vilification.

This tone of civility continues as Luther proceeds to offer some guidelines for convincing Jews of the truth of Christianity. "We would also
like to do a service to the Jews on the chance that we might bring some
of them back to their own true faith, the one that their fathers held. To
this end, we will deal with them further and suggest for the benefit of
those who want to work with them a method and some passages from
Scripture that they should employ in dealing with them."[17] Clearly, the
Jews of the present deny Christian truth, as they have done for a very
long time by the sixteenth century. Nonetheless, reflected here is a sense
that the potential still exists for changing the minds of at least some Jews
and a commitment to providing guidance for an enhanced effort to confront Jews – intellectually and sympathetically – with Christian truth.

Luther was of course deeply committed to dismantling the superstructure of Church doctrine and bringing Christians and Christianity back
to Scripture itself and the direct realities of the lifetime of Jesus and his
teachings. He felt that the Jews as well should attend to simple biblical texts and their essential message. This urging is already present in
his discussion of Isaiah 7:14 and the term `almah`. It lies at the heart of
his directives for bringing Christian truth to the Jews. For Luther, the
key to convincing Jews of their errors involves adducing direct biblical
testimonies and juxtaposing these testimonies to the obvious realities of
postbiblical history.

Luther begins the proposed argumentation to Jewish contemporaries
with Genesis 49:10, a verse we have seen quoted regularly by Christian

thinkers to Jews.[18] Luther combines this verse with the realities of Jewish history from the days of Jesus down through the succeeding centuries. "In the first place, that the current belief of the Jews and their waiting upon the coming of the Messiah is erroneous is proven by the passage in Genesis 49:1–12.... This passage is a divine promise, which cannot lie and must be fulfilled unless heaven and earth were first to pass away. So the Jews cannot deny that for nearly fifteen hundred years now, since the fall of Jerusalem, they have had no scepter, that is neither kingdom nor king. Therefore, the *shiloh* or Messiah must have come before this fifteen hundred year period and before the destruction of Jerusalem."[19] In light of the discussions of this crucial verse we have already encountered, Luther's treatment is rather simplistic. However, since he is deeply opposed to what he perceived as medieval casuistry in Church doctrine and exegesis, he tended to avoid intricacies of interpretation and to elicit what he genuinely believed to be the straightforward meaning of biblical texts such as Genesis 49:10.

Luther shows some awareness of alternative Jewish views of Genesis 49:10, including the notion that it was a reference to Jewish exile in Babylonia. He counters this alternative in a number of interesting, albeit not original, ways. The first is to claim that all through Babylonian exile Jews did have genuine rulers. This string of genuine Jewish rulers, however, came to an end with Herod, which means that the real loss of the Jewish scepter came long after the Babylonian exile and in fact at the time of the advent of Christ. A second counterargument involves the suspension of prophecy. All through the Babylonian exile, Jews benefitted from the insights provided by their prophets, who reassured them that their exile would end shortly. "But for these last fifteen hundred years they have had no prophet to proclaim that they should again be free. God would not have permitted this state of affairs to continue for such a long time, since he did not on that occasion permit it for such a short time."[20] Were the exile in which the Jews currently find themselves not the ultimate exile predicted by the patriarch Jacob, God would not have left the Jews bereft for such a long time of the guidance of their prophets; the lack of such prophets makes clear that the current Jewish exile is the one predicted in Genesis 49:10.

Luther's argument from Genesis 49:10 moves from the negative – evidence of Jewish losses – to the positive. According to Luther, there is in the prophecy of the patriarch Jacob not only a prediction of the loss of Jewish authority; there is also a prediction of the glory of the new ruler and order. "The prophecy says that the nations shall be gathered to or be subject to this *shiloh*. Now I ask the Jews: When was there ever such a man of Jewish ancestry to whom so many nations were subject as this Jesus Christ? David was a great king, and so was Solomon; but their kingdom never extended beyond a small portion of the land of Syria. This Jesus, on the contrary, is accepted as a lord and king throughout the world." Luther adduces a number of further Jewish rulers from antiquity and argues that none of them can match the range of the authority and power of Jesus.

Luther cites his conclusion in this regard in a strong and direct way, but once again without a hint of the contumely with which his 1543 essays are replete. "It is amazing that the Jews are not moved to believe in this Jesus, their own flesh and blood, with whom the prophecies of Scripture actually square so powerfully and exactly, when they see that we gentiles cling to him so hard and fast and in such numbers that many thousands have shed their blood for his sake. They know perfectly well that the gentiles have always shown greater hostility toward the Jews than toward any other nation and have been unwilling to tolerate their dominion, laws, or government. How is it then that the gentiles should now so reverse themselves as to willingly and steadfastly surrender themselves to this Jew and with heart and soul confess him king of kings and lord of lords, unless it be that there is here the true Messiah, to whom God has made the gentiles friendly and submissive in accordance with this and numerous other prophecies?"[21] Luther argues here for the historic lack of popularity of the Jews, but juxtaposes that negative with the positive emphasis on the fact that Jesus, who has achieved such acclaim among the gentiles, was obviously a Jew. The interplay of the negative and the positive in this argument is striking.

In the closing sentence of this last claim, Luther cites "this and numerous other prophecies." He proceeds immediately to adduce one of these prophecies, namely Daniel 9:24–27, another passage we have encountered regularly throughout this study. As noted, these few verses are extraordinarily difficult to parse. Once again, however, Luther treats these difficult verses rather simplistically, cutting to what he sees as the core meanings embedded therein. He opens by indicating that Daniel 9:24–27 is "where Gabriel speaks to Daniel in the plainest terms about Christ."[22] However, he does acknowledge that these verses hardly constitute the "plainest terms." "God help us! This passage has been dealt with so variously by both Jews and Christians that one might doubt whether anything certain can be derived from it!"[23] Undaunted by the multitude of exegetical approaches, Luther charges ahead to reach the essence of the divine message delivered by the angel Gabriel. He draws two over-arching conclusions: The first is that Gabriel "is speaking here of the rebuilding of Jerusalem after the Babylonian captivity."[24] The second is that "Gabriel can surely be referring only to the destruction of Jerusalem, which subsequently took place under the Roman emperor Titus about the thirtieth year after the ascension of our Lord."[25] Thus, despite the exegetical uncertainties and disagreements, the time frame of the Gabriel message is clear: it begins with the return from Babylonian captivity and concludes with the destruction of the year 70. Given this time frame, argues Luther, the messianic message can relate only to Christ.

Luther was well aware that the Daniel passage had produced endless exegesis by Jews and Christians. He now addresses this exegesis in the following terms: "It is true that the Jews long ago began to feel the pressure of this mighty flood of evidence and have anxiously defended their position with all manner of preposterous glosses." Once again, present-day Jews are portrayed – calmly – as finding refuge in strained exegesis. For Luther, whose central battle on the Christian front involved repudiation of what he saw as the strained and ultimately preposterous Catholic exegesis that had proliferated during the medieval centuries, attacking the legacy of Jewish exegesis was hardly difficult or daunting. He was used to carrying on such battles and was convinced that ultimately the plain truth of Scripture would carry the day, that both Christians (his major concern) and Jews – when confronted reasonably with the plain biblical truth – would acknowledge it. Luther adduces some of the Jewish approaches to Daniel 9:24–27 and refutes them, leaving the conclusion that the divine message that predicts Christ in the "plainest terms" cannot possibly be denied.

Luther indicates that there are many further biblical verses that prove conclusively the messianic role of Jesus. He then urges a reasonable educational approach to dealing with Jews. They must be addressed lovingly (recall Augustine) and in stages. All issues must not be introduced immediately and in one fell swoop. "If the Jews should take offense because we confess our Jesus to be a man and yet true God, we will deal forcefully with that from Scripture in due time. But this is too harsh for a beginning. Let them first be suckled with milk and begin by recognizing this man Jesus as the true Messiah; after that they may drink wine and learn also that he is true God."[26] Given Luther's 1543 writings, this is rather amazing. Here, Luther relates to the Jews civilly, indeed compassionately, recognizing the difficulties they will encounter in accepting Christian truth and urging patience and a multistage missionizing effort.

In this earliest essay, Luther presents a contrasting view of the Jewish present and the Jewish future – the former largely negative and the latter highly positive. His Jewish contemporaries are beset by more than a millennium of intransigent misinterpretation of biblical truth. This shortcoming should by no means be grounds for hatred and contempt. Rather, it serves as an educational challenge – indeed an educational challenge not unlike the challenge of educating the Christian population of Europe out of its misguided Catholic interpretation of biblical truth. The required educational effort must be undertaken, above all, with patience and understanding. Moving Jews to undo many centuries of error will be an arduous task, but one that can be achieved when undertaken properly. Implicit in this view of the Jewish present is an optimistic perspective on the Jewish future. If Christians can muster the energy and the patience to address the Jews properly, then the Jewish future can be one of achievement of truth and fulfillment of the Pauline vision of the regrafting of the Jewish branch onto the olive tree.

What is needed for this effort is Christian love and patience, and this need is addressed by Luther in this early essay in two ways – first by invoking the Jewish past in order to engender positive feelings toward Jews and then by contrasting the required approach to the Jews with the misguided Catholic alternative. The first objective relates directly to the allegations that set the essay in motion. As we have seen, Luther argues that he has never denied the doctrine of Virgin Birth and advances a number of proofs for the truth of this doctrine. The doctrine posits that Christ had to be born of a human mother and divine impregnation. That human mother – Luther insists, in consonance with traditional Christian thinking – was a first-century Palestinian Jewess, making Jesus' human element Jewish. Furthermore, all Jesus' early followers were likewise Jews, first Palestinian Jews and subsequently diaspora Jews as well.

Luther advances this argument very early on in the essay. "When we are inclined to boast of our position, we should remember that we are but gentiles, while the Jews are of the lineage of Christ. We are aliens and in-laws; they are blood relatives, cousins, and brothers of our Lord. Thus if one is to boast of flesh and blood, the Jews are actually nearer to Christ than we are, as St. Paul says in Romans 9[:5]. God has also demonstrated this by his acts, for no nation among the gentiles has he granted so high an honor as he has to the Jews. For among the gentiles there have been raised up no patriarchs, no apostles, no prophets – indeed very few genuine Christians either. And although the gospel has been proclaimed to all the world, yet he committed the Holy Scriptures, that is the law and the prophets, to no nation except the Jews."[27] As Luther himself indicates, this is all very Pauline. For Luther, these Pauline reflections serve a very useful purpose. They are intended to provide the justification for requiring Christians to undertake the arduous educational program that Luther proposes for dealing with – that is converting – Jews. Christians reminded of the past greatness of the Jews would be reinforced in their effort to summon up the strength and the patience required to undertake the monumental task of overcoming their lengthy intransigence and bringing them to the truth.

The final objective of the essay is to contrast the correct path to converting Jews with the erroneous and ultimately unchristian efforts of his Catholic opponents. Failure as regards the Jews is, for Luther, yet one more indication of the misguided directions pursued by the popes and their followers. It is on this note that he opens his discussion of the Jews and that he closes it as well. Early on, after indicating that he will prove that Christ was a Jew born of a virgin and suggesting that this might win over some Jews, he says the following: "Our fools, the popes, bishops, sophists, and monks – the crude asses' heads – have hitherto so treated the Jews that anyone who wished to be a good Christian would almost have had to become a Jew. If I had been a Jew and had seen such dolts and blockheads govern and teach the Christian faith, I would sooner have become a hog than a Christian."[28] The kind of invective launched by Luther later on against the Jews is here directed against the leadership of the Roman Catholic Church.

From this invective, Luther proceeds to a more focused discussion of the errors of the Roman Catholic Church vis-à-vis the Jews. "They [the leaders of the Church] have dealt with the Jews as if they were dogs rather than human beings; they have done little else than deride them and seize their property. When they baptize them, they show them nothing of Christian doctrine or life, but only subject them to popishness and monkery. When the Jews then see that Judaism has much stronger support in Scripture and that Christianity has become a mere babble without reliance on Scripture, how can they possibly compose themselves and become right good Christians? I myself have heard from pious baptized Jews that, if they had not in our day heard the gospel, they would have remained Jews under the cloak of Christianity for the rest of their days."[29] In this more considered passage, Luther's criticisms herald the positive approach he espouses in the essay – the effort to confront Jews with Scriptural verses in a measured way that would enable the Jews to integrate slowly and fully their new grasp of truth.

At the close of this essay, Luther once again contrasts his proposed program with the misguided efforts of the Catholic leadership. "I would request and advise that one deal gently with them and instruct them from Scripture; then some of them may come along. Instead of this, we are trying only to drive them by force, slandering them, accusing them of having Christian blood if they don't stink, and I know not what other foolishness. So long as we thus treat them like dogs, how can we expect to work any good among them?"[30]

In this closing passage, Luther introduces the economic and social realities of late medieval European Jewish life. "When we forbid them to labor and do business and have any human fellowship with us, thereby forcing them into usury, how is this supposed to do them any good? If we really want to help them, we must be guided in our dealings with them not by papal law, but by the law of Christian love. We must receive them cordially and permit them to trade and work with us, that they may have occasion and opportunity to associate with us, hear our Christian teaching, and witness our Christian life. If some of them should prove stiff-necked, what of it? After all, we ourselves are not all good Christians either."[31] Luther introduces the realities of late medieval Jewish life, with a focus on problematic economic specialization and social distancing from Christians. He does not use these contemporary Jewish realities as the grounds for harsh criticism; rather, he urges ending the negative pressures on Jewish life. The ultimate purpose of removing these constraints is so that Jews might get to know directly Christians and Christianity and be attracted. Once again, the ominous element in this sympathetic portrait is that it is predicated on the eventual objective of bringing Jews into the Christian fold.

Thus, an essay sparked by allegations of heresy on Luther's part led to a careful discussion of Jesus' genealogy, which eventuated in positive comments on the Jewish past, sympathetic observations on the shortcomings of the Jewish present, and optimism as to a Jewish future that would involve acceptance of Christianity. Clarification of Jesus' genealogy evoked a very positive view of the Jewish past. The fact that Jesus was born a Jew meant for Luther the need to acknowledge past Jewish greatness and to keep that greatness firmly in mind. His view of his Jewish contemporaries is calm and reasonable. They are religiously in error and socially problematic; however, the fault is hardly theirs. Jewish economic and social deformities have been forced upon them by misguided Catholic treatment. Warmer and more sympathetic treatment will expose them to Christian life and draw them toward it. Proper Christian teaching, that is, emphasis on plain and direct biblical truth, will destroy their defenses and bring them to slow but steady understanding of undeniable Christian truth. In effect, the religious error of the Jews is the same as that of the Catholic Church; both fail to attend to the simple and direct meaning of Scripture. Reflected here on Luther's part are appreciation for the greatness of the Jewish past, measured criticism of the Jewish present, and optimistic hopes for the Jewish future.

Fifteen years after his first extended treatment of the Jewish issue, Luther turned his attention once again to the Jews. This second essay – *Against the Sabbatarians* – was three quarters of the way chronologically toward Luther's last and virulently anti-Jewish compositions, written in 1543. It is, however, much closer in substance and tone to the earlier *That Jesus Christ Was Born a Jew* than to the 1543 diatribes. There is in this second composition none of the violent hostility of the later pieces. To be sure, some of the warmth of the earlier essay is no longer in evidence either. Especially noteworthy is the absence of the encomia to the Jewish past that were so striking in the 1523 essay, although the intense admiration for and invocation of the Hebrew Bible remains. Nonetheless, even though this second essay was sparked by alleged misbehaviors on the part of some Jews, Luther maintains his focus on the religious problem of Jewish misreading of the clear message of the Bible, with the implication – less overtly stressed than previously – that the key issue in dealing with Jews is refutation of their misguided exegesis of the Hebrew Bible and thus their reeducation.

The stimulus to this second essay was quite different from the issue that sparked the writing of the first. In the case of the first essay, the issue was internal and Christian, namely allegations that Luther had been guilty of denying the doctrine of Virgin Birth and the need to refute these allegations. The 1538 composition resulted directly from Jewish activities. "You informed me that the Jews are making inroads at various places throughout the country with their venom and their doctrine and that they have already induced some Christians to let themselves be circumcised and to believe that the Messiah or Christ has not yet appeared, that the law of the Jews must prevail forever, that it must be adopted by all the gentiles, etc. Then you inquired of me how these allegations are to be refuted with Holy Scripture."[32] Luther identifies here a sequence of Jewish claims, and he will proceed to provide the requested refutations of these claims.

It is striking that Luther presents this report of successful Jewish proselytizing without exploding into fury. It is true that he was asked to provide counterarguments to the Jewish claims and did. However, given what we know of the 1543 Luther, it is noteworthy that he did not erupt into violent castigation of Jews who would behave this way. He was asked to provide intellectual responses, and he did so.

The very first ploy on Luther's part was to explain more fully than he had done earlier the basis for the Jewish intransigence he had previously noted. His explanation is interesting: "In the first place, the Jewish people have become very stubborn because of their rabbis. As a result, they are difficult to win over."[33] Luther had earlier noted intransigence as a key characteristic of present-day Jews and had urged sympathy for this intransigence and a commitment to relentless educational effort. Now, he identifies the root of this intransigence and makes an almost predictable observation. "Even when one persuades them out of Scripture, they retreat from the Scripture to their rabbis and declare that they must believe them, just as you Christians (they say) believe your pope and your decretals."[34]

Thus, the problem with late medieval Jews is precisely parallel to what Luther projects as the problem with late medieval Christians. In both cases, the plain truth of Scripture has been perverted by misguided religious authorities, thereby leading astray in similar ways both Christians and Jews. The response to this deplorable situation is likewise parallel: Both groups must be constantly exposed to biblical truth, until it begins to make the desired inroads into the minds and hearts of misled believers, both Christian and Jewish. In his 1523 essay, Luther pointed regularly to Jewish error, but his criticism of errant and intransigent Jews was rather restrained. As he identifies the root of the Jewish intransigence and error in the rabbis and points to a parallel with Christian error, we can understand the restraint better. If both Christians and Jews are afflicted with the same problem, then castigation of the Jews in some especially intense way hardly seems warranted.

Having identified the problem and the solution – the errant leadership of the rabbis and a relentless focus on biblical truth, Luther proceeds to provide the guidance his correspondent had requested. The request had identified three Jewish claims that had to be refuted: "that the Messiah or Christ has not yet appeared, that the law of the Jews must prevail forever, that it must be adopted by all the gentiles." Luther, however, saw these three issues as intimately related one to another and skillfully weaves together his refutations of the three Jewish claims. Ostensibly, Luther begins with the issue of Jewish law and the Jewish claim that this law must prevail forever. For Luther, historical realities serve as the decisive refutation of this claim. "The Jews have been living away from Jerusalem, in exile, for fifteen hundred years, bereft of temple, divine service, priesthood, and kingdom. Thus their law has been lying in the ashes with Jerusalem and the entire Jewish kingdom all this time. They cannot deny this, for it is proven clearly and emphatically by their wretched situation and experiences and by the place itself, which is even today called Jerusalem and which lies desolate and devoid of Jews before the eyes of all the world. However, they cannot observe Moses' law anywhere but in Jerusalem – this they themselves know and are forced to admit."[35]

The reality of lengthy Jewish exile, which Luther had already emphasized in his 1523 essay, serves to rebut Jewish claims about the eternality of Jewish law; this reality also had served and continues to serve Luther as a key argument in his case that the Messiah has already come, and he quickly segues to this issue. For Luther in this essay as in the prior one, the most obvious truth for the prior advent of the Messiah is the lengthy Jewish exile. God had promised in the Bible redemption, but there are no signs of this redemption among the Jews. This can only mean – according to Luther – that the redemption has in fact taken place, with a different human community enjoying its benefits.

Luther examines at some length the claim made by Jews that they remain in exile because of their sins and that, when expiation of these sins is complete, they will be redeemed.[36] He concludes that Jews cannot in fact identify such an exile-causing sin or even combination of sins. The notion of God sending off the Jews into this exile without any reasonable explanation for its remarkable length is, for Luther, incomprehensible and unacceptable. This can only mean that God, who is always true to his promises, has in fact fulfilled the promise of redemption, that this redemption involves the coming of the Messiah, and that the Jews have been passed over in this redemption. "He [God] assures them that he will never fail because of their sins in his promise to send the Messiah and to preserve the throne of David forever. It follows incontestably that one of the following two things must be true: Either the Messiah must have come fifteen hundred years ago, or God must have lied (may God forgive me for speaking so irreverently!) and has not kept his promise."[37] The only reasonable alternative is the first – the Messiah has obviously come already. Thus, by pointing to the lengthy Jewish exile, which had already played such a dominant role in Luther's initial essay on the Jews, Luther addresses two issues simultaneously: He has advanced a persuasive argument against the eternality of Jewish law and a persuasive argument against the Jewish contention that the Messiah has not yet come.

Luther asserts this obvious conclusion and uses it to make further observations on present-day Jews. "The Messiah has come, and God's promise has been kept and fulfilled. They, however, did not accept or believe this, but constantly gave God the lie with their own belief, etc. Is it any wonder that God's wrath destroyed them together with Jerusalem, temple, law, kingdom, priesthood, and reduced these to ashes, that he scattered them among all the gentiles, and that he does not cease to afflict them as long as they give the lie to the divine promise and fulfillment and blaspheme them by their unbelief and disobedience? For they should have accepted the new covenant (as promised by Jeremiah) from the Messiah and received him. He was commissioned to teach them properly concerning the throne of David, the priesthood, the law of Moses, the temple, and all things."[38]

Here, Luther clarifies further his perceptions of the Jewish past and Jewish present. The early period of the Jewish past was truly distinguished, as he had argued in his previous statement on the Jews. Although he does not overtly repeat his praise for the early Jews in this second essay, it is nonetheless reflected in his ongoing reverence for the Hebrew Bible, which God vouchsafed to the early Jews. In this later essay, Luther focuses more fully on the second and negative stage of the Jewish past, which has continued down into the Jewish present. The Jews made a fatal error in failing to recognize – from clear Scriptural teachings – that Jesus was the promised Messiah and that his teachings represented the true meaning of prior biblical prediction and guidance. Instead, the Jews of the second stage of the Jewish past and of the present attend to the misguided teachings of their rabbis, who – like their papal counterparts – lead their followers astray.

Having utilized the lengthy Jewish exile to show that the doctrines of the eternality of Jewish law and the future advent of the Messiah are both erroneous, Luther returns to say more about the former Jewish doctrine. He mounts a number of further arguments against the notion of the eternality of Jewish law, citing biblical sources that proclaim that Jewish law would eventually be suspended. More interesting is his lengthy consideration of the Hebrew term *le-`olam*, which is often used in biblical passages with respect to aspects of the law and which Jews claim to mean "forever." Luther, who had made some observations in his earlier essay on the Hebrew term *`almah* in Isaiah 7:14, discusses at length the meaning of the term *le-`olam*, concluding that it does not in fact mean "forever."

Luther ends this discussion of the eternality of the law in normally decisive fashion, certain of his reading of the Hebrew Bible. "Now let us consider whom it is more reasonable for us to believe, the faithful and truthful God or the false and lying Jews? God declares that Moses' covenant will not endure forever, but that it will terminate at the time of the Messiah. The Jews assert that it will endure forever and will never terminate. Thus to the Jews God must ever be a liar. And yet they wonder why they suffer such miserable exile. They insist that they are in the right and God is in the wrong."[39] This is an intensification of Luther's projection of Jewish error. Convinced of the accuracy of his reading of Scripture, Luther concludes that the Jews – who read the Bible differently from the way he does – are in fact disagreeing not with Martin Luther, but with God himself.

At this point, Luther introduces very briefly Jewish claims derived from the New Testament. Citing Matthew 5:17–20, Jews claim that Jesus indicated that he had not come to abolish the law. This claim arouses Luther's scorn. "If at this point they try to escape and blaspheme, saying: 'Your Jesus himself stated that he had not come to abolish the law, not a jot, not a letter of it, etc.,' you must answer that that they should stick to the passage in Jeremiah [Jeremiah 31:32, which speaks of a new covenant] and give a correct and thorough answer [to the Christian claims based upon this passage]. Since they do not believe our Jesus at all, they cannot appeal to him. They must either refute Jeremiah or defend themselves against him with plausible reasons and valid statements."[40]

The third issue raised by his correspondent involves Jewish law and gentiles. This leads Luther to consideration of the Ten Commandments, which Jews advance as an indication of the binding quality of Jewish law for all of humanity. In response, Luther argues that the Ten Commandments are in fact binding on all humanity, but that they do not constitute a genuine part of the law of Moses. "If the Ten Commandments are to be regarded as Moses' law, then Moses came far too late, and he also addressed himself to far too few people, because the Ten Commandments had spread over the whole world not only before Moses but even before Abraham and all the patriarchs. For even if Moses had never appeared and Abraham had never been born, the Ten Commandments would have had to rule in all men from the very beginning, as they indeed did and still do."[41] Luther then proceeds through the Ten Commandments to show that all of them have been accepted by the totality of humanity from time immemorial. This perspective on the early role of Israel in the socialization of humanity differs markedly from that of Eusebius.[42]

Luther closes his essay by turning once again to the central argument he has adduced for the prior advent of the Messiah and the abrogation

of Jewish law. This central argument lies in the fifteen hundred years of
Jewish exile, which – for Luther – can mean nothing other than divine
rejection of the Jews. He ends by pointing to numbers and their significance. "If we reckon the time exactly, we find that their present exile
under the Roman Empire is lasting longer than their former state and
government in the land of Canaan. Anyone may figure the time from the
exodus from Egypt to the final destruction of Jerusalem, under which
they still live, and he will arrive at the sum of approximately fifteen hundred and ten years. At present, they have not lived many fewer years in
exile; and in the end this will become a far longer period of time, since
they neither have had nor will they have any prophet or prophecy regarding their exile's end." There was initially happy Jewish fortune in the
Land of Israel; however, the loss of good fortune set in motion by the
failure to acknowledge Jesus is well on the way to exceeding the period
of good fortune. This is a striking closing statement of the two stages of
the Jewish past.

Whereas the focus of Luther's first essay was early Jewish virtue and
the resultant need to reach out to Jews and educate them, the focus of this
essay is Jewish religious claims and their refutation. Luther addresses each
of the three Jewish claims on which he had been asked to provide guidance. In the process, he clarifies further his view of the Jewish past and
present, not relating in any significant way to the Jewish future. The early
Jewish past remains glorious, although outright praise for it is noticeably
absent. At a critical juncture in the past, Jews misread the advent of Jesus
and have suffered for this misreading ever since. Luther avoids dwelling on
the role of the Jews in the Crucifixion, which is another interesting aspect
of the lack of vituperation in this second essay. Nonetheless, the failure
of the Jews to recognize Jesus was monumental, resulting in their exile,
which has lasted for a millennium and a half. The length of this exile means
again for Luther that redemption has already dawned and that the Jews
have been bypassed in this redemption as a result of their own error. This
error in the past has been maintained by the rabbis, who – like their papal
counterparts – guide their followers into continued error. The corrective, in
Luther's eyes, is straightforward and again parallels the cure for Christian
error. Jews must be confronted with the biblical truth that they cannot
deny. This biblical truth obviates any danger from the religious claims they
advance to Christians; to the extent that Jewish defenses could be penetrated by biblical truth, Jewish conversion would be stimulated as well.

Throughout this essay, Luther's tone remains restrained and moderate. He avoids inciting animosity by citing damaging New Testament

passages that highlight virulent Jewish opposition to Jesus; he is content simply to point to Jewish failure to acknowledge Jesus' messianic role. At no point does he break out into harshness, even though the occasion for the essay was Jewish proselytizing among Christians. Nothing in the tone of this statement prepares us for the virulence that Luther would exhibit in a series of essays five years later.

In 1543, Luther wrote a series of lengthy and vicious attacks on the Jews, which included proposals for drastic anti-Jewish measures on the part of the political authorities. Oberman's claim that there was in these harsh compositions no change in Luther's fundamental stance on Judaism and Jews – since assertion of Christian truth and denial of Judaism appears throughout his essays – is correct.[43] There was in fact continuity in the specifics of Luther's religious argumentation based on the Hebrew Bible, including a focus on the very same verses recurrently cited in his earlier essays. New in 1543 were abandonment of the commitment to proselytizing among the Jews; the shift in focus from religious disagreement to socioeconomic critique; the nearly exclusive focus on the negative aspects of Jewish present, past, and future, with no reference whatsoever to the positive elements noted in his 1523 essay; and the programmatic implications of this overwhelmingly negative perspective on the past and – especially – present of the Jews. Because his 1543 essays are so lengthy, rambling, and repetitive, I have decided to focus on the earliest and most important of them, his extremely long and demeaning *On the Jews and Their Lies*.[44]

On the Jews and Their Lies begins with precisely the issue that had sparked the 1538 essay. In the earlier essay, a correspondent had indicated Jewish proselytizing successes among Christians and had asked Luther to provide counterarguments with which to rebut the Jewish missionizing argumentation, which he did, without reacting emotionally to the report. Now, five years later, Luther reports the same phenomenon, but reacts quite differently. "I had made up my mind to write no more about the Jews or against them. But since I learned that these miserable and accursed people do not cease to lure to themselves even us, that is the Christians, I have published this little book, so that I might be found among those who opposed such poisonous activities of the Jews and who warned the Christians to be on their guard against them. I would not have believed that a Christian could be duped by the Jews into taking their exile and wretchedness upon himself. However, the devil is the god of the world, and wherever God's word is absent he has an easy task, not

only with the weak but also with the strong."[45] Ostensibly, this essay was
to reprise the theological argumentation presented five years earlier. As
we shall see, however, Luther ranges far more broadly, moving from the
sphere of religious difference to the panoply of dangers that contemporary Jews allegedly present. Warning Christians to be on guard against
the Jews suggests subtly the eventual breadth of this essay. Introduction
of the devil sounds an ominous note.

Opening on the theological plane, Luther indicates that he is fully
familiar with Jewish exegesis of Scripture, can learn nothing from what
his Jewish contemporaries might teach, and will not waste energy on
quarreling with them. Surprising is his next statement: "Much less do
I propose to convert the Jews, for that is impossible."[46] This is of course
the same Martin Luther who had urged twenty years earlier a serious
and concerted effort to convert German Jews, with a relatively high level
of optimism. Now, that effort is totally abandoned, out of recognition
that it is hopeless. Luther explains his loss of confidence in the conversion project in the following terms: "They have failed to learn any lesson
from the terrible distress that has been theirs for over fourteen hundred
years in exile. Nor can they obtain any end or definite terminus of this,
as they suppose, by means of vehement cries and laments to God. If
these blows do not help, it is reasonable to assume that our talking and
explaining will help even less."[47] Luther had emphasized the significance
of lengthy Jewish exile back in 1523, but it had not brought him to
abandon his hopes for conversion; now, in 1543, he concludes that no
argument could be stronger than Jewish suffering and that preaching to
Jews is thus hopeless. This constitutes a major strategic retreat from his
1523 essay.

With talking to the Jews out of the question, Luther proceeds to indicate that he will now talk *about* the Jews, for the benefit of the German
people. The 1523 essay had proposed a plan for talking to Jews and
converting them; the 1538 essay had advanced guidelines for rebutting
Jewish religious claims, in the process still providing useful information
for talking to Jews as well; in 1543, the focus is entirely talking about
Jews and providing information that will be useful to the German people
in their encounters with Jews, in the religious sphere and well beyond
the religious sphere. This new and broader objective opens the way for
Luther to sketch a total portrait of the Jews, all their shortcomings, and
what should be done about them – which is precisely what he proceeds to
do in this essay. He spells this out clearly at the very end of the essay. "My
essay, I hope, will furnish a Christian (who in any case has no desire to

become a Jew) with enough material not only to defend himself against the blind, venomous Jews, but also to become the foe of the Jews' malice, lying, and cursing and to understand not only that their belief is false but that they are surely possessed by all devils."[48] In this essay, there is no attempt to provide theological arguments for use with the Jews or theological counterarguments to Jewish religious claims; there is a far broader effort to present information useful for protecting Christians in multiple ways against contemporary Jews, who constitute the threatening allies of the devil.

The objective of this essay – providing Christians a sense of precisely who contemporary Jews are and the dangers they present – constitutes a striking departure from the more limited religious concerns of Luther's earlier essays and leads to a remarkable reversal in tone. In 1523, Luther had railed against the Catholic Church for its misguided policies that focused on denigration and mistreatment. He had argued that this Catholic focus had eliminated any possibility of attracting the Jews into the Christian fold: "We are trying only to drive them by force, slandering them, accusing them of having Christian blood if they don't stink, and I know not what other foolishness. So long as we thus treat them like dogs, how can we expect to work any good among them." Now, having abandoned any hope of converting Jews, Luther himself resorts to invective as harsh as or even harsher than the Catholic denigration he had earlier criticized and proposes programs much crueler than those encouraged by the medieval Catholic Church.

Luther's long essay divides into three segments: (1) a mini-treatise on Jewish arrogance; (2) a return to the theological issue of the advent of the Messiah, which he had already treated in 1523 and 1538; (3) a closing section in which he describes at length Jewish anti-Christian calumnies and behaviors and the policies they necessitate. The middle segment focuses on the Jewish past; the opening and closing segments focus on the Jewish present. For our purposes, it is useful to begin with the middle section of the essay and examine Luther's evolving views of the Jewish past and then proceed to the first and third sections and analyze his changing views of the Jewish present.

The middle section of *On the Jews and Their Lies* reopens the issue of advent of the Messiah, which Christians know has already taken place and which – according to Jews – lies yet in the future. "Now we come to the main subject, their asking God for the Messiah."[49] In this section of his essay, Luther returns to precisely the same arguments and the same biblical texts he had utilized in his earlier essays. For Luther (as for many medieval Christian thinkers), the length of Jewish exile clearly indicates that Jewish hopes for a Messiah yet to come are pointless. God would not have left them in exile for such a long time if their redemption was yet to come. Especially striking to Luther was the lack of prophecy during this long exile. The length of Jewish exile and the lack of prophecy can mean for Luther only one thing: God, who had promised redemption and is scrupulously faithful in fulfilling his promises, has in fact already delivered the promised redemption, which is enjoyed by those who worship Jesus as the true Messiah. This argument runs throughout Luther's essays of 1523, 1538, and 1543.

In 1523, Luther had chosen – for a variety of reasons – to focus in Pauline fashion on the blessings conferred by God on the early Israelites/Jews. In that essay and the 1538 essay, he nonetheless noted that the divine gift of redemption bestowed upon gentiles, rather than Jews, reflects the critical Jewish shortcomings of the second and error-ridden phase of the Jews' past. The decisive Jewish error was of course the failure to acknowledge Jesus as the divinely predicted and divinely dispatched Messiah, which was the key to the shift in the gift of redemption from the Jews to the gentiles and thus a foundational element of all Christian thinking. In his earlier essays, Luther had grounded his argument from lengthy Jewish exile in a number of biblical passages, with heavy emphasis on Genesis 49:10 and Daniel 9:21–24. In this sense, there is no significant change from the earlier essays to those of 1543. What does change, however, is his treatment of the Jewish past and its shortcomings. The earlier essays had advanced – in relatively mild fashion – the notion of a key error in the Jewish past, that is the failure to acknowledge the true Messiah. In his 1543 essay, Luther treats at great and damning length this key Jewish error.

We have noted that Luther in his earlier essays refrains from citing the most condemnatory passages of the New Testament, content simply to highlight the Jewish failure to recognize Jesus as Messiah without introducing the inflammatory imagery of the Jewish role in the Crucifixion. This restraint disappears in the 1543 essay, in which Luther points to the Crucifixion recurrently. Already in his opening section on Jewish arrogance, he begins by highlighting Jewish pride in descent from Israel. In the course of his attack on this pride, Luther says the following: "I hold that, if their Messiah, for whom they hope, should come and do away with this boast and its basis, they would crucify and blaspheme him seven times worse than they did to our Messiah; and they would also say that he was not the true Messiah, but a deceiving devil."[50] The

Crucifixion – notably absent in his earlier essays – moves immediately front and center in 1543.[51]

In the middle section of his essay, during his extended treatment of Daniel 9:21–24, Luther dwells at length on the interactions between Jesus and his Jewish contemporaries. The opening error of the Jewish leaders was misguided expectations. As a result of Jesus' miracles, "the Jews hoped that now, after the loss of the scepter, Shiloh had come. But the chief priests, the rulers, and their followers took offense at the person, since he did not come as a mighty king but wandered about as a poor beggar."[52] This rejection set off a dynamic of mutual disdain, with Jesus upbraiding the Jews and the Jews dismissing him. "Now the fat was really in the fire; they [the Jews] grew wrathful, bitter, and hateful, and ranted against him; finally they contrived the plot to kill him. And that is what they did; they crucified him as ignominiously as possible."[53] Previously, Luther had located the decisive sin of the Jewish past in the failure to recognize Jesus, without exacerbating this sin by pointing to the Jewish role in the Crucifixion. Now, the rhetorical negativity of the Luther position is intensified and the Jewish role in the Crucifixion is highlighted.

In this middle section of *On the Jews and Their Lies*, Luther fills out extensively his portrait of past Jewish error, beyond their rejection and crucifixion of Jesus. He discusses at considerable length the history of the Jews from Herod onward, beginning with Herod himself. "Josephus writes that Herod razed the temple of Haggai [i.e., the second Jerusalem temple], because it was not sufficiently splendid, and rebuilt it so that it was equal or superior to the temple of Solomon in splendor.... Herod had not been commissioned by God to build it, but did so as an impious enemy of God and his people, motivated by vanity and pride, in his own honor.... Herod certainly did not merit much grace for tearing down and desecrating the temple that had been commanded, built, and consecrated by the word of God and then presuming to erect a much more glorious one without God's word and command."[54] According to Luther, even apart from Herod's destruction and rebuilding of the Second Temple, it had been repeatedly desecrated by external forces and internal Jewish misdeeds. Among the external forces sullying the Second Temple were the Seleucid ruler Antiochus and the Roman ruler Caligula. Luther describes at length the more damning spiritual desecration inflicted on the Second Temple by various forms of Jewish wickedness.

Luther eventually focuses on some of the well-known Jewish groupings of the Second Temple period, especially the Sadducees. "The real abomination of all abominations, the shame of all shames, is this: that at the time of this temple there were several chief priests and an entire sect that were Sadducean, that is Epicurean, who did not believe in the existence of any angel, devil, heaven, hell, or life after this life. And such fellows were expected to enter the temple, vested with the priestly office and in priestly garments, and sacrifice, pray, and offer burnt offerings for the people, preach to them, and rule them!"[55] According to Luther, the Sadducees were actually Epicureans, denied all the fundamental tenets of religious life, and nonetheless played a central role in temple life and in the administration of Jewish affairs.

This excoriation of the Jews of the Second Temple, who were responsible for the rejection and crucifixion of Jesus, leads Luther to reflect on the contrasting virtues of the pagans of antiquity and their philosophers. "How much more honorably do the pagan philosophers, as well as the poets, write and teach not only about God's rule and about the life to come, but also about temporal virtues. They teach that man by nature is obliged to serve his fellow man, to keep faith also with his enemies, and to be loyal and helpful, especially in time of need." The virtues of the pagan thinkers contrast strikingly with the vices of the Jews. "Indeed, I believe that three of Aesop's fables, half of Cato, and several comedies of Terence contain more wisdom and more instruction than can be found in the books of all the Talmudists and rabbis and more than may ever occur to the hearts of all the Jews."[56] This paean of praise to the pagans contrasts strikingly with Eusebius's denigration of the pagan world and encomium to the role of the Israelites/ Jews in civilizing all of humanity.[57]

The errors of the Jews of the past did not cease with their rejection of Jesus as Messiah. Immediately after rejecting and crucifying the true Messiah, the Jews of the first century saw in their midst a number of messianic pretenders, whom they blindly followed with disastrous results. Luther projects the first Jewish revolt, which began in the year 66, as a failed messianic outburst. Luther relates this revolt directly to first-century messianic fervor among the Jews, adding into the mix the ongoing Jewish hatred for Jesus and his followers. "When they had executed this false Messiah (that is the conception they wanted to convey of him), they still did not abandon the delusion that the Messiah had to be at hand or nearby. They constantly murmured against the Romans because of the scepter. Soon, too, the rumor circulated that Jesus, whom they had killed, had again risen and that he was now really being proclaimed openly and freely as the Messiah. The people in Jerusalem were adhering to him, as well as the gentiles in Antioch and everywhere in the country. Now they really had their hands full. They had to oppose this dead Messiah and his followers, lest he be accepted as resurrected and as the Messiah. They also had to oppose the Romans, lest their hoped-for Messiah be forever bereft of the scepter. At one place a slaughter of the Christians was initiated, at another an uprising against the Romans. To these tactics they devoted themselves for approximately forty years, until the Romans finally were constrained to lay waste country and city."[58] The Jewish error in failing to acknowledge Jesus was thus compounded by the persecution of his adherents and rebellion against the Romans, all related to mistaken Jewish messianic conceptions.

According to Luther, the sad story did not end there. The humiliation of defeat in conjunction with the flourishing of Christianity caused the Jews to maintain their messianic delusions, which eventually erupted in the revolt led by Simon bar Cochba and supported by the important Rabbi Akiba. Luther describes fully the background to the uprising and its results. This was yet another Jewish disaster, with its roots in misguided messianic expectations. Although these Jews were correct in their sense that the Messiah had been predicted to arrive at this point in time, they were misguided in their sense of who the Messiah would be and what he would achieve. This misreading of the Messiah resulted – according to Luther – in the rejection of Jesus, persecution of his followers, hopeless revolt against Rome, terrible persecution and suffering, and an ongoing commitment to the maintenance of the very errors that had laid them low. Present-day Jews are the heirs of this woeful history.[59]

In concluding his discussion in this middle section of his essay of four key biblical texts that predict the Messiah, Luther makes an overall summary statement. For Luther, Jewish misreadings of these four key biblical texts are not to be seen as errors; rather, they are lies, the lies that in part give the essay its title. According to Luther, this penchant for lying extends well beyond the four biblical texts cited. "We will limit ourselves for the time being to these four texts – those of Jacob, David, Haggai, and Daniel – wherein we see what a fine job the Jews have done this fifteen hundred years with Scripture and what a fine job they still do. For their treatment of these texts parallels their treatment of all others, especially those that are in favor of us and our Messiah. These of course must be accounted as lies, where they themselves [believe they] cannot err or be mistaken. However, they have not acquired a perfect mastery of the art of lying; they lie so clumsily and ineptly that anyone who is just a little observant can easily detect it.... The example of the Jews demonstrates how easily the devil can mislead people, after they once have digressed from the proper understanding of Scripture, into such blindness and darkness that it can be readily grasped and perceived by natural reason, yes even by irrational beasts."[60] Once again, biblical truth is the key to true religious and indeed to all human life, and Jews have misread biblical truth from the days of Jesus down to the present. Anyone with simple natural reason can readily discern their errors/lies.

In this propensity to lie, the Jews are joined by two other groups on the sixteenth-century scene – the Catholics and the Muslims. "As S. Paul declares in Romans 11, we must fear God and honor his word as long as the time of grace remains, so that we do not meet with a similar or worse fate [similar to or worse than that of the Jews]. We have seen this happen in the case of the papacy and of Muhammad."[61] Jewish errors/lies attach them to an unholy trinity of forces, all of whom have suffered from the same tendency to misread the record of God's revelation to humanity. As noted by many scholars, Luther was obsessed toward the end of his life by an apocalyptic sense of the burgeoning power of the devil, supported by the allied forces of the papacy, the Islamic world, and the Jews.[62]

Although this portrait of the Jewish past is damning, Luther's depiction of the Jewish present, sketched in the first and third sections of *On the Jews and Their Lies*, is even harsher. The first section of the essay is devoted to Jewish arrogance and its sources. Luther identifies four sources for this arrogance: Jewish pride in descent, circumcision, the law, and the land of Canaan. All four elements contribute to the distorted and outrageous Jewish sense of self, which leads inevitably to the denigration of all others. Christians must be aware of this arrogance and be on guard against it. "Therefore be on your guard against the Jews, knowing that, wherever they have their synagogues, nothing is found but a den of devils in which sheer self-glory, conceit, lies, blasphemy, and defaming of God and men are practiced most maliciously and vehemently, just as the devils themselves do. And where you see or hear a Jew teaching, remember that you are hearing nothing but a venomous basilisk who poisons and kills people by fastening his eyes on them."[63] The earlier Luther's concern with theological argumentation – either to be used directly against the Jews themselves (1523) or by Christians in refuting Jewish claims (1538) – has given way to a far broader picture of Jews and the dangers they present. Mere engagement with Jews is dangerous, as they – like the basilisk – can poison and kill simply by fastening their eyes on others.

The arrogance of the Jews depicted in the first section of the essay and the hatred of all others it purportedly inspires lead smoothly to the third section of *On the Jews and Their Lies*, which argues at length that the Jewish propensity for lying extends beyond Scripture into lying about Christianity and Christians. Reflected in this section is the growing awareness of Jewish sources accumulated in western Christendom from the thirteenth century on. Luther was familiar with this literature and deploys his knowledge to full advantage in the third section of his essay. He adduces a series of Jewish calumnies against Jesus and an even lengthier series of calumnies against Mary. These reports of Jewish calumnies were intended to arouse Christian rage against the Jews, and they surely did so.[64]

The Jewish slanders about Jesus and Mary adduced by Luther lead in a natural way to Jewish slanders against the followers of Jesus and Mary. "Now such devilish lies and blasphemy are aimed at the person of Christ and his dear mother; but our person and that of all Christians are also involved. Because Christ and Mary are dead and because we Christians are such vile people to honor these despicable, dead persons, they also assign to us our special share of slander."[65] According to Luther, ongoing Jewish messianic delusions result in aspirations for wholesale killing of Christians upon the advent of the Messiah for whom they still pray. "That is to say that he [God] is to kill and exterminate all of us Goyim through their Messiah, so that they can lay their hands on the land, the goods, and the government of the whole world. And now a storm breaks over us with curses, defamation, and derision that cannot be expressed with words. They wish us that sword and war, distress and every misfortune may overtake us accursed Goyim."[66]

Luther quickly moves from Jewish anti-Christian prayers and intentions to the realm of anti-Christian Jewish behavior. "They [the Jews] have been blood-thirsty bloodhounds and murderers of all Christendom for more than fourteen hundred years in their intentions and would undoubtedly prefer to be such with their deeds. Thus they have been accused of poisoning water and wells, of kidnapping children, of piercing them through with an awl, of hacking them in pieces, and in that way secretly cooling their wrath with the blood of Christians, for all of which they have often been condemned to death by fire."[67] Here, Luther has abandoned theological argumentation and moved to a total portrait of contemporary Jews, their desires, and their behaviors and to the Christian need to guard against the multiple dangers accruing from Jewish presence.

Like Friar Alphonso de Espina, Luther moves from the allegations of Jewish misdeeds to the decisive evidence for this charge, that is the governmental reactions of expulsion. "Thus they were banished from France (which they call Tsorfath., from Obadiah [20]), which was an especially fine nest. Very recently, they were banished by our dear Emperor Charles from Spain, the very best nest of all (which they called Sepharad, also on the basis of Obadiah). This year they were expelled from the entire Bohemian crownland, where they had one of the best nests, in Prague. Likewise, during my lifetime they have been driven from Regensburg, Magdeburg, and other places."[68] The hatefulness of the Jews that Luther has labored to illustrate is decisively proven – for him – by these expulsions.

Although the accusation that Jews murder their Christian neighbors is the direst in Luther's litany of allegations, he concludes with Jewish economic persecution of Christian contemporaries. "They let us work in the sweat of our brow to earn money and property, while they sit behind the stove, idle away the time, fart, and roast pears. They stuff themselves, guzzle, and live in luxury and ease from our hard-earned goods. With their accursed usury, they hold us and our property captive. Moreover, they mock and deride us because we work and let them play the role of lazy squires at our expense and in our land. Thus, they are our masters and we are their servants, with our property, our sweat, and our labor. And by way of reward and thanks, they curse our Lord and us! Should the devil not laugh and dance if he can enjoy such a paradise at the expense of us Christians. He devours what is ours through his saints, the Jews, and repays us by insulting us, in addition to mocking and cursing both God and man."[69] Again, Luther has radically reversed a prior position. In 1523, he had excoriated the Catholic Church for policies that forced the Jews into usury; now usury has become a treasured Jewish activity, through which Jews exploit the Christian majority and become in effect its masters, once more in service to their master, the devil.

This horrific depiction of contemporary Jews builds on strong medieval foundations. During the Middle Ages, allegations of Jewish murder and anger over Jewish moneylending emerged and accelerated. Slowly, these claims made their way into constructions of the Jewish present, as we have seen, especially in the previous chapter. Christian thinkers began to connect this image of the Jewish present to the series of expulsions that began toward the end of the twelfth century and to advance the expulsions as evidence for Christian awareness of and reaction to these alleged Jewish crimes. Although it is doubtful that the rulers who expelled their Jews did so out of a sense of these purported Jewish crimes, it is likely that, in the complex thinking that underlay the decision to expel Jews, the hope of winning approbation among the populace that had come to believe in these allegations played a role.

Expulsion was the harshest step against Jews countenanced in medieval Catholic Europe, out of the ongoing influence of the Augustinian view of the necessary place of Jews in Christian society. Freed from the constraints of the Roman Catholic Church, Luther made new and radical proposals for the treatment of Jews in light of their enmity and crimes; these proposals included setting fire to their synagogues and burying and covering with dirt whatever might not burn; razing the homes of Jews as well, since they pursue in their homes the same aims as in their synagogues; confiscation of all Jewish books; prohibiting teaching by their rabbis; abolishing safeguards on the highways; prohibiting Jewish usury and sequestering Jewish silver and gold, to be used for the support of sincere converts to Christianity; forcing young and strong Jews to labor and earn their bread by the sweat of their brows. Ultimately, all this leads to expulsion, to ridding Christendom once and forever of its Jewish scourge.

Toward the end of his essay, Luther turns in two directions. He enjoins the political leaders to fulfill their responsibility for the well-being of the societies over which they preside. This means carrying out the proper program he has enunciated with respect to the Jews, culminating in expulsion. Luther is well aware that these authorities enjoy considerable benefit from their taxation of the Jews, but they should bear in mind the source of the funds they extract from their Jewish subjects, which come directly from the exploited Christian masses. Responsible political leadership involves repudiation of such tainted funds and ending harmful Jewish presence. Luther, deeply distrustful of popular uprising, insists that the requisite anti-Jewish steps be initiated by the authorities and that the Christian populace refrain from any anti-Jewish activity, beyond demanding of their rulers fulfillment of their obligations.

Second, Luther turns to the religious and educational leadership of Christian society. "And you, my dear gentlemen and friends who are pastors and preachers, I wish to remind very faithfully of your official duty, so that you too may warn your parishioners concerning their [the Jews'] eternal harm, as you know how to do."[70] This turn to the pastors and preachers clarifies Luther's view of his own role in writing this and the other essays of 1543. He has fulfilled the key obligation of the preacher, as he conceives it. He has warned all of Christian society of the dangers – religious and well beyond religious – presented by the Jews.[71] To be sure, the kernel of the Christian-Jewish dispute lies in the realm of theology, and Luther addressed the theological issues in his earlier essays. This Christian-Jewish extended, however, far beyond the limited realm of theology. The dispute was in fact a religious war, with Jews utilizing

every weapon at their disposal – blasphemies, curses, murder, and economic exploitation – in their struggle against the Christian enemy. It was
crucial for Christians to grasp the nature of this unremitting battle, and
it was the obligation of pastors and preachers – starting with Martin
Luther himself – to educate their flocks to the struggle and to their enemy.
The trinity of enemies that Luther cites throughout – Muslims, Catholics,
and Jews – are alike in that all three are essentially religious opponents
who have evolved into total and lethal adversaries.

Martin Luther serves a number of useful purposes as the concluding
chapter of this study. In the first place, he provides the fullest example
of one and the same individual taking a number of alternative positions
on the Jewish present, past, and future. Although there is a consistent
thread that runs through all his essays, namely the core theological dispute between Christians and Jews, with the former correct and the latter
misguided, much else changes as we move with Luther from 1523 to
1543. The stunning evolution of Luther's views indicates just how malleable Christian perceptions of the Jewish present, past, and future can
be, for it is precisely Luther's constructions of the trajectory of Jewish
history that evolves most markedly from 1523 to 1543.

In addition, the evolution of Luther's perceptions of Jewish history
also reveals how dependent these constructions are on the shifting contexts within which they are created. From 1523 to 1543, the Jews of
Germany did not change in any appreciable way, and – broadly speaking – Germany's Christian majority did not change either. Rather, Luther's
personal vantage point was altered, as he experienced Jews differently
and as he assessed Christendom and its enemies in new ways. For a variety of reasons, Luther came to see his Jewish contemporaries as immune
to missionizing and thus unredeemable. He also came to focus more fear-
fully on the forces ranged against the true Christianity he felt himself to
be preaching.[72] This new perspective on the Jews shifted his perceptions
of the Jewish past and – more striking yet – of the Jewish present. He
muted the favorable elements he had earlier highlighted, and he focused
on negatives he had earlier suppressed or underplayed.

The impact of context can be seen in Luther in two quite different
ways. In 1523, aware of a more fluid religious environment, Luther was
able to envision new possibilities with respect to the Jews, hoping that
they might be moved out of their historic intransigence and drawn into
the new-style Christianity that he was pioneering. Also at this early time,
he was able to utilize the Jews as a cudgel with which to beat the Roman

Catholic Church, pointing to its foolish and counterproductive policies vis-à-vis Jews. The passage of time, the ongoing intransigence of the Jews, and the seemingly associated dangers from Islam and the Catholic Church altered Luther's views of Jewish present, past, and future in a starkly negative direction. He increasingly saw Jews as incorrigibly opposed to Christianity, indeed as part of a threatening trinity of oppositional forces. These new circumstances led to the construction of a different and more negative Jewish past and present, with significant policy implications. By 1543, his changing views had produced the most virulently negative construction of Jewish present, past, and future we have encountered.

Luther's alternative constructions of the trajectory of Jewish history were important for subsequent Western history. As European society evolved during the succeeding centuries, new constellations of forces emerged, and these new constellations created new projections of the Jewish present, past, and future and new possibilities for Jewish existence. In some cases, these new constellations opened positive options, like the religious fluidity Luther envisioned in 1523; in other cases, they created positive possibilities utterly devoid of religious grounding, which Luther could not even have imagined. In unfortunate ways, the tensions and anxieties produced by rapid change brought to the fore majority fearfulness, which often focused on Europe's Jewish minority. The later Luther view of the Jews, their history, and the dangers they purportedly represented eventually fanned the flames of subsequent anti-Semitic thinking in highly destructive ways. Luther's 1543 writings powerfully reinforced the innovative medieval popular perceptions of Jewish enmity and danger as a potent danger to Christianity and Christian society.

Notes

1 This emphasis is especially notable in the recurrent treatments of the Reformation by Heiko Oberman. See *The Roots of Anti-Semitism in the Age of the Renaissance and Reformation*, trans. James I. Porter (Philadelphia: Fortress Press, 1984); *Luther: Man between God and the Devil*, trans. Eileen Walliser-Schwazbart (New Haven: Yale University Press, 1989); *The Reformation: Roots and Ramifications*, trans. Andrew Colin Gow (Edinburgh: T&T Clark, 1994); and *The Two Reformations: The Journey from the Last Days to the New World*, ed. Donald Weinstein (New Haven: Yale University Press, 2003).

2 There has been an efflorescence of Luther biographies of late. In addition to the important Oberman study noted just now, see Richard Marius, *Martin Luther: The Christian between God and Death* (Cambridge, MA: Harvard University Press, 1999); Martin Marty, *Martin Luther: A Penguin Life*

(New York: Penguin Books, 2004; *Penguin Lives Series*); Michael A. Mullett, *Martin Luther* (London: Routledge, 2004; *Routledge Historical Biographies*); Derek Wilson, *Out of the Storm: The Life and Legacy of Martin Luther* (New York: St. Martin's Press, 2007); Robert Kolb, *Martin Luther: Confessor of the Faith* (Oxford: Oxford University Press, 2009; *Christian Theology in Context*).

3 I will cite the Luther texts from the fifty-five-volume *Luther's Works*, ed. Helmut T. Lehmann and Jaroslav Pelikan (55 vols.; St. Louis, Concordia Press, 1955). The 1523 essay can be found at 45:195–229.

4 Ibid., 47:57–98.

5 His three major essays are all available in English translations. The first and best known of these 1543 essays is "On the Jew and Their Lies," in ibid., 121–306 (note the length of this essay). "On the Ineffable Name of God" is now available in Gerhard Falk, *The Jew in Christian Theology: Martin Luther's* Vom Schem Hamphoras, *Previously Unpublished in English, and Other Milestones in Church Doctrine Concerning Judaism* (Jefferson, NC: McFarland, 1992); the third essay is "The Last Words of David," available in Henry Cole, trans. *Select Works of Martin Luther* (2 vols.: London: W. Simkin and R. Marshall, 1826), 2:177–335. Because of its renown and its range, I shall focus on the first of these essays.

6 All modern biographers cited in nn. 1 and 2 address the shift, assessing it differently.

7 The authors cited in n. 1 all show awareness of the post-Holocaust setting of their analyses.

8 Oberman, *The Roots of Anti-Semitism*, 45.

9 See Chapter 4.

10 Note that I am not suggesting that Luther provides us with a look further forward into the period of toleration of alternative religious perspectives.

11 *Luther's Works*, 45:199.

12 Ibid., 200.

13 Ibid., 202.

14 While I normally cite Hebrew Bible translations from the Jewish Publication Society translation, I have deviated here in order to highlight Luther's reading of the verse.

15 *Luther's Works*, 45:203–204.

16 Ibid., 213.

17 Ibid.

18 See especially Eusebius (Chapter 3) and the *Pugio fidei* (Chapter 6).

19 *Luther's Works*, 45:213.

20 Ibid., 215.

21 Ibid., 220–221.

22 Ibid., 221.

23 Ibid.

24 Ibid., 222.

25 Ibid.

26 Ibid., 229.

27 Ibid., 201.

28 Ibid., 200.
29 Ibid.
30 Ibid., 229.
31 Ibid.
32 *Luther's Works*, 47:65.
33 Ibid.
34 Ibid., 66. When the Talmud was attacked in medieval Europe, as noted in Chapter 6, a standard line of Jewish defense was to compare it to Christian canon law.
35 *Luther's Works*, 47:66.
36 This is the position taken by the sixteenth-century Jewish chronicler Joseph *ha-Kohen* in his widely circulated `*Emek ha-Bakha*.
37 *Luther's Works*, 47:73.
38 Ibid., 73–74.
39 Ibid., 88.
40 Ibid.
41 Ibid., 89.
42 See Chapter 3.
43 See n. 8.
44 For English versions of all three essays, see n. 5.
45 *Luther's Works* 47:137.
46 Ibid.
47 Ibid., 138.
48 Ibid., 306.
49 Ibid., 176.
50 Ibid., 141–142. The closing theme of Jewish accusations again the Messiah is central to the third section of the essay.
51 Recall Friar Alphonso's highlighting and dramatizing of the Crucifixion in Book III of the *Fortalitium fidei*, noted in the previous chapter.
52 *Luther's Works* 47:232.
53 Ibid.
54 Ibid., 224–225.
55 Ibid., 227.
56 Ibid.
57 See Chapter 3.
58 *Luther's Works* 47:232–233.
59 Ibid., 234–237. Recall Friar Raymond Martin's parallel views, grounded in Jewish sources, as described in Chapter 6.
60 Ibid., 253.
61 Ibid.
62 Again noted by all the authors cited in nn. 1 and 2.
63 *Luther's Works* 47:172.
64 Recall Luther's praise for Jews in his 1523 essay, which was intended to encourage Christians to reach out to Jews sympathetically.
65 *Luther's Works* 47:263.
66 Ibid., 264.
67 Ibid., 264–265.

68 Ibid., 265–266.
69 Ibid., 266.
70 Ibid., 274
71 Once more, the parallel to Friar Alphonso and his sense of the preacher's responsibility is striking.
72 This is much the same fearfulness that animated Friar Alphonso.

Epilogue

As concern over dangerously destructive Christian teachings about Judaism and Jews emerged in the wake of the Holocaust, the initial focus was on the Gospels, their portrayal of the Jewish role in the Crucifixion, and the impact of this portrayal over the ages. The depiction of total Roman innocence and total Jewish guilt in the most dramatic episode in the Gospel accounts of the life of Christ has resonated down through the centuries. For many Christians, the Gospel depiction of Jewish culpability for the Crucifixion captured the essence of Judaism and Jewishness. Jews of all times were considered to be consumed by the hatred of Christ and Christianity and to bear responsibility for insistence on the death of Jesus. Indeed, according to Matthew, the Jews of Jerusalem who demanded his death accepted full responsibility for themselves and their descendants. Some modern observers – seeking to understand the wellsprings of the hatred and fear that moved so many Europeans toward committing genocide and so many other Europeans toward acceding passively to the genocide – highlighted this imagery, in the process implicating Christianity in the Holocaust.[1]

This conclusion led to a wrenching question: Is Christianity at its core antisemitic (utilizing the term in this spelling as I have used it throughout this book as a designation for radical and dangerously provocative anti-Jewish thinking)? This led to a further query: Would it be possible to purge Christianity of its purported antisemitism without doing violence to essential Christian beliefs? Put in other terms, could Christianity be freed of its allegedly antisemitic essence and still remain Christianity? These questions were pressing and painful, especially to many liberally and univeralistically oriented Christians.

With the passage of time, the focus on the Gospel narratives and their harmful message has been subjected to further scrutiny, and alternative perspectives have emerged. Some observers began to question whether the portrayal of Jewish opposition to Jesus might really have provided the backdrop and grounding for modern anti-Semitic thinking and Nazism. While the Gospel depiction of Jewish opposition to Jesus was damning and had the potential over the ages to enrage believers in Jesus and his mission, the modern anti-Semitic movements went to great lengths to dissociate themselves from earlier and religiously grounded anti-Jewish thinking. How might the Gospel portraits have convinced anti-Semites and Nazis that Jews constituted a serious threat to contemporary European civilization? That the Gospel depictions might have engendered negative perspectives on Jews made sense; that they would have projected Jews as a contemporary and imminent danger to nineteenth- and twentieth-century Europe did not.

In addition, observers uncomfortable with the focus on the role of the Gospels in anti-Semitism and Nazism noted that the Gospel portrayal of the Jewish role in the Crucifixion did not constitute a statement as to the essence of Jewishness in first-century Palestine. The Gospel portrait of first-century Jews was complicated in multiple directions, and I have examined these complications in some detail in Chapter 1. The accounts of the Crucifixion do highlight the reluctance of the Romans to decree execution upon Jesus, which meant that responsibility was placed squarely upon the Jews. That said, Matthew's depiction of the Jews willingly and in fact aggressively accepting responsibility for the death of Jesus upon themselves and their descendants was mitigated to a significant extent by the theologically grounded necessity of Jesus' death and resurrection recurrently noted throughout all the Gospel accounts.

Beyond this theological complication as regards the Crucifixion, there is in the Gospels mitigation of Jewish guilt on a purely human level as well. In contradistinction to Matthew's portrayal of defiant Jewish acceptance of culpability for the death of Jesus, Luke depicts Jesus himself indicating that the Jewish actions were undertaken in error and should be forgiven, and the Luke narrator shows the Jewish crowd chastened – rather than exhilarated – by the spectacle of Jesus' execution. While Jewish responsibility for the Crucifixion is projected by all the Gospels, the human tenor of this responsibility varies, ranging from vicious delight (especially in Matthew) to conflicted concern (especially in Luke).

Equally important, the Gospels portray Jesus' contemporaries and their reactions to him in settings other than the climactic scene of the

Crucifixion, which after all involved only a small number of Jews. Although there is an overall sense of Jewish rejection of Jesus and his message, Jews are by no means portrayed as unanimously opposed to him. All Jesus' followers are Palestinian – indeed largely Galilean – Jews. The Gospels further suggest that, left to their own devices, most Jews who encountered Jesus were convinced of his divine mandate. Opposition to Jesus is described in the Gospels as the result of unremitting resistance on the part of the Jewish leadership. However, even that leadership is depicted as mixed in its reactions to Jesus. Some leaders heard Jesus' message and accepted it. Thus, fierce and violent resistance to Jesus was not a core feature of Jesus' Jewish contemporaries. Human behavior in general is always complex, and the reactions of Palestinian Jewry to Jesus were no exception.

To be sure, the portrait of intense and successful lobbying for Jesus' execution constitutes the dramatic highlight of the Gospel narratives and tends to overshadow the more nuanced realities depicted in the Gospels and grasped by numerous ancient and modern students of the New Testament. Nonetheless, while popular sensibility may well have been overwhelmed by the drama of the Crucifixion, careful Christian readers of the Gospels over the ages have been fully aware of these complications and have thus established complex and nuanced perspectives on Judaism and Jews.

I have argued that, in order to best appreciate the complexity of these perspectives, it is useful to track Christian constructions of the entire trajectory of Jewish history, that is the Jewish present, the Jewish past, and the Jewish future. I have urged this approach because I believe it encourages the fullest possible sensitivity to nuance. On the one hand, all Christians must express fundamental negativity to their Jewish contemporaries, since these Jews continue to reject the truth of Christianity. For most Christian thinkers and most Christian believers, the truth of Christianity is overwhelming, and non-Christians with an open mind should acknowledge this truth. Jews in particular should be the most responsive non-Christians of all, since so many Christian truth claims are grounded in the Hebrew Bible, which Jews venerate and study assiduously. Jewish failure to accept Christian truth elicits regularly Christian bewilderment and condemnation.

At the same time, however, Christian perspectives on the Jewish past are in many instances quite positive. Moving beyond the Gospels, we have seen this in Paul, Eusebius, and Augustine. In all three, the setting of the large and heterogeneous Roman Empire – as opposed to the closed

and tension-ridden context of Roman-controlled and heavily Jewish
Palestine – expanded and complicated consideration of the place of the
Jews on the human scene. Whereas in first-century Palestine Jews were
the majority and the opponents of Jesus, in the enormous Roman Empire
Jews and Christians were both tiny minorities. Christian thinkers looking
out over the pagan majority of the empire could readily see the advantages that Jews enjoyed over their pagan contemporaries. Although they
did not grasp the full truth of Christianity, Jews did comprehend the
fundamental reality of one God in the universe and understood the core
demands of that one God for dignified human living.

Awareness of the heterogeneity of humanity fostered acknowledgment
of the distinguished past of the Jewish people, who had been the first
human beings to bring awareness of one universal deity to humanity.
Paul, Eusebius, and Augustine all acknowledge and applaud this major
Jewish contribution to the human race. Beginning with Paul, the sense
emerged that the remarkable Jewish contribution to humanity, which
undergirded the special mission of Jesus, would ensure for the currently
misguided Jews abundant reward at the end of days. Thus, the Jewish
future, as well as the Jewish past, was projected positively by Paul and
Augustine. These central figures from late antiquity were fully cognizant
of the negative portrayal of Jews in the Gospels, but were equally aware
of the positive elements as well. At the same time, they did not limit their
appraisal of Jews to their own contemporaries or to the contemporaries
of Jesus; they considered the deep past of the Jews and the outlook for
the distant Jewish future.

The more positive postures of Paul, Eusebius, and Augustine reinforce
the sense gleaned in Chapter 1 of the complex perspectives of the Gospels
on Judaism and the Jews, which were embraced and adopted by these
careful readers. In addition, they themselves constituted authoritative
interpreters and disseminators of Christian belief. This is certainly the
case for Paul, whose writings form an essential part of the New Testament
corpus. To be sure, the pronouncements of Paul and their complexity pale
before the intensity of the Gospel narratives and their dramatic tale of
the Crucifixion. Nonetheless, Paul was unquestionably an authoritative
voice in the evolution of Christianity. Although not an element in the
New Testament, Augustine became the dominant formulator of Christian
beliefs and policies from the age of the Church Fathers. His pronouncements on the widest possible range of issues – including Judaism and
Jews – set forth official Church doctrine from the fifth century throughout the Middle Ages and down to the present.

The complexity of the Gospel narratives themselves and of the views of Paul and major Church Fathers like Eusebius and especially Augustine has raised questions as to the long-term influence of the anti-Jewish views bequeathed from antiquity. As these questions multiplied, the attention of those concerned with the impact of Christian thinking on anti-Semitism and the Holocaust shifted to a later period and an alternative venue. Increasingly, recent students of Christian anti-Jewish stereotypes have discerned in medieval Europe the emergence of extremely negative, dangerous, and influential imagery of Judaism and Jews.

The environment that spawned this imagery was radically different from the richly diversified Roman Empire of Paul, Eusebius, and Augustine. Medieval western Christendom was a highly homogeneous Christian society. In most areas, the Jews constituted the only legitimately dissenting minority; moreover, in the northern areas of medieval western Christendom the Jews were newcomers and resented as such. These problematic features of Jewish life focused societal attention on the Gospel accounts of historic Jewish enmity. The combination of historic Jewish enmity and problematic contemporary circumstances produced projections of regular Jewish blaspheming of Christian *sancta*, of Jewish economic activities designed to harm the Christian majority, and of murderous Jewish inclinations and actions. In the process, the Jews were transformed in the minds of many medieval Europeans into an active oppositional force, indeed a grave danger to the well-being of Christian society.[2]

This medieval "Christian" anti-Jewish imagery – it has been urged by a number of scholars – was a dominant factor in modern anti-Semitism and Nazism. There was continuity in geographic venue between the medieval anti-Jewish imagery and the thinking of the modern anti-Semites, as Europe was home to both. The Christian nature of this imagery was not theologically grounded, which would have been important to the anti-Semites' desire to distance themselves from traditional religious antipathies. The medieval imagery was Christian in the sense only that it was created and propagated in an overwhelmingly Christian environment. Arguably, it was reinforced by the Gospel imagery of the murderous Jewish role in the Crucifixion, but this popular reading of the Crucifixion narrative ran counter to the more nuanced interpretations of Paul and the major Church Fathers. The set of pernicious medieval popular perceptions made its way into the folk memory of European society and from there emerged in the nineteenth and twentieth centuries to form the ideological core of the anti-Semitic and Nazi claims that Europe's Jews constituted a lethal threat to European society and had to be defeated in an epic battle between two powerful forces.

To be sure, the more positive views of Jews adumbrated by Paul, Eusebius, and Augustine were by no means absent from the medieval European scene. Church leadership, committed to careful reading of Scripture – including the Gospels – and to veneration of the Church Fathers, regularly opposed the popular stereotypes. In this effort, they by and large enjoyed the support of the temporal authorities. Together, these two pillars of society managed to minimize the violence perpetrated upon medieval Europe's Jews, although their success was far from total. The effort by the ecclesiastical and temporal authorities to dispel the popular stereotypes was far less successful, and the negative popular imagery that emerged became deeply embedded in the consciousness of medieval and modern Europe.

Medieval and early modern Christian thinkers normally followed the official Church position on Judaism and Jews, as formulated for example by Augustine. This official position stipulated that Jews should enjoy full rights to live peacefully and securely within Christian society. Jews should suffer no untoward violence to person or property and should never be forced to abandon their Jewish religious faith. To be sure, Jews duly convicted of transgressing the laws of society could be brought to justice and suffer the penalties duly imposed by the authorities. Under normal circumstances, however, Jews were to live undisturbed. Put differently, Jews enjoyed fundamental rights to life and property in medieval Christian society.

These protections were regularly guaranteed to European Jews by a lengthy sequence of medieval popes.[3] Ecclesiastical protection involved more than simply formal declarations. Regularly, high-ranking churchmen intervened on behalf of Jews whom they perceived unfairly treated in one of many ways. Jews were keenly aware of the formal protective doctrine and of the energetic interventions by churchmen. As a result, Jews recurrently turned to Church leaders for protection when threatened. We have noted one striking instance of ecclesiastical protection provided to Jews in the face of danger. When popular distortions of the core crusading message, which had done considerable harm to Jews during the course of the First Crusade, resurfaced on the eve of the Second Crusade, Bernard of Clairvaux stepped in and reaffirmed decisively the traditional Church policy of safety and security for the endangered Jews.[4]

To be sure, the ringing statement of protection promulgated by Bernard of Clairvaux included an empirical judgment, along with restatement of traditional Church doctrine and policy. Bernard made an important assessment of the Jews of Europe in the middle of the twelfth century. In his view, these Jews had come to accept their subjugated status in Christian society and lived peacefully and docilely among their Christian neighbors. This subservient Jewish behavior translated into activation of the normal protections guaranteed to Jews by the Church. Indeed, it was in addition an act of Christian piety to treat kindly non-Christians prepared to live peacefully and docilely in Christian society.

This empirical conclusion was contested, however, by Bernard's influential contemporary, Peter the Venerable. Peter's assessment of twelfth-century Europe's Jews was radically different. In his view, the opposition expressed by the Jews of first-century Palestine to Jesus was maintained by their descendants eleven hundred years later, in the form of active and blasphemous repudiation of the religion founded by Jesus. In Peter's view, the Jews of twelfth-century Europe were consumed by the same hatred that had moved their ancestors more than a millennium earlier to demand the crucifixion of Jesus. The Church guarantee of safety for Jews had to be honored; however, appropriate penalties could and should be imposed on the Jews for their ongoing hostility.[5] Peter's empirical conclusions were much more negative than those of Bernard, but far less radical than those of his contemporaries who were convinced that twelfth-century Jews regularly murdered their Christian neighbors. Peter introduces us to the broad phenomenon illuminated in the second half of the book – slow acceptance by European intellectual leaders of the negative perspectives germinating among the masses.

Friar Raymond Martin utilized new data for reconstructing the past and future of the Jews.[6] With access to rabbinic literature as a result of the expanding intellectual horizons of thirteenth-century Europe, Friar Raymond and his colleagues gathered rabbinic sources, translated them carefully, and used them to fashion an elaborate, rabbinically grounded case for the truth of Christianity. In the process, Friar Raymond also constructed an innovative portrait of Jewish history, based on Jewish sources. Both the Jewish past and the Jewish future are portrayed in negative hues. This portrait contrasts sharply with the more appreciative stances of the Jewish past and future advanced by Paul, Eusebius, and Augustine.

Friar Alphonso de Espina reflects a yet later stage in the evolution of medieval western Christendom.[7] The bellicosity and confidence of the twelfth and thirteenth centuries had dissipated considerably by the fifteenth century, although western Christendom had not yet fractured, as it would shortly thereafter. By the fifteenth century, thinkers like Friar

Alphonso were in a far more defensive mode, deeply concerned with the dangers threatening the fortress of Christian faith. Prominent among these dangers were internal heretics, composed heavily according to Friar Alphonso of former Jews now living within the Christian majority of Spain. Likewise prominent among the dangers to the fortress of Christian faith were the Jews of Spain, who occupied a median position. They were not members of the Christian majority, but they constituted a significant and threatening minority element within Spanish society. Indeed, Alphonso accords more attention to the Jewish danger than to all other dangers combined.

Friar Alphonso introduces into his depiction of the Jewish dangers the popular slanders that had been generated by the European Christian populace for two centuries. This acceptance of the popular anti-Jewish slanders is noteworthy. Prior high-ranking churchmen had rejected the popular anti-Jewish claims; Friar Alphonso now accepted them and depicted them in great detail in his manifesto. In his view, the Jews of Spain constituted a mortal danger to Spanish society: Their usury threatened the foundations of the Spanish economy; their blasphemy of Christianity was insufferable; and their murderousness threatened each and every Spanish Christian.[8]

Even in the face of these dangers, Friar Alphonso remained committed to the traditional safeguards for Jewish life established by the Church. He did not highlight the dangers emanating from the Jews in order to arouse anti-Jewish violence. Rather, he wished to activate the legitimate techniques for dealing with Jewish misdeeds. As noted, Jewish rights in Christian society did not translate into *carte blanche* for misbehavior. Individual Jews accused of crimes were to be investigated and – if found guilty – punished appropriately. Large-scale Jewish misbehaviors were likewise to be carefully investigated. If the allegations of serious misbehavior were substantiated, Jews were not to be subjected to violence; rather, such broadly offending Jews were to be removed from Christian society.

This legitimate response to wide-ranging and incorrigible Jewish misdeeds was already well established in western Christendom by the fifteenth century. Beginning with a trickle of expulsions in the late twelfth century, rulers in the more advanced westerly sectors of northern Europe, for example, England and France, began to expel their Jews *en masse* by the end of the thirteenth century. Expulsion was viewed as a legitimate and appropriate response to large-scale Jewish harmfulness; it by no means contravened the traditional Church doctrine of protection for

Jews in Christian society. In effect, Friar Alphonso was laying out the case for Jewish misdeeds and urging the rulers of Spain to follow the laudable precedent set by earlier European Christian kings. The Spanish authorities should expel Spain's Jews and thus rid the kingdom of the multiple dangers they posed to Spanish society.

Martin Luther ushered in a new era in European history in general and in perspectives on Europe's Jews in particular.[9] Luther's criticism of the Church did not break truly new ground. Over the preceding centuries, numerous reformers had accused the Church of rejecting the simple and pure religious vision of Jesus of Nazareth in favor of increasingly legalistic, aristocratic, and philosophic complications that led to distortion and abandonment of the teachings of Christ himself. What was unique to Luther was his ability to disseminate his views broadly and effectively, largely as a result of the printing press, and to gain political backing and protection. The leadership of the sixteenth-century Church was unable to mobilize loyal temporal authorities to displace Luther's protectors, as their medieval predecessors had done. Thus, Luther was able to articulate his disagreement and survive, in the process fracturing the unity of western Christendom irrevocably.

Early on, as we have seen, Luther – while of course convinced of the error of his Jewish contemporaries – took the more benign position associated, for example with Augustine of preaching to them. Indeed, Luther was convinced that his preaching had significant possibilities of success. In the first place, his knowledge of Hebrew would serve him well. Jewish audiences could not dismiss him out of hand, taking the stand that he had no direct access to the Hebrew Bible they venerated. In addition, he claimed that the Church had so mistreated the Jews that they as a result could reasonably do nothing other than reject its overtures. By treating Jews with dignity (in a manner reminiscent of Augustine), Luther was convinced that he could make genuine inroads into the Jewish community, in the process highlighting the superiority of his vision over that of the established Church. The danger in this conviction was that failure to win over Jews in this new way might well explode into animosity, which is precisely what happened.

Luther's early and more positive writings are grounded in a sense of the contemporary Jewish capacity for change. If approached properly, Jews would listen to the Christian message delivered by Martin Luther and accept it. This hopeful perspective on the Jewish present led Luther to emphasize the richness of the Jewish past, beginning with the reality that Jesus himself was a Jew. For the early Luther, as for Paul and

Augustine, this fundamental reality conferred great dignity on Jews of all eras. The Jewish role in the Crucifixion is muted. Luther's conviction of potential Jewish acceptance of his message constituted a positive perspective on the Jewish future as well.

By the end of his career, Luther had turned vehemently against the Jews whom he had once hoped to convert. In the process, he accepted and projected all the popular slanders that had evolved in medieval Christian Europe. Jews were involved in incessant blaspheming of Christianity and Christians; they were inflicting serious suffering on the Christian populace of Europe through their harmful usury; most significantly, they threatened the lives of Christians through their propensity to anti-Christian violence and murder. Given the centrality of Luther and his views in the new Europe taking shape, adoption and promulgation of these medieval stereotypes was profoundly damaging to the modern European imagery of Judaism and Jews. Not surprisingly, the shift in the assessment of his Jewish contemporaries led Luther to a reexamination of the Jewish past as well. The Jewish past – earlier painted in positive colors – was now reconstructed in the most negative terms possible. Given Jewish resistance to his message, the Jewish future was obviously bereft of hope.

By setting himself up against the ecclesiastical superstructure erected by the Church of late antiquity and the Middle Ages, Luther was in a position to dismiss the prior ecclesiastical position on the Jewish right to safety and security in Christian society, and he did so. Convinced of the damage that Jews inflicted on Christian society, Luther called for attacking them, for burning down their synagogues and homes, and for depriving them of all the traditional safeguards that had protected them. The process of insisting on a return to Scripture meant, on the one hand, refocusing on the dramatic and dangerous portrayal of the Jewish role in the Crucifixion; on the other hand, it freed Luther from the constraints on anti-Jewish behaviors that had been so vital to Jewish survival all through the Middle Ages.

The harmful stereotypes generated in medieval western Christendom flowed from popular perceptions of medieval Jewish circumstances, arguably reinforced by simplistic reading of the dramatic Gospel accounts of the Crucifixion and the Jewish role in it. The leadership elite of medieval Europe read the Gospel narratives more carefully and absorbed key doctrinal and policy perspectives adumbrated by Paul and the Church Fathers. As a result, this leadership elite insisted on more balanced comprehension and treatment of medieval Europe's Jews.

At the same time, the intellectual elite could hardly remain totally resistant to the popular canards. Slowly, some of the intellectual leaders of medieval Europe absorbed the popular slanders, and their writings became vehicles for further embedding these slanders in European consciousness.[10] Arguably, Martin Luther represented the most extreme example of this absorption of popular imagery, as he at the same time dismantled the medieval ecclesiastical safeguards that had protected Europe's Jewish minority. Given Luther's role in the major changes that overtook Europe during the early modern centuries, the dignity he conferred on the popular canards by including them in the angry denunciation of his Jewish contemporaries did incalculable damage. Confirmation of these allegations by a figure as towering as Martin Luther accorded them great authority and a position from which they could influence significantly the subsequent thinking of modern Europe. Luther's broad recasting of the Jewish present, past, and future was of enormous significance to modern European Jewish fate.

Anti-Judaism was well established within the Church of antiquity. Ancient thinkers and sources described Jews who remained opposed to accepting Christianity in negative terms. However, the overall trajectory of Jewish history was depicted by these thinkers and sources in balanced fashion, with a combination of positive and negative perspectives on the Jewish past and the Jewish future. Under the special circumstances of medieval Europe and its Jewish minority, a new sense of Jews as both religiously opposed to Christianity and socially and economically dangerous to Christian society evolved at the popular level. This intense popular loathing and fear was eventually absorbed by some of the medieval Christian intelligentsia, who portrayed the Jewish present, past, and future in starkly negative hues. The harsher medieval constructions of the overall trajectory of Jewish history played a significant role in laying many of the foundations for modern anti-Semitism. These medieval thinkers thus served as a destructive conduit between the anti-Judaism of antiquity and the anti-Semitism of modernity.

Notes

1 See the Prologue.
2 For some of this literature, see again the Prologue.
3 See the sequence of such documents – the so-called *Constituio pro Judeis* – in the collection of papal documents with English translations edited by Solomon Grayzel and Kenneth Stow, *The Church and the Jews in the XIIIth Century* (Philadelphia and New York: Dropsie College and Jewish Theological Seminary, 1933–1989).

4 See Chapter 5.
5 Ibid.
6 See Chapter 6.
7 See Chapter 7.
8 Ibid.
9 See Chapter 8.
10 I have spoken repeatedly of the slanders becoming part of the folk memory of Europe, which constitutes a somewhat nebulous vehicle of transmission, although still a powerful one. In addition, Sara Lipton's *Dark Mirror* – cited in the Prologue, n. 14 – shows that these slanders were visually and more concretely preserved and transmitted through works of medieval European art. Thus, the writings examined in this book constitute yet a third vehicle for the transmission of the medieval canards – like the medieval art a tangible vehicle – into the modern West.

Index